6/95

THE KREMLIN AND
THE SCHOOLHOUSE

THE KREMLIN AND
THE SCHOOLHOUSE

Reforming Education in
Soviet Russia, 1917–1931

LARRY E. HOLMES

INDIANA UNIVERSITY PRESS
Bloomington and Indianapolis

The paper used in this publication meets the minimum requirements of American
National Standard for Information Sciences—Permanence of Paper for Printed
Library Materials, ANSI Z39.48-1984.
∞™

Manufactured in the United States of America

Library of Congress Cataloging-in-Publication Data

Holmes, Larry E. (Larry Eugene), date
    The Kremlin and the schoolhouse : reforming education in Soviet
Russia, 1917–1931 / Larry E. Holmes.
        p.   cm. — (Indiana-Michigan series in Russian and East
European studies)
    Includes bibliographical references and index.
    ISBN 0-253-32847-0
    1. Education—Soviet Union—History—20th century.   2. Education
and state—Soviet Union—History—20th century. 3. Educational
change—Soviet Union—History—20th century.   I. Title.   II. Title:
Kremlin and the school house.   III. Series.
LA831.8.H65   1991
370'.947—dc20   91-8380

1   2   3   4   5   95   94   93   92   91

For Bobby and Sheena

Until now, we have studied the
history of movements; we have not
studied sufficiently the history of
resistance. . . . The resistance of attitude
in place is one of the great factors
of slow history.
　　—E. Labrousse in *L'Histoire Sociale*

CONTENTS

Part Four. Cultural Revolution, 1928–1931

ACKNOWLEDGMENTS

I am indebted to many organizations. The University of South Alabama has provided several grants through its Research Committee and Research and Public Policy Council. The Russian and East European Center at the University of Illinois has assisted through its Slavic Reference Service, the Summer Laboratory, and the Independent Scholars Program. My gratitude goes to the National Endowment for the Humanities for several travel to collections grants and to the Kennan Institute for Advanced Russian Studies for a short-term grant and a research scholarship. Research in Moscow was supported by a grant from the International Research and Exchanges Board (IREX), with funds provided by the National Endowment for the Humanities and the United States Information Agency. None of these organizations is responsible for the views expressed.

I am grateful to many librarians who contributed their time and knowledge: David Kraus and Grant Harris of the Library of Congress, and the Slavic bibliographers at the University of Illinois, especially June Pachuta. Their counterparts in Moscow at the Lenin Library, Fundamental Library of the Social Sciences, and Central State Archives were equally as helpful. The staff at the Library of the Academy of Pedagogical Sciences (Ushinka) in Moscow made their facility a productive and pleasant place in which to work. My thanks for the welcome extended at the Institute of General Pedagogy of the Academy of Pedagogical Sciences by Z. A. Mal'kova, Z. I. Ravkin, M. N. Skatkin, and E. D. Dneprov. At IREX, Carley Rogers and Mary Kirk offered advice and encouragement.

Mark Kulikowski has consistently provided a list of recent Soviet publications on the subject of Soviet education. A number of colleagues have commented on earlier versions of the current work: Ben Eklof, Timothy Edward O'Connor, Richard Stites, Harley Balzer, James C. McClelland, Margaret K. Stolee, Christine Hinshaw, Oskar Anweiler, Patrick Alston, Pinkhas Agmon, Peter Reddaway, and Ralph Fisher, Jr. Ralph Fisher graciously provided me with some of his notes on the Young Communist League. Ben Eklof has been immensely helpful in suggesting changes in style and content. His published work on education in late tsarist Russia has clarified many of the issues relevant to my study. Sue Walker edited the entire manuscript. All errors of fact and judgment are, of course, mine.

My major professors represented something special about the craft: Raymond Flory, the joy of history; Oswald P. Backus, the love of scholarship; Herbert J. Ellison, the importance of originality and clarity of expression. During the early 1970s, Elizabeth Martin, Don Hendren, Howard Mahan, Herbert J. Ellison, A. Taber Green, and Melton McLaurin came forward on my behalf to demonstrate that academic freedom is more than a slogan. A. P. Zakharova has been a devoted friend and a source of inspiration for this work from its inception.

My family has watched while the attention it deserved went instead to the officials, teachers, parents, and pupils who dominate the pages to follow. It gives me great pleasure to thank them each, Sheena, Bobby, and Heather, for allowing me the independence necessary for an undertaking of this sort.

NOTE ON TRANSLITERATION

I have used the Library of Congress system with several exceptions. Proper names are spelled as they usually appear in English. The ending "ii" in proper names is always rendered as a "y."

INTRODUCTION

When I first decided to write a history of primary and secondary schools in Soviet Russia, it seemed a simple task. An examination of familiar sources—from State laws and Party decrees to speeches of officials—would reveal the essential features of the subject from the Kremlin to the classroom. My expectations betrayed a vision largely limited to political history. I presumed that in little more than a decade Moscow could dictate educational policy and classroom practice. It has been an exciting venture to discover that it was not so simple.

This study maintains that decision-making was a multi-dimensional process in which many institutions, social groups, and ideas conflicted in a complex way. The Commissariat of Enlightenment (Narkompros), the Communist Party, the Young Communist League, and the technical lobby proposed their own educational programs. They quickly discovered that they were not alone; there was a troubling social dimension to their efforts. Practice did not conform to policy. Neither local departments of education, teachers, parents, nor pupils responded as officials in Moscow had hoped. This resistance below significantly influenced discussions above and new policies that followed.

The relationship between teachers and the Commissariat of Enlightenment is of special importance to this study. Narkompros devised a radical curriculum for making schools agents of grand social change, but teachers refused to cooperate in the critical area under their control—the classroom. Their stubbornness became a major consideration at Narkompros and contributed first in the mid-1920s and again in 1931 to reshaping policy in the image of practice.

My work builds upon the historiography that precedes it. During the late 1950s and early 1960s, Soviet historians made outstanding contributions to the field. *Ocherki po istorii sovetskoi shkoly i pedagogiki, 1921–1931* (Moscow, 1961) by F. F. Korolev, Z. I. Ravkin, and T. D. Korneichik and monographs by Korolev, Ravkin, and P. I. Pidkasistyi emphasize the intellectual, ideological, and political content of central policy.[1] They only occasionally refer, however, to problems of implementation and its signficance.

The same can be said of German scholarship. Oskar Anweiler led the way with his masterful *Geschichte der Schule und Paedagogik in Russland vom Ende des Zarenreiches bis zum Beginn der Stalin-Aera* (Berlin, 1964). His study, Anna Gock's *Polytechnische Bildung und Erziehung in der Sowjetunion bis 1937* (Berlin, 1985), and the work of Marianne Krueger-Potratz on disputes among Soviet educational theoreticians provide much information, but little sense of what a classroom was and how it affected Moscow's decisions.[2]

A number of useful studies are available on the first Commissar of Enlightenment, A. V. Lunacharsky. Those by Robert C. Williams and Timothy Edward O'Connor stress the ideological and intellectual content of Lunacharsky's vision to the exclusion of how developments below and a related clash of opinions above may have altered his views on education.[3] Sheila Fitzpatrick began to address these issues in *The Commissariat of Enlightenment: Soviet Organization of Education and the Arts under Lunacharsky, October 1917–1921* (Cambridge, 1970).

Fitzpatrick's subsequent study, *Education and Social Mobility in the Soviet Union, 1921–1934* (Cambridge, 1979), places education squarely in its larger institutional and social dimension. Competing groups within Narkompros, the Young Communist League, and economic agencies fought over policy; teachers and parents questioned the use of schools to transform society. Yet Fitzpatrick's work has its conceptual limits. Concern for education as a vehicle for social mobility leads to a focus on vocational and higher education and on the creation by fiat of a proletarian intelligentsia. There is little of the primary and secondary school classroom and its influence on decisions made in Moscow.

The current discussion of educational reform in the Soviet Union adds special significance to this study. For the opponents and defenders of an authoritarian educational system, the 1920s have become a battleground. As it did seventy years ago, contemporary Soviet educational literature abounds with the views of many of the names that dominate the pages to follow: Lunacharsky, N. K. Krupskaya, P. P. Blonsky, S. P. Shatsky, V. N. Shul'gin, and M. V. Krupenina. Once again, reformers demand that the school take the lead in changing (restructuring) society. They argue that the classroom should promote individual initiative, and that pupils, teachers, parents, and the local community should participate in the development of a school's curriculum. There are echoes of the call to deemphasize marks and subjects. Of greatest importance, reformers insist that teachers participate in devising new policies. Only then can decisions conform to the availability of material resources and to the abilities of teachers.[4] I will return to this rebirth of the 1920s and the relationship between the Soviet past and present in the conclusion.

The present work examines school education from the dual perspectives of Moscow and the school. In so doing, it uses familiar sources published in the capital in new ways. One such item is the Narkompros weekly, *Ezhenedel'nik Narkomprosa,* later renamed *Biulleten' Narkomprosa.* Many of its entries disclose what authorities thought they knew about developments below and how they responded to them. This journal, Narkompros circulars, and the extensive collection of curricula and syllabi at the Library of the Academy of Pedagogical Sciences in Moscow provide the information necessary for following modifications of policy in response to outside pressure.

A different world than that depicted in Moscow's publications emerges upon examination of previously ignored regional and local publications. Until the late 1920s, provincial departments of education displayed a remarkable degree of independence in their journals, curricula, and syllabi. Reacting sooner than Moscow to resistance from teachers, they adjusted policy and urged Narkompros to do the same. Another neglected source, the newspaper of the teachers' union, *Uchitel'skaia gazeta,* found that teachers, local officials, and common Russians rejected central dictate. The newspaper often presented this unflattering reality in the form of cartoons submitted by its staff and by teachers. Several of these items are reproduced in the pages that follow.

The influence of practice on policy cannot be authenticated by referring only to resistance below and policy shifts in apparent response to it. The opportunity to document such a relationship came with access to the Narkompros archives, which reveal Narkompros's growing awareness of what transpired in the classroom and its determination to reach an accommodation with it.

My work is limited in scope. Schools in a non-Russian area or in a specific location in the Russian Republic might be examined to discover their own ways of coping with Moscow's directives and problems facing the schools. The potential value of the choice, I suspect, would depend primarily on availability of archival documents. Experimental schools that purportedly applied the radical curriculum of the 1920s merit study to determine the reasons for their sustained effort, for the level of any success attained, and for the influence they may have had on schools nearby. Finally, when Party archives are opened, scholars will learn much more about the Party's response to perceived and actual developments below.

Four parts follow. The first, second, and fourth conform to generally acknowledged periods in Soviet history: 1917–1921, 1921–1928, and 1928–1931. The third focuses on the late 1920s to emphasize the compromises reached at that time among competing educational interests.

The thematic organization of each part necessitates some sacrifice of chronological continuity. In an effort to focus on the reciprocal relationship between policy and practice, each part interweaves a discussion of the two. Brief chapters (chapters 3 and 10) present the educational program of Narkompros's institutional competitors, the Young Communist League and the technical lobby. Chapter 11 assesses the school system from several Soviet perspectives. It serves as a conceptual bridge spanning moderate curricula adopted at the close of the New Economic Policy and the changes that followed during the Cultural Revolution. A compromise between Narkompros and teachers in 1926 and 1927, a development of great significance to this study, further convinced some Soviet authorities that the school system had failed the revolution. Subsequent policies destroyed that compromise and its promise for the future.

Part One.

The Idea and the Reality, 1917–1921

Get into line. Shake out the banners.
And sing revolutionary Hosannas.
Into the sun and trumpets, carrying flowers.
And the road seemed clear ahead to the
    Commune.

How could he know, with his Cossack top-
    knot,
so easily deciding life in advance,
that for us it wasn't going to be so simple:
how know the weight and mass of the
    complications?

—Evtushenko, "Zima Junction"

Absence of Central Funding

"A fastidious bride or . . . seven years without requital." The suitor is Lunacharsky representing Narkompros (Narkompros is written on his jacket); the bride, G. Ia. Sokol'nikov, commissar of Finance (Narkomfin is written on his dress). The bride remains unmoved by the suitor, who pleads his case in front of a safe labeled "finances."

SOURCE: *Uchitel'skaia gazeta,* no. 2 (74) (January 14, 1926), p. 1.

I.

A NEW SCHOOL FOR A NEW SOCIETY

Many Bolsheviks believed the October Revolution heralded the beginning of a new era in human history. It took an immense faith in themselves and their ideology to face so boldly the challenges that lay immediately ahead. The Commissariat of Enlightenment (Narkompros) sought nothing less than a reshaping of human behavior and society through education. The ideology that ignited this grand undertaking would long sustain it in the face of difficult material conditions and opposition from parents and teachers.

An Ideology of Education

Bolsheviks were not alone in embracing new ideas and approaches. In the late nineteenth and early twentieth centuries, Charles Darwin, Karl Marx, William James, Sigmund Freud, and Friedrich Nietzsche challenged old assumptions about human nature and society. They emphasized human dependence on impersonal forces as well as the capacity of humans to control their environment. Pedagogy was no less in ferment. Here the result was more uniform—an optimistic belief in the ability of the school to mold pupils into active agents capable of changing their community and nation. Edward Thorndike, Georg Kerschensteiner, John Dewey, and Maria Montessori called for an education appropriate to the child's interests and relevant to the surrounding community. They advocated the study of hygiene, domestic science, and manual and industrial arts, sought less reliance on subjects isolated one from the other, and rejected classroom drill and harsh codes of conduct.[1]

These same ideas were expressed in Russia by N. I. Pirogov, P. A. Kropotkin, K. D. Ushinsky, L. N. Tolstoy, I. I. Gorbunov-Posadov, K. D. Ventssel, and S. T. Shatsky.[2] After 1917, Krupskaya, Lunacharsky and other prominent figures in the Commissariat of Enlightenment hoped to devise policies to match. Unlike many of their progressive Russian and Western colleagues, however, they opposed instruction in religion, nationalism, and "bourgeois" morality. Moreover, they insisted that the school's primary function was the complete transformation of society. Narkompros wanted nothing less than a world of fundamentally-altered structures and values.[3]

Marxism supplied much of the inspiration for the new Soviet school and the persevering commitment to its transformationist role. Although Marx and Engels wrote no separate treatise on education, they proposed locally controlled public schools which would offer a secular and free education to all children regardless of class.[4] Their vision of a highly industrialized society emphasized the special importance of labor training, but left some of their followers in doubt as to what was meant. Engels called for an "industrial education"; Marx spoke of the need for "technical instruction, both theoretical and practical," and for the "early combination of production labor with education."[5]

Marx and Engels were more precise when it came to discussing the ultimate purpose of education. They insisted that schools become agents for the remaking of *all* human beings. Public education in a socialist society would mirror and shape a glorious future, free of prejudice and alienation of the individual from his or her own labor. By teaching and by example, Engels asserted in 1847, the school could abolish social classes and end the antagonism between town and country.[6] In 1869, Marx made the point in a dialectical fashion. "On the one hand, a change of social circumstances is required to establish a proper system of education. On the other hand, a proper system of education is required to bring about a change of social circumstances."[7]

It was quite a legacy to leave to any Marxist educator—an exciting canvas of the future done in sweeping strokes of various hues, not all of them distinct. It failed to specify the degree to which labor instruction was to be polytechnical or more specialized, i.e., technical or frankly vocational.[8] If, when discussing education, Marx and Engels thought of a peaceful transformation of society, they were not so sure when it came to other subjects. On these occasions, they often resorted to a vastly different vocabulary of class warfare and violence. Future Marxists, therefore, might reach different conclusions about the role of schools in a socialist society.

So it was in the infant Soviet Republic. The first Commissar of Enlightenment, Anatoly Vasil'evich Lunacharsky, believed that the school should become in its structure, curriculum, and student body a microcosm of a future classless society. The educational system would lead to a cultural awakening among all citizens and create a new order, the image of the school writ large. Other Bolsheviks, especially those outside the Commissariat of Enlightenment, demanded that schools become partisan agents of the dictatorship of the proletariat.

Conflicting Visions

Born in 1875, the son of a government official, Lunacharsky graduated from a gymnasium in Kiev and studied philosophy under Richard Avenarius at Zurich University. Lunacharsky concluded that ideology was valuable insofar as it could inspire people to change themselves and their environment. His first volume of *Religion and Socialism,* published in 1908, stated that Marxism, as a scientific religion, possessed such lofty powers. Driven by emotional and ethical fervor, its converts, the proletariat, would metaphorically become God, save themselves, and create a new world. Lenin objected to Lunacharsky's "God-building" as an underestimation of the importance of political power. Lunacharsky clung tenaciously to his beliefs and bolted from the Bolshevik ranks in 1908, not to return until August 1917.[9]

A bureaucrat neither in training nor in spirit, Lunacharsky nevertheless welcomed the opportunity to head Narkompros, vent his own commitment, and inspire the same from others. He put it eloquently at the Third Congress of the Young Communist League (Komsomol) in October 1920. The Soviet school would create a new person—informed, sensitive, useful, and thoroughly imbued with the human and communist spirit.[10] "Our first and basic credo is to create a real united labor school; this must be our catechism."[11] Less than a year later, Lunacharsky enthusiastically declared that the school would "take fresh, small hearts and bright, open, little minds [and make], given the right educational approach, a true miracle ... a real human being."[12] Teachers were, therefore, "living through the miracle of humanity's transformation" and theirs was a "sacred calling."[13] The same speech referred to a school open to all children as "really a non-class school."[14] Despite ensuing disappointments, Lunacharsky retained this faith in education until the end of his tenure as commissar in 1929. When the First Five-Year Plan glorified economic change, Lunacharsky still insisted on the creation of a "new kind of human being" as an essential prerequisite for economic and political progress.[15]

In difficult times, Lunacharsky looked excitedly to the future. His assistant at the Commissariat, Nadezhda Konstantinovna Krupskaya, helped him to do so. Born in 1869 in St. Petersburg, the daughter of a military officer, Krupskaya completed a women's gymnasium in 1887, where she remained a teaching assistant until 1891. A Marxist from about 1890, she met Lenin four years later and married him in Siberian exile in 1898. Education remained one of her consuming interests. She was widely read on the subject, and completed her own significant work, *Narodnoe obrazovanie i demokratiia* (Public Education and Democracy), in 1915. Appointed the first Deputy Commissar of the new Commissariat of Enlightenment, she resigned the post in May 1918, but stayed on as an active member of the Commissariat's collegium. In 1921, she became the official most responsible for development of school curricula. In this capacity she founded an important periodical, *Na putiakh k novoi shkole* (On the Paths to the New School), which she edited until its demise in 1933.

Krupskaya's view of education was more politicized than Lunacharsky's. She insisted that schools transmit political propaganda—a view consistent with her Commissariat post as head of the Chief Committee for Political

Education (Glavpolitprosvet). Yet, like Lunacharsky, Krupskaya believed the school should serve as a "model of the future classless society."[16] When the First Five-Year Plan promoted a virulent notion of class struggle, she held that the school as an institution promised something different. In 1929, she labelled efforts to expel children of hostile class elements as a "throw-back to the Middle Ages."[17] Schools were to be open to all children because "we stand for a classless society."[18]

The founder and head of the Bolshevik Party, Vladimir Il'ich Lenin, approached social change and education in a manner different than Lunacharsky and Krupskaya. He looked to political power rather than enlightenment as the primary means for making the future. Lenin emphasized the practicality of his argument in *What Is to Be Done,* and its ideological orthodoxy in a 1914 essay on Marx.[19] The 1917 revolution, the Civil War, and foreign intervention reinforced his preoccupation with politics. While Lunacharsky and Krupskaya turned to creating a society free of conflict, Lenin remained immersed in a struggle over power.

On several occasions, Lunacharsky and Lenin presented contrasting points of view in the same forum. At the First All-Russian Congress of Enlightenment in August 1918, Lunacharsky spoke metaphorically of schools as temples dedicated to the abolition of class culture and the creation of a humane society.[20] Two days later, Lenin countered that education was an extension of politics. "We openly declare that it is ... hypocritical to say that the school is outside of life, outside of politics."[21] Lenin proceeded to equate schooling with the acquisition of useful technical skills and knowledge, rather than with cultural regeneration. Two years later, on October 2, 1920, at the Third Komsomol Congress, Lunacharsky referred to the school as a brotherhood for the teaching of a human and communist spirit.[22] That same day, Lenin asked delegates to undertake the disciplined study necessary for the development of industry, agriculture, and electrification.[23]

Lenin understood the importance of changing people's attitudes. Frederic Lilge has pointed to Lenin's disdain for ineffective political indoctrination.[24] The differences separating Lenin from Lunacharsky and Krupskaya, therefore, were a matter of emphasis. Like them, he could conceive of social transformation through attitudinal change. In late 1920 and early 1921, Lenin spoke of labor unions as "schools of communism," in which the proletariat is taught the proper skills and attitudes. Near the end of his life, he thought of the Party's highest organs in like fashion. Faced with an uncooperative majority on the Central Committee, Lenin proposed adding workers who would grow on the job, acquire both knowledge and culture, and put an end to the "cancer of bureaucratism."[25] But for Lenin, in the final analysis, political power coupled with technology would best propel Russia forward. In his last years, he turned to electrification as the agent for the transformation of nature and society.[26] His introduction to I. I. Skvortsov-Stepanov's *Electrification of the Russian Republic in Connection with the Transitional Phase of the World's Economy* (Moscow, 1922) promoted the book's use in every classroom.[27] This was education as it should be, directly in the service of grandiose economic change. Lenin too could dream.

All these contrasting dreams among Bolsheviks reflected a diversity in Russian visionary thought that went beyond differences of opinion over Marxism. Richard Stites points out that for years, a utopian current calling for popular and spontaneous action from below coexisted with an equally utopian notion of an ordered society imposed from above. Socialism combined elements of both.[28] James C. McClelland finds similar trends within the Bolshevik Party from 1917 to 1921—utopianism and revolutionary heroism. The former advocated a psychological transformation of the masses as a prerequisite for building socialism; the latter, a crash program of economic development for the same purpose.[29] Lunacharsky and Krupskaya represented the first; Lenin tended toward the second. It was questionable whether these competing currents could coexist within the same political party. The extent to which they both survived to dominate discussions of school policy was remarkable indeed.

II.

IN SEARCH OF A POLICY

A New System

The Commissariat of Enlightenment wasted no time in opening an assault on all forms of alleged ignorance. Its attack came on a wide front—from nurseries to universities in the regular school system to vocational schools and institutions for adult education. Enjoying the brief luxury of devising policies to suit philosophy rather than reality, Narkompros adopted the most ambitious projects. The Soviet of People's Commissars (Sovnarkom) gave it the opportunity to proceed by ordering the transfer of elementary, secondary, and higher educational institutions to the Commissariat's jurisdiction.[1]

At one end of the educational spectrum, Narkompros planned a network of preschool institutions and special schools for the mentally and physically handicapped.[2] At the other, it abolished all fees and entrance examinations at higher educational institutions, so that anyone sixteen years of age could now enter.[3] In 1919, Narkompros further encouraged workers and peasants to seek a higher education by creating the first of many preparatory workers' faculties (rabfaks). To highlight its importance, Lunacharsky and M. N. Pokrovsky, Deputy Commissar of Enlightenment and Party historian, attended the opening ceremonies.[4]

At the primary and secondary school level, Narkompros took dramatic initiatives and expected equally dramatic success. It began with a "Declaration on the United Labor School," signed by Lunacharsky and published in *Pravda* on October 16, 1918, and a "Statement on the United Labor School," approved earlier on September 30 by the All-Russian Central Executive Committee.[5] These two documents introduced the United Labor School as the critical element in a single system "from the kindergarten to the university, serving as one school, one uninterrupted ladder."[6] Narkompros announced it would replace all vocational schools, gymnasiums, realschulen, lower and higher elementary schools, and commercial schools with a single co-educational institution. This new school would consist of an elementary division of five years and a secondary division of four years.[7] Whereas the constitution of the Russian Republic, adopted on July 10, 1918, promised a free education for children of workers and the poor peasantry, the Commissariat's Declaration promised free and compulsory schooling for *all* children eight to seventeen years of age.[8] To entice and keep the young, schools were to provide free paper, pencils, hot breakfasts, shoes, clothing, and physical examinations.[9] As a further incentive to parents and children of the poor, the Commissariat's Department for the United Labor School introduced a mild form of discrimination in 1919. It recommended that these children be assigned to schools housed in the buildings of former secondary institutions, while children of the well-to-do might be placed in the sparer surroundings of former elementary schools.[10]

Narkompros harbored no illusions about the extent to which local communities could support schools financially. It initially planned that Moscow shoulder the burden.[11] However, Narkompros expected active local involvement so that education could achieve its broad social objectives. Within days of the October revolution, all schools were transferred to the jurisdiction of local soviets.[12] In early 1918, Lunacharsky hoped to arouse community interest by creating special educational soviets to administer local schools. Opposed to a diminution in the authority of its regular soviets, the Commissariat of the Interior succeeded in limiting Narkompros's new creation to an advisory role.[13] Undaunted, Narkompros found another way to stimulate local initiative. It mandated that the governing body of each school— the school council—include workers and peasants as well as teachers and senior pupils.[14] The Commissariat even planned for the creation of advisory councils of workers within its own central apparatus. A brief appearance was made by at least one council associated with the Extramural Department.[15]

Methods

Narkompros issued a flurry of directives to annihilate the distinction between physical and mental labor that Marx had found so abhorrent; to make learning a joyful and relevant exercise; and to produce well-rounded, energetic, and politically loyal citizens. It began with the Declaration and Statement on the United Labor School, each of which proclaimed the dawn of polytechnical and labor education. These terms had not been uniformly understood, but for the moment, disputants reached a broad consensus.[16] Polytechnical education came to mean the physical, psychological, intellectual, aesthetic, and social development of children—and not preparation for a specific trade. Narkompros would not allow any technical education before the age of fourteen.[17] Labor meant activity in a school workshop, school garden plot, or factory as a means of becoming acquainted with conventional technology and techniques of agricultural and industrial production. Inside the classroom and beyond, children would learn as active participants— caring for plants and animals; working with cardboard, wood, metal, or leather; and operating tools and machines. The same approach extended to other subjects. Nature walks were critical to biology; excursions to social studies; and modelling, drawing, and singing to the fine arts.

Subjects lost much of their significance in a rush to center instruction around the more relevant areas of labor, nature, and society. For the elementary grades, the Declaration proclaimed an end to "boundaries separating subjects . . . [by means of] lessons amounting to one great almost undifferentiated subject: a working knowledge of the natural and social environment surrounding the child."[18] It allowed language, science, mathematics, and the social sciences to be taught in the secondary grades only as long as the primary concern remained the study of "human culture in connection with nature."[19]

Narkompros believed that self-motivation and self-discipline could replace compulsory measures at school. Lunacharsky banned marks; the Declaration abolished entrance, promotion, and graduation examinations, homework, and all forms of punishment.[20] Pupils gained the right to send representatives to the school's administrative organs and to select by lot their own group leaders for clean-up, games, choirs, and orchestras. Thus liberated from the shackles of the past and freed from adult authority, pupils would react responsibly.[21] Such was the Narkompros faith in human nature and in the power of the new school.

A New Curriculum

While Narkompros required new methods, it avoided dictating the specific content of education. In 1918 and 1919, it refrained from issuing a weekly timetable, nor did it release syllabi in the usual sense. Rather, it prepared general non-obligatory guidelines with scant concern for content. Draft syllabi issued in 1918 did little more than suggest the study of local and contemporary issues.[22] History classes acquainted pupils not with facts but with "the spirit of each epoch";[23] the study of language centered around classroom use of the local dialect, the performance of plays and songs, and the inscription of objects pupils themselves made;[24] and natural sciences focused on the care of plants and animals.[25] Narkompros suggested a school museum to assist instruction in local speech and the natural sciences.[26]

Even these timid efforts provoked criticism. Members of the Commissariat's Department for the United Labor School and Department of School Reform opposed guidelines for any subject.[27] However, Narkompros continued to prepare them, publishing a new set in 1919 under the title "Materials for Educational Work in the Labor School." Although somewhat more detailed than drafts of the preceding year, the "Materials" remained brief and non-obligatory attempts to encourage activity methods and to promote relevance. The publication for mathematics, only sixteen pages in length, dismissed a "volume of knowledge as [having] no real significance for the school; far more important is the method by which the material is studied."[28] Its authors almost apologized for this modest effort when they observed that schools need not designate a specific number of hours for mathematics or teach it as an independent subject.[29] Arithmetic meant measuring a nearby field, calculating the volume of various containers made at school, and charting the growth of production and population.[30] Aesthetics sought to inspire a love of music, beginning with folk songs, and an appreciation for the collective (the choir and orchestra).[31] For art, Narkompros suggested that pupils make a virtue out of necessity by manufacturing their own paints and brushes.[32] The guideline for nature study (mirovedenie) urged activity in a garden, field, or shop.[33]

The model curriculum and syllabi released in 1920 continued the appeal for an activities-oriented course of study.[34] The art syllabus for the secondary school suggested an acquaintance with "material culture," defined as a working knowledge of the materials, instruments, and methods of production.[35] The study of history was limited to developments leading to the 1917 revolution.[36] The language syllabus, however, revealed a willingness to pay more attention to content. It listed specific skills to be taught for each elementary grade in reading, writing, and speech.[37] The curriculum recommended a specific number of hours for the instruction of individual subjects in the second through the ninth grades. Approximately 40 percent of the time would be devoted to mathematics and science, and a similar block was set aside for the humanities and social sciences.[38]

Many provincial departments of education shared Moscow's concern for relevance and activity methods. The "General Tasks and Plan of Study" released in late 1918 by the Moscow Department of Education cautioned against the study of language and mathematics for their own sake. The basic subject should be "not language or arithmetic but life, the surrounding world."[39] Instructions from the Viatka and Malmyzh departments of education in 1918 contrasted the teaching of a body of knowledge with an approach stimulating a child's curiosity and powers of observation.[40] The Malmyzh program for elementary schools advised against a history of tsars and wars, preferring instead a focus on the struggle against autocracy.[41] In 1919, the Penza Department of Education limited its effort to a republication of Narkompros's "Materials for Educational Work in the Labor School."[42] One year later, the Novonikolaevsk Department of Education argued against grammar study at the expense of "living speech" and the local vernacular.[43]

Other departments of education were not so cooperative. Some demanded a more systematic approach, while others favored less concern for content. In the fall of 1918, the Petrograd Department of Education released a model plan combining new and traditional features. It recommended that schools function seven days a week, with two days (Thursday and Sunday) devoted to non-academic pursuits (dramatic productions, excursions, singing, and sports). A traditional program was suggested for the remaining five days. The department issued a timetable specifying the number of weekly hours allotted to eight subjects in grades two through five, and to sixteen subjects in grades six through nine. It included instructions for teaching an ever-expanding volume of skills and knowledge, culminating in the eighth and ninth grades with a specialization in either the humanities or natural sciences and mathematics.[44] In sharp contrast, the Moscow Department of Education's model program of 1920 rejected conventional subjects in the first three grades in favor of thematic study, aesthetic training, games, and handicrafts.[45]

The Commissariat of Enlightenment and its departments of education recommended policy. It was a simple matter of debate, decree, curricula, and expectation of change to follow. As it turned out, teachers and parents were not so cooperative, and Narkompros would prove incapable of controlling either them or events.

III.

IN SEARCH OF A SCHOOL AND A PUBLIC

The Commissariat's plans derived from an optimistic estimate of the means at its disposal and the plasticity of the people it hoped to transform. It possessed the vision; before it lay the immense task of finding the teachers, parents, pupils, and materials to make it reality.

While the Declaration on the United Labor School acknowledged serious shortages, it hoped that more funding and a massive teacher training program would make the new school possible.[1] The situation turned out to be worse than expected. No one had anticipated the devastation that accompanied the Civil War. Most important of all, Narkompros leaders woefully underestimated the extent of popular resistance to its policies.

The Past

The naiveté dominant at Narkompros stemmed, in part, from its leaders' focus on the future. An irreverent attitude toward history reflected the self-image of the Narkompros leadership—individuals challenging the past and storming the future. While it inspired bold action, this innovative spirit led to an exaggerated sense of the novelty of the Commissariat's policies. As a result, Narkompros failed to use recent developments to full advantage.[2]

Attempts to extend educational opportunities to the entire population, regardless of class status, gender, or national origin, had begun prior to the revolution. From 1900 to the beginning of World War I, the number of elementary schools and their pupils more than doubled. Also seeing impressive growth were gymnasiums offering either Greek or Latin or both, realschulen with a modern secondary curriculum, and urban schools. A dramatic increase in funds was allotted to education by the Ministry of Education, rural organs of local government (zemstvos), and municipalities. By 1914, educational support was provided by an unprecedented 4.4 percent of the State's budget, and over 30 percent and 13 percent came from all zemstvo and municipal budgets, respectively. In matters of curriculum, increased attention went to mathematics, science, and modern foreign languages. Manual labor became a subject of interest, valued for its contribution to the development of the well-rounded individual.[3]

The Commissariat's control over all types of schools proceeded along lines established by the Provisional Government's transfer of vocational and elementary schools receiving State funds to the Ministry of Education. Plans for local control of education matched what many teachers, principals, and a growing portion of the educated public had been advocating since 1900. On the eve of the October Revolution, the Provisional Government's State Committee for Education prepared a bill permitting boards of community leaders, parents, and senior pupils to administer secondary schools. Finally, the Commissariat's proposal for a single educational system reflected currents evident from the turn of the century. A number of such schemes came from the Ministry of Education, the last and most comprehensive of which was issued in 1916 by Count Paul N. Ignatiev, the Minister of Education. It proposed a single secondary school consisting of a junior division with a three-year common curriculum, and a four-year senior division with classical, humanities, and natural sciences tracks.

The Commissariat intended a bold departure from the past. Its concept of a united labor school outstripped anything contemplated earlier. With one sweep of the proletariat's collective hand, Narkompros sought to create a single path from the nursery to the university. Neither the Declaration, nor the Statement on the United Labor School, nor early Sovnarkom decrees allowed for vocational schools to compete with the United Labor School. Similarly, the Commissariat intended to accelerate developments by: banning Greek, Latin, and religious instruction; placing reliance on activity methods and labor training; allowing extensive local control over schools; and requiring nine years of compulsory education. In the context of Russian history, only the efforts of individual reformers and their experimental schools provided a historical basis for such ambitious policies.

Narkompros was inspired by the work of Stanislav Teofilovich Shatsky (1878–1934). A graduate of a classical gymnasium and Moscow University, Shatsky found instruction at both places boring and irrelevant. Committed to providing the next generation with a different experience, he organized a summer colony for juvenile boys near Moscow in 1905. A club and kindergarten were added the next year. The "Settlement," as the entire enterprise came to be known, attracted private donations as well as funds from the Ministry of Education. However, municipal authorities forced its closure in 1908. Shatsky responded by forming in Moscow a Society for Children's Life and Leisure that included a kindergarten and elementary school. In 1911, he added a children's summer colony, "The Cheerful Life," in Kaluga, which, with the help of funds from the Ministry of Education, included kindergartens, schools, and facilities for adult education. Here, as in earlier efforts, Shatsky insisted on developing each individual's aesthetic, mental, and physical abilities. The colony combined academic subjects with excursions, gymnastics, metalwork, bookbinding, sewing, farming, animal husbandry, and kitchen and janitorial duties.[4]

But Shatsky was no Bolshevik. It was a measure of the difficulty facing Lunacharsky that he could not initially count on Shatsky, who spurned the offer of a post at Narkompros.[5] Shatsky later reported that he withdrew to his work, distrustful of the Bolsheviks because of his educated background, his opposition to mixing education with politics, and his belief that the Communist Party was bent on destruction.[6] However, two years later, Shatsky and Narkompros joined forces when his colony became the Commissariat's First Experimental Station.[7] By the mid-1920s, the Station encompassed two secondary schools, fifteen elementary schools, four kindergartens, and a two-year teachers college (technicum).

The Present

Shatsky's experimental school was an important but isolated venture. Narkompros had visions of transforming all schools at once, but it found that first it had to save them from total collapse. Despite substantial progress in education since 1900, Narkompros inherited a terrible situation. In 1913, over 60 percent of the population over eight years of age could neither read nor write.[8] Between 1914 and 1917, funding of elementary education by the Ministry of Education and zemstvos decreased; increased spending on secondary education went primarily to raise teachers' salaries, which actually declined because of inflation. Many schools suffered from shortages of paper, books, ink, and pencils.[9] The 1917 Revolution and the Civil War created more shortages. Equally as devastating, class warfare and military conflict betrayed the rosy vision of human nature cherished by Narkompros and brutalized the very people and institutions it had hoped to ennoble.

Lunacharsky discovered that not only Shatsky regarded Bolsheviks as thugs. Officials and staff at the Ministry of Education refused to work for the new Commissariat. The Petrograd and Moscow branches of the All-Russian Teachers Union went on strike. Many instructors in Moscow remained off the job until March.[10] In other areas, local soviets and Party officials used the Commissariat's call in February 1918 for election of teachers to harass those who stayed in the classroom. Teachers frequently were not paid the salaries promised them, yet Narkompros expected them to revise their instruction in the face of tremendous obstacles.

Narkompros's own survey in 1919 discovered that teachers were not aware of plans for the new school.[11] That same year a report from Tver noted that they remained ignorant of new methods.[12] Confronted with the same problem in Western Siberia, the Novonikolaevsk Department of Education dispatched its representatives to European Russia to buy some of the new pedagogical literature.[13] Years later, a secondary teacher, A. Tolstov, reported that even when materials from the center arrived, it was no cause for rejoicing. The Commissariat's programs and explanatory notes were printed on poor gray-blue paper with dozens of lines missing. Even when read with care, the content tended to confuse most teachers. Many of the first books on the labor school had the same effect.[14]

Teachers refused to introduce anything like the new curriculum, even when they understood it. Some of them simply did not want the added burdens involved;[15] many lacked the experience and training necessary for a new approach. Detailed surveys of Ul'ianovsk and Novgorod provinces in 1920 revealed that about half of the teachers were twenty-five years of age or younger and had four years of experience or less, while 70 percent had never attended a higher educational institution or received any kind of pedagogical training. In Novgorod, 18 percent had not advanced beyond a seminary (secondary school).[16] Surveying its own activity during the three years since the revolution, Narkompros admitted that the nation's instructors, especially in the secondary schools, were incapable of creating the new school.[17]

Those instructors who attempted progressive methods ran the considerable risk of antagonizing the local population, especially in rural areas. Parents opposed any departure from a traditional presentation of reading, writing, and arithmetic, subjects deemed far more useful than aesthetic training and excursions.[18] Adults sometimes displayed aggressive initiative, but not as Narkompros had hoped. Instead, they rushed to the defense of religion. Efforts by teachers to remove religion from the classroom provoked threats of physical violence.[19] In December 1918, parents surrounded a school in Spasskoe, a village not far from Nizhnii Novgorod, demanding to take their children home because the Antichrist was on his way to rob pupils of their crosses.[20] Parents at other schools called upon teachers to accompany children to church and collect money for the church's coffers.[21]

When given the opportunity to become acquainted with Narkompros plans, teachers raised serious professional objections. On the eve of the 1918 school year, a commission of Malmyzh teachers insisted on a curriculum for elementary grades that assigned a precise number of hours per week for each of seven subjects. Taking Narkompros rhetoric to task, they equated a "pursuit of an encyclopedia of knowledge" with superficial instruction, and objected to phraseology critical of memorization and the study of grammar.[22]

In the summer of 1919, Krupskaya witnessed Narkompros's ineffectiveness when she visited teachers, parents, and schools during a six-week trip through the Volga-Kama region. She discovered that in cases where teachers and officials might have sympathized with educational reform, appropriate instructions from higher authorities were not forthcoming, or, if sent, were never received. Ignorance of the labor school prevailed in many cases.[23] One particular instance distressed her. In Osa, a town with 12,000 inhabitants, the local department of education received instructions from Perm' provincial authorities, demanding to know how many schools were under its jurisdiction, to be classified by the pre-revolutionary categories of seminaries, gymnasiums, and realschulen.[24] In another case, military authorities occupied school buildings while barracks nearby remained empty.[25] Krupskaya's mood went from bad to worse when she found that most teachers resented Bolshevik rule and Narkompros's plans. They opposed innovations in teaching methods and the curriculum, scorned labor as a subject, and refused to share authority with their pupils or the local population.[26] Those few instructors who did favor Narkompros's initiatives could not elicit public support nor could they find time to recast their own instruction while burdened with the anti-illiteracy campaign and other civic duties.[27] When Krupskaya asked about icons found hanging in schools, teachers explained that the religious objects were left there to avoid irritating the local populace.[28]

Material Conditions

Krupskaya should not have expected better results, if for no other reason than Narkompros could not support the very people it called into action. The best-intentioned, the most imaginative and courageous of teachers could not overcome the lack of material support. Narkompros did not possess the funds necessary to provide any kind of education, progressive or otherwise. In 1920, it released a sobering account of its brief tenure. Narkompros managed to boast that its share of the total State budget had risen from about 6.5 percent in 1918 to 11 percent in 1920, an increase from three billion to 114 billion rubles, making Narkompros the fourth-best funded commissariat in the Russian Republic.[29] But it observed that these promised funds frequently never reached their destination, and the Commissariat did not know what the State actually distributed to schools and teachers.[30]

Public education lacked materials essential to basic instruction. A 1919 investigation of 323 schools in 23 provinces, surveys carried out late the following year at schools in Novgorod and Orlov provinces, and a yearbook for the 1920/21 school year prepared by the Central Statistical Administration revealed horrendous shortages of everything imaginable. Urban and rural schools badly needed teachers, space, furniture, laboratory instruments, paper, pencils, notebooks, textbooks, visual aids, shops, gardens, food for both pupils and teachers, kerosene, and firewood.[31] The 1920 Narkompros account admitted that over a period of six months, the Commissariat could provide only one pencil for sixty pupils, one quill pen (pero) for twenty-two, one fountain pen (ruchka) for twelve, one notebook for two, and one inkwell for 100.[32] Such conditions required heroic measures: teachers and pupils manufactured ink from sugar beets and wrote on whitewashed walls with coal or on old posters with charred ends of sticks.[33] Schools in the capital fared no better, lacking fuel, space, pencils, and books.[34] A report in 1919 indicated that Moscow's schools provided breakfasts for pupils and teachers, but an appraisal a year later found that much of the food was inedible and refused by hungry children.[35] Narkompros officials experienced many of these same difficulties. At work, they ate a thin, clear broth pretentiously called soup.[36] During the winter of 1919, members of the Commissariat's Section for Professional Education wore coats while working in their cold offices. On their way out each day, they grabbed a stack of pre-revolutionary documents to fuel a handwarmer (burzhuika) at home, their only source of heat.[37]

Labor training remained an empty promise because of shortages of materials, tools, and machines. Krupskaya came across a school with a sizable plot of land, but no horse or plow with which to work it.[38] The Novgorod study lamented that schools with space for shops had no equipment.[39] Narkompros had hoped that factories would give schools these items and provide senior students with opportunities for a practicum. Neither proved possible. Industry and entire urban areas had their own, more immediate, goal—survival. During the Civil War, one-fourth to one-third of the population left many cities in search of work and food. By August 1920, Moscow had lost one-half and Petrograd two-thirds of their inhabitants. Under such circumstances, surviving factories were not inclined to equip schools or to take on the nuisance, at its best, of introducing pupils to the workbench.[40]

Narkompros could not create any kind of inspection network to encourage teachers to adopt a new outlook. Of the three inspectors it dispatched in 1918, two disappeared and the third misunderstood his instructions.[41] Although the situation had improved somewhat three years later, many inspectors refused to visit schools.[42] They had good reason. Like many of the teachers they were expected to help, they went hungry and did not receive their pay in full or on time. They also lacked the means of transportation to get from one district to another.[43] Their problems began before they reported for duty. In 1921, a young student in one of the courses that trained inspectors wrote to Narkompros requesting a blanket, or materials to make one, so that he might endure life in his inadequately heated room.[44] Only the passage of time could make the thought of such experiences bearable. Years later, school inspector N. Naumov waxed sentimental about his work in 1919 and 1920. He reported how, in the autumn, he covered his route "barefoot, with stick in hand and boots slung across my shoulders, [stopping] to rest in a picturesque place."[45]

Failure

In its own defense, Narkompros pointed to official statistics indicating that the number of elementary and secondary schools and their enrollments remained constant, perhaps exceeding slightly the pre-war totals.[46] These figures poorly reflected reality. Many schools barely functioned, if at all. Surveys in 1919 and 1920 found that schools did not open until the end of October or as late as December because of shortages, hunger, and epidemics. At least one-third of the schools functioned poorly during the winter months.[47] Pupils stayed away in droves because of epidemics, a search for food, the distance from home to school, and work at home. Absenteeism was especially telling during spring planting, when anywhere from 40 to 70 percent of the students failed to attend.[48] Skeptical of the benefit of labor at school, parents preferred that children work at home. Krupskaya encountered one school, apparently fortunate enough to have a garden plot and requisite equipment, resorting to hired labor.[49]

The much heralded educational soviets failed to develop. Krupskaya looked for them during her journey and eventually concluded that they did not exist.[50] Labor training, when it was offered at all, was often limited to such tasks as cleaning and repairing the school, hauling water, and collecting firewood.[51] Narkompros had encouraged the performance of such chores, but only as components of a larger package of more complex assignments in a shop, school, garden, or factory.[52] By this standard, Narkompros could point to few successes, and those were largely limited to the area of handicrafts.[53] It took a group of Malmyzh teachers to observe that such a simple "labor task" as tracking at home the amount of daylight over a year's time proved impossible because most families did not possess clocks.[54]

Narkompros directives notwithstanding, schools remained what they had been before the revolution. Teachers relied on the familiar mix of homework, dictation, marks, pre-revolutionary textbooks, and coercion.[55] Schools with an unusual amount of supplies and equipment adhered to this norm.[56] In Tver province, institutions retained their pre-revolutionary labels of lower elementary schools, gymnasiums, and realschulen. It was more than poetic license, for they refused to implement coeducation or to end religious instruction.[57]

Two examples illustrate the extent to which classroom instruction defied Narkompros intentions. In early 1919, the *Biulleten'* of the Moscow Department of Education featured a ringing indictment.[58] It came in the form of a letter, "Is It Really Necessary," from a woman who, upon hearing of the new education based on a child's "creativity and initiative," had placed her son in school. The results disappointed her. She complained that teachers assigned huge quantities of homework, much of it amounting to copying pages from a text, and required standard arithmetical exercises. Rarely did pupils sing or perform gymnastics, but they recited prayers after lessons. Her son was tired and bored with it all. Two years later, a Narkompros investigation of a State children's home revealed that the "old methods," the "old programs of the gymnasium," and, overall, the "old school" dominated. Language study focused on grammar; arithmetic on multiplication tables; and history on biographical, political, and military facts in chronological order. The report put the situation in the best possible light by concluding that "the impression of the school is a positive one if one ignores school lessons."[59]

Narkompros began with plans for nine years of universal education; it had to settle for considerably less. Of all children eligible for the elementary grades, only 25 percent of the boys and 40 percent of the girls were attending school in Novgorod in 1920.[60] A report released by Narkompros in 1925 reaffirmed what had been well known previously—that throughout the Russian Republic from 1919 to 1922 universal elementary education was nothing more than a fantasy. On the average, children received only 2.4 years of education (2.3 in rural and 3.1 in urban areas).[61] In rural schools one-third of all students did not advance to the second grade; in urban areas, 17 percent did not do so. Only 23 percent of the boys and 15 percent of the girls who entered the first grade in rural areas completed four years of education. In urban regions, slightly more than half of both genders finished a four-year course.[62]

This modest success, however, came only after many pupils repeated one or more grades. In 1920, one out of five pupils in elementary schools was taking a grade for a second time.[63] Their tenacity, a source of great hope, proved nevertheless to be a costly venture at a time when public education had few resources at its disposal.

The Declaration on the United Labor School typified the effort of the

Commissariat of Enlightenment from 1917 to 1921. A charming but rambling document, its plans ran rudely afoul of reality. Shortages, hunger, disease, a climate of violence, and the resistance of teachers and parents prevented implementation of the Commissariat's program and imperiled the philosophy behind it.

By 1920, Narkompros could point with pride to its vision, still largely intact, but not to any substantial realization of it. Not unexpectedly, Narkompros would have to endure serious criticism.

IV.

NARKOMPROS UNDER SIEGE

The Commissariat of Enlightenment found itself challenged at all levels. Below, local departments of education issued curricula that departed from central guidelines, while teachers adhered to traditional methods preferred by parents. Above, economic agencies, organized labor, and the Young Communist League attacked Narkompros for ignoring technical and vocational training. By 1920, the Soviet of People's Commissars (Sovnarkom), the Party's Central Committee, and Lenin criticized Narkompros. It was they—and not teachers and parents—who forced changes in policy.

The Technical Lobby

From November 1917 to the middle of 1919, Sovnarkom supported Narkompros's demand for jurisdiction over all schools, including those offering vocational instruction.[1] Sovnarkom's effort was vital, for the Commissariat experienced difficulty with agencies reluctant to lose control over vocational schools. What might have been a jurisdictional dispute became much more because of Narkompros's attempted closure in 1918 of all courses and schools designed to provide technical or professional instruction to youth aged seventeen or under.[2] Criticism quickly followed from other commissariats, the labor union leadership, the Supreme Economic Council (Vesenkha), and the Young Communist League (Komsomol). They made a compelling case, pointing to a shortage of skilled workers and to the need for providing youth with technical training relevant to their place of employment. In defiance of central policy, labor unions, factories, and local departments of education sponsored schools for working youth, offering part-time instruction, usually for two hours a day, six days a week.[3]

Narkompros begrudgingly compromised. In the autumn of 1918, it accepted schools for working youth as an accomplished fact. One year later, Lunacharsky conceded that vocational schools may provide a trade useful to a particular locality.[4] Narkompros had little choice but to share jurisdiction over these schools with representatives of the technical lobby, first in a State Committee for Professional-Technical Education and then in a Section for Professional-Technical Education. When, in 1920, Sovnarkom ordered a reorganization of the Commissariat of Enlightenment, it upgraded the Section into a Main Administration for Professional-Technical Education (Glavprofobr) to administer vocational schools, special courses, technicums, and higher educational institutions.[5]

An unwelcome addition, Glavprofobr threatened Narkompros's system and the philosophy behind it. Its expanding network of vocational schools admitted students under seventeen years of age who had not completed nine years of education. Worse yet, from Narkompros's perspective, Glavprofobr proposed to modify the polytechnical program at the regular schools.[6] In late 1920, it announced it was preparing curricula keyed to particular branches of industry for the senior division of the secondary school (grades eight and nine). And it announced plans to transfer the division to technicums for an even more specialized course.

Glavprofobr harbored notions of a network of vocational schools to replace Narkompros's polytechnical secondary school. It found a possible prototype in the school for working youth. Glavprofobr began by devising a standard program of academic and technical training for these schools. Then, in early 1920, it proposed their reorganization into a network of factory apprenticeship schools (fabrichno-zavodskoe uchenichestvo). General academic subjects were to relate to the type of industry with which the apprenticeship school was affiliated. This part of the curriculum might include the history of labor, the history of the appropriate branch of industry, or the study of industrial management.[7] By late 1920, these schools remained small in number, but for supporters of vocational education, their potential as rivals of regular secondary schools was significant.[8]

Young Communist League

Komsomol bitterly contested Narkompros's program for educating urban youth. At its initial congress (October 29 to November 4, 1918) the complaint was made that Narkompros made no effort to educate young workers. However, Komsomol limited its own program to organizing reading huts, libraries, orchestras, and courses.[9] The following year, a more aggressive Komsomol demanded that Narkompros redirect resources designated for the United Labor School to schools for working youth.[10] At the League's Second Congress in October, O. L. Ryvkin, a member of Komsomol's Central Committee, urged Narkompros to accept these schools as the single system for educating the new generation. The Congress agreed.[11] Neither Ryvkin nor Komsomol specified, however, just how much specialized training should be offered. One delegate complained that Ryvkin had not indicated what a school for working youth was; another commented that Ryvkin proposed the training of narrow specialists.[12] While Ryvkin denied this, he again neglected to specify the degree of occupational training permissible. The Third Komsomol Congress (October 2–10, 1920) was no less ambivalent. It endorsed the new factory apprenticeship school, while criticizing Glavprofobr's plans for specialized training.[13]

Despite vagueness on substantive matters of curriculum, Komsomol offered the factory apprenticeship school as a substitute for regular secondary schools. Its congresses pointed to the painfully obvious: Narkompros guidelines and instructions to the contrary, existing secondary schools offered a traditional curriculum presented by a "petty bourgeois teaching staff to a petty bourgeois audience."[14] Working-class youth either avoided the schools, or, if they attended, absorbed ideas hostile to proletarian interests.[15] Ryvkin put it bluntly: the United Labor School remained a "bourgeois school masked by the label 'united and labor'."[16]

Response

Under intense pressure, Narkompros made concessions part of a defense of its polytechnical program. The Declaration on the United Labor School had launched the effort by allowing for a degree of "special technical education" for pupils aged fourteen and older.[17] In 1919, the Commissariat's Sector for Social Training considered tracks (uklony) in physics-mathematics, the natural sciences, and humanities for the secondary school.[18] Later that year, Lunacharsky declared that Narkompros was not opposed to differentiation (furkatsiia), broadly defined, in the senior grades.[19] The following January, the Narkompros Collegium's "Declaration on Professional-Technical Education" acknowledged a need for technical training of youths aged fourteen and older.[20] Yet several months later, Lunacharsky limited the effect of these concessions in a major address to the Young Communist League.

That October, Lunacharsky went before the Third Komsomol Congress to defend the United Labor School and to launch an attack of his own.[21] He charged that socialism would not be built by chasing lofty economic goals before the completion of a cultural revolution. The task of schools was not to produce engineers or experts, but well-rounded persons with a strong commitment to socialism. Calling upon religious metaphors to help make his point, Lunacharsky proclaimed that a polytechnical school should be like a brotherhood in which a child could rise above a petty bourgeois background. A vocational school, on the other hand, was "the Fall (grekhopadenie)." Rejecting in principle occupational training for youth, Lunacharsky spoke of Glavprofobr's doom "in the comparatively distant future."[22] He closed as he had begun. There should be "only one system," providing nine full years of general education.[23] Later that month, Lunacharsky mentioned that Glavprofobr could be Narkompros's stomach, but not its head or heart.[24]

The Party's Involvement

Debate over the secondary school dominated proceedings of the First Party Conference on Education, December 31, 1920, to January 4, 1921. Its 134 voting and 29 non-voting delegates included members of the Narkompros Collegium and representatives from Glavprofobr, the Ukrainian Commissariat of Enlightenment, the cultural departments of labor unions, and the Eighth Congress of Soviets, then in session.[25]

Lunacharsky once again combined compromise with a reaffirmation of Narkompros's plans for secondary education. He did so by presenting his own version of theses prepared by Krupskaya, who was ill and unable to attend.[26] She made no concession to vocational training for Soviet youth under seventeen years of age. The Commissar, however, acknowledged that as an "economic (khoziaistvennyi) commissariat [Narkompros] must consider the nation's pressing economic needs" and allow a modicum of technical instruction of pupils after their fifteenth birthday. It was not enough. A majority of the delegates went well beyond Lunacharsky's concessions to adopt Glavprofobr's program. Their resolutions condemned secondary schools "as a bourgeois vestige," demanding in their place factory apprenticeship schools and technicums. They even wanted the sixth and seventh grades to provide instruction in skills relevant to nearby industrial enterprises.[27]

Lunacharsky seemed uncharacteristically pleased with the outcome. Krupskaya, feeling betrayed, asked Lenin to intervene.[28] Lenin had already become involved with a resolution presented to the Party's Central Committee the previous December and, with hurried comments, marked "private, a rough draft and not to be publicized" on an earlier version of Krupskaya's theses. After the conference, Lenin moved aggressively. It was Lenin at his best—impatient, petulant, and sarcastic, but also sensitive to the issues and personalities involved.

With difficulty, Lenin came to support vocational training for adolescents. He began by proposing to the Central Committee on December 8 a "merger of secondary schools (or their senior grades) with vocational-technical education."[29] His comments on Krupskaya's theses suggested the merger might

include the sixth and seventh grades of the junior division.[30] Following the
First Party Conference on Education, his statements became more precise.
Through the Central Committee's instructions of February 5, 1921, and his
own article five days later in *Pravda,* Lenin echoed the conference's demand
for vocational training for youths fifteen to seventeen years of age.[31] He did
so reluctantly, labelling the measure "a temporary and practical expedient
necessitated by the country's poverty and ruin."[32]

Narkompros took some satisfaction from Lenin's remarks. He had dis-
tanced himself from proposals to create a permanent vocational alternative
to the secondary school. Krupskaya claimed that Lenin and the Central
Committee had endorsed the polytechnical principle,[33] yet she must have
understood that their involvement limited Narkompros's initiative and set a
precedent for interference in educational matters. Lenin in fact took this
opportunity to clarify his differences with Narkompros over the curriculum.

Lenin wanted less talk of innovative methods and more concern for traditional content. He demanded syllabi for general courses in vocational
schools: "If there are no such syllabi yet, Lunacharsky is to be hanged."[34]
In following months he condemned Narkompros (and the First Party Conference on Education) for indulging in "general arguments and abstract
slogans."[35] Lenin wanted employment of experienced teachers and preparation of detailed syllabi, lesson plans, and textbooks.[36]

Compromise

Narkompros had little choice but to reach a compromise with its powerful
critics. Early in 1921, the Main Administration for Social Training (Glavsotsvos), the Commissariat's arm responsible for general education, prepared
a curriculum for the upcoming academic year.[37] It remained non-obligatory
and did not include a timetable, as had the curriculum of the previous year.
Accompanying syllabi, however, recommended a systematic approach to traditional subjects. Narkompros overcame its squeamishness about grammar,
called for the reading of literary classics, and recommended survey courses
on the history of Russian language and literature. Detailed instructions were
included for the study of mathematics (including algebra and geometry),
physics, chemistry, and biology. The biology syllabus for the secondary grades
began with the comment that it may be too difficult for the teacher.[38] The
program for social studies, despite its focus on broad socio-economic trends,
presented material on the history of the Russian state in chronological order.[39]
At the same time, Narkompros approved vocational instruction for pupils
fifteen to seventeen years of age by ordering a transfer of the eighth and
ninth grades to technicums to be carried out over the next two years.[40]

Once again, events overcame intentions. The 1921 curriculum and syllabi
were ready for publication by early September; Narkompros expected that
they would be printed within two to three weeks, but the State Publishing

House did not manage to have them ready until six months later, at the end of the academic year.[41] The campaign for technical education foundered as a result of inadequate funds and a top-heavy, ineffective bureaucracy. The number of vocational schools more than doubled from September 1920 to July 1921, while the number of technicums more than tripled.[42] This rapid growth exacerbated already severe shortages of teachers, textbooks, equipment, and opportunities for practicums. Schools managed as best they could, irrespective of central directives. As in the regular system, local variations ruled the day.[43]

The dream of a thriving network of vocational schools was as unrealistic as Narkompros's vision for a united labor school. Glavprofobr, the Young Communist League, and Lenin, critical of Narkompros for wishful thinking, found themselves guilty of the same. In 1921, the Supreme Economic Council attempted to solve the problem with another layer of bureaucracy. It created a special bureau to assist Glavprofobr "in the preparation of skilled personnel for industry."[44] New agencies on top of old proved as ineffective as philosophical statements in bringing about practical results.

Resistance by teachers and parents had not forced Narkompros to revise its program. The story was much different when objections were raised by Lenin, the technical lobby, and the Young Communist League. Yet, developments in the classroom were not without significance to the debate in the capital. Komsomol criticized the continuing dominance of traditional content and methods; Lenin favored the instructional methods preferred by teachers. He did not, however, share the views of most teachers and parents concerning the overall purpose of schooling. Like Narkompros, the Young Communist League, and Glavprofobr, he believed that educational institutions should reshape reality.

It was small consolation to Narkompros that its most prominent antagonists shared its aggressive instincts and its frustrations. By 1921, the Commissariat of Enlightenment found that it had a policy still searching in vain for a school, a public, and support from state and party organs. Leaders at Narkompros nevertheless retained their spirit as they prepared more curricular changes.

Part Two.

Change and Permanence in the 1920s

Everything unusual prevents people from living the way they would wish. Their aspirations, when they have such, are never for fundamental change in their social habits, but always simply for more of the same. The basic theme of all their moans and complaints is: "Don't stop us from living the way we're accustomed!"
— From Gorky's eulogy to Lenin, 1924

Ему снились страшные сны: как это комплексировать?

The Complex Method

"He had nightmares: how to teach all this by the complex method?" Teachers could not cope with the complex method and other elements of the progressive curriculum of the 1920s.

SOURCE: *Uchitel'skaia gazeta,* no. 26 (149) (June 24, 1927), p. 3.

V.

NEP AND THE
PROGRESSIVE CURRICULUM

In early 1924, the Commissariat of Enlightenment received a request from administrators of a school asking permission to name their institution after Lunacharsky. Responding energetically, Narkompros called for an investigation of the school's methods of instruction before bestowing such a distinguished title.[1]

The incident exemplified the aggressive mood at Narkompros. While the party engineered a calculated retreat with the New Economic Policy (NEP), Narkompros remained determined to compel, if need be, a transformation of school and society. In difficult circumstances, it still chose to remake reality rather than adjust to it.

Struggle for Survival

The NEP turned a bad educational situation into a disaster. Beginning in 1921, the concern for a balanced budget ended all pretense of central funding of schools and the limited support that had followed.[2] What few funds Moscow now assigned to education went for professional and technical training, especially in higher educational institutions. This pattern of expenditure continued the pre-revolutionary bias toward more prestigious and narrowly expedient forms of instruction. Schooling was such a low priority that the government of the Russian Republic spent more on political training (politprosvet) than on primary and secondary schools.[3]

While Moscow's financial commitment declined, local governments struggled under the burden dumped on them. Throughout the 1920s, they assigned only 12 percent of their total budget to primary and secondary schools, not enough to meet teachers' salaries. The problem was not just a lack of revenue. One writer pointed out in the Narkompros journal *Narodnoe prosveshchenie* that during the 1920s, state support of industry and agriculture increased at a much faster rate than support of education.[4] From 1925 to 1926, the portion of the budget in Leningrad province devoted to education fell from 19.3 to 16.3 percent.[5] An embittered Lunacharsky complained that when the State increased minimum salaries for teachers, local governments reduced other expenditures to avoid spending more on schools.[6] Narkompros tried shaming local governments into action by pointing out that in pre-revolutionary times zemstvos had devoted 31 percent of their budgets to education.[7] It was to no avail.

Inadequate funding wreaked havoc with the educational system. Between 1920 and 1924, the total number of schools and teachers decreased, and enrollment in primary grades fell by about 30 percent.[8] Schools in Moscow fared no better. In the space of one year, from 1921 to 1922, their number declined by 38 percent.[9] The system recovered somewhat during the mid-1920s, but even as late as 1928, the number of schools and teachers remained below the corresponding figures for 1920. Total enrollment was only slightly higher.[10] It was a slow recovery, and it came at the expense of one of Narkompros's most cherished pledges.

A Lesser Evil

Narkompros had initially abolished all school fees and promised free distribution of books, food, footwear, and clothing. It soon discovered that it could not find, let alone give away, most of these items. With the budgetary restraints of the NEP, it also had to accept that it could not guarantee free schooling. In September 1921, Sovnarkom took the first step toward the reintroduction of fees by calling upon parents to consider self-taxation (samooblozhenie), which it defined as voluntary contributions of materials.[11] Narkompros condemned a measure that it knew meant the imposition of obligatory payments. It proposed instead a local educational tax collected primarily from the well-to-do. Local authorities disliked the idea and suggested that Moscow shoulder the burden of any new taxes.[12] For all concerned, fees emerged as the lesser evil; they could be levied as needed by a department of education, village commune, or school. Narkompros accepted the inevitable, meanwhile urging schools to limit their dependency on this source of income.[13]

Narkompros made another concession. In August 1922 it permitted departments of education as well as individual schools to sign contracts with a cooperative, union, or state agency for financial support.[14] In many localities, resulting agreements stemmed the decline in the number of schools, perhaps saving 30 percent of them.[15] As of April 1, 1923, contractual arrangements supported more than 33 percent of the primary schools in the Russian Republic.[16] Many schools relied on them for the remainder of the decade.[17]

It was not a solution that pleased Moscow. School fees damaged the credibility of Communist rule by denying Soviet youth a free and equal opportunity for education. With local authorities setting payments, anything but an egalitarian and uniform system emerged. Ability to pay determined who could attend school and affected the quality of instruction. In 1924 and

1925, fees ranged from as low as 25 kopecks a month at a primary school to as much as 200 rubles a year in the secondary grades. Among all schools, the number of pupils attending free of charge varied from 25 to 95 percent, with the average reported as 35 percent.[18] By the mid-1920s, 32.5 percent of the revenue for secondary schools came from fees, a figure higher than the pre-revolutionary 28.2 percent.[19] Some schools also charged for extra-curricular activities.[20] Parents who could afford it paid for tutorials or special evening classes. The practice had become so popular by 1924 that the Commissariats of Enlightenment and Interior limited such instruction to no more than three children at a time and to teachers registered to do so.[21] Admitting failure four years later, Narkompros reissued the same edict.[22] Narkompros received equally disturbing news about a contract system that permitted arrangements between teachers and parents for thinly-disguised private schools.[23]

The Soviet state found itself in the uncomfortable position of supporting, while at the same time rhetorically condemning, privatization of the school system. In 1922, when Narkompros first allowed contracts, it disingenuously repeated an earlier prohibition on private elementary and secondary schools.[24] That December, while approving fees, the Tenth Congress of Soviets did the same.[25] Because statutes prohibited the removal of pupils whose parents refused to pay, the State prosecuted the offending adults.[26] Some schools saved it the trouble by illegally removing children for non-payment.[27] Hoping to stem the worst of these abuses in 1926 and 1927, Narkompros and the Soviet government abolished fees in the primary grades and restricted their use at the secondary level.[28] These measures, however, only added to a school's financial woes.[29]

Heroic Measures

Fees could not compensate for the inability at all levels of the government to support primary and secondary schools.[30] Horrendous shortages continued throughout the decade. Schools lacked fuel for heating and lighting, pencils, paper, tools, and books.[31] One district in 1925 possessed only one pencil and one notebook for each pupil for a three-month period.[32] A report from Nizhnii Novgorod province complained that enough texts were on hand to satisfy only 8 to 10 percent of the demand in secondary schools.[33] The heroic measures of the immediate post-revolutionary period continued. Pupils used pieces of coal or chalk to write on pans, desks, or a stove at school. When paper was needed, pages ripped from old journals had to do.[34] Teachers assigned whatever motley collection of old and new texts they could find.[35] The resultant confusion, perhaps, was better than having no reading matter at all. But even the most imaginative of teachers could not cope when books that arrived at the school were, inexplicably, in Japanese, Chinese, or Latin, or when most texts that came were for mathematics.[36] In such cases, teachers used pages from these books to insulate windows for the winter.

Other schools closed during the winter for lack of fuel.[37] Out of necessity, some teacher repreparation courses included practicums on the production of academic materials at home and school.[38] In 1925, Lunacharsky reported to Sovnarkom that 50 percent of all school buildings were in need of repair.[39] He could have provided an even more devastating picture, for in the mid-1920s, government agencies used school facilities for other than educational purposes.[40] A high percentage of schools, especially in urban areas, operated in two or even three shifts. This was the practice in half the urban schools in the USSR, and in Moscow alone, over 90 percent did so.[41] One shift following on the heels of the other necessitated an abbreviated school day for pupils but a lengthened one for teachers. In the mid-1920s, the Moscow Department of Education reduced the school week from thirty-six to thirty hours, while raising the teaching load from eighteen to twenty-four hours.[42]

The Commissariat could not help the large number of children who desperately needed the barest necessities of life and medical treatment. In the mid-1920s, scarlet fever and malaria remained serious problems in schools in the Moscow region.[43] Narkompros often took note of the plight of the wandering homeless children (besprizorniki), admitting its helplessness before their staggering numbers. It could only appeal for help from any and all State agencies, from the Commissariat of Agriculture to the Supreme Economic Council.[44]

Narkompros Militant

Faced with immense difficulties, Narkompros exhibited a devotion to its ideals, perhaps even an obstinacy of purpose. The first to practice his own belief that commitment could move history, Lunacharsky continuously held aloft the ideal of the "non-class school" creating a "new kind of human being."[45] Krupskaya proved similarly stubborn, tirelessly keeping alive the idea of educational soviets.[46] Narkompros refused to surrender its intentions to provide all children with a primary and secondary education, to distribute shoes, clothes, books, and hot breakfasts, and to help each school acquire its own garden plot and shop.[47] Not content with these formulas, it now insisted on a curriculum more radical than anything devised earlier.

This aggressiveness in curricular matters accompanied important organizational changes at Narkompros. In 1921, the State Academic Council (Gosudarstvennyi Uchenyi Sovet, or GUS), heretofore with jurisdiction primarily over higher education, assumed responsibility for instructional content, materials, and methods in primary and secondary schools. This task fell to one of the Council's six new sections, the Pedagogical Section, headed by Krupskaya. Its members included, among others, Pokrovsky, Shatsky, P. P. Blonsky (psychologist and author of *Trudovaia shkola* [The Labor School]), and M. M. Pistrak, a Narkompros official since 1918 and head of the experimental Lepeshinsky School Commune in Moscow.[48]

The Section began its work inauspiciously enough by endorsing the 1921 curriculum submitted earlier by Glavsotsvos. The approval masked serious differences of opinion within the Section. Privately, some critics found the curriculum too broad and urged a more decisive turn toward systematic instruction. A majority in the Section thought otherwise. They wanted less attention paid to traditional subjects and more to the study of labor, the local area, and contemporary life.[49] Their preference for the experimental pervaded the Section's new and appropriately named journal, *Na putiakh k novoi shkole* (On the Paths to the New School), edited by Krupskaya. Its first issue carried articles by Krupskaya, Shatsky, and Blonsky exhorting teachers to adopt an active, relevant, and labor-oriented curriculum. Their appeals came none too early, for an impatient Pedagogical Section had already launched just such a course of study. Faced with resistance below, Krupskaya and a majority at the Section determined to compel reform. As one member put it on September 15, 1921, "without the center's instructions, the school will return to the past."[50]

The Section began by enhancing its own authority over the schools. In the autumn of 1921 it announced that local educational departments, schools, and teachers could no longer dismiss Moscow's syllabi.[51] Three years later, the State Academic Council required the submission of all local curricula and syllabi to the Pedagogical Section for review.[52] At the same time, schools were told to regard the Section's syllabi as an "obligatory orientation." The following year, the Section required that its programs be implemented in the first two grades of the elementary school and the first grade of the secondary school (the fifth grade overall). It planned to devise elaborate and obligatory syllabi for other grades so that by 1928 a uniform progressive curriculum would prevail throughout the Russian Republic.[53] A comparable attitude developed at Narkompros toward textbooks. In 1922, the Commissariat's Collegium declared that by January 1, 1924, only the State Academic Council, and not local officials, could approve texts for publication.[54]

Centralization of curricular authority paralleled changes in the administration of each school. A "Statute for the United Labor School," confirmed by the Russian Republic's Sovnarkom on December 18, 1923, dispensed with governance by consensus of pupils, teachers, and community. It concentrated power in the hands of the local department of education and in its appointee, the school director.[55] The school council survived, but in emasculated form. The director could block its decisions until a final resolution by the local department, and could act independently in "exceptional cases" so broadly defined as to cover virtually any aspect of school life. Furthermore, the new Statute altered the composition of the council to reflect the interests of those institutions now empowered to send representatives to it: Party organs, labor unions, the local soviet, and the Young Communist League. Similar changes occurred in the structure of Committees for School

Welfare. As originally proposed in 1922, each committee was to consist of three to ten persons elected at a general meeting of parents. One year later, a new statute added the school director and representatives selected by the women's department (zhenotdel) of the Communist Party, the Young Communist League, and the teachers union.[56]

The Complex Method

"These are orphans," Al'khen answered . . .
"Children of the Volga region?"
Al'khen stopped short.
"The terrible legacy of the tsarist regime?"
Al'khen spread his hands as if to say
that one can't do anything given such a legacy.
"Coeducation . . . by the complex method?"

For Narkompros and its Pedagogical Section, the complex method became just what I. Il'f and E. Petrov implied it might be in their popular novel, *Dvenadtsat' stul'ev* (The Twelve Chairs), first published in 1927. Through a method attributed with near mystical powers, schools could achieve the lofty goals assigned to them.

In 1918, the American educator William Heard Kilpatrick published an essay, "The Project Method," setting forth "the purposeful act," not separate disciplines, as most relevant to contemporary life.[57] His proposal captured the imagination of policy-makers at the Commissariat of Enlightenment. The complex method was one prominent result.[58] Instead of traditional subjects, the method focused on an assortment of themes arranged under the rubrics of nature, labor, and society. A topic under study on a particular day would relate to the theme of the week, which, in turn, would correspond to major topics of the month and year. Themes were selected to deal successively in each grade with larger geographic areas and more difficult concepts. In elementary school, pupils focused on the most familiar and concrete elements of nature, labor, and society (seasons of the year, domestic chores, the family) while those in the higher grades examined more general and abstract fare (world geography, the economy, Russian government).[59]

For the Pedagogical Section, the complex was much more than a method; it represented all that progressive education in a socialist society could hope to be. Whereas the traditional array of subjects divided the world into false categories for the memorization of irrelevant bits of information, an appropriate selection of themes demonstrated the interconnectedness of the real material world of labor, society, and nature. "Instead of the study of subjects," the Pedagogical Section declared in its 1923 instructional letter on the complex method, "we require the study of life itself."[60] In a publication sponsored by the Section, one enthusiast claimed that no psychological basis existed for a presentation of separate subjects because children wanted to examine life as a whole.[61] The method had the added potential of mandating use of the progressive arsenal at Narkompros's disposal: activity methods, excursions, aesthetic training, acquisition of basic agrarian and industrial skills, and community projects. At home, school, factory, and farm, teachers and pupils would join with doctors, agronomists, peasants, and workers to benefit school and society.

Specific themes centered on: the importance of education; hygiene; the collection of material for a school museum or a "living corner" of plants and small animals; nature walks; decoration of the classroom; or the examination of electrification, religious prejudice, and the alliance (smychka) of the proletariat and peasantry. For the fall theme "October Revolution," pupils conducted interviews with participants, prepared posters and decorations for celebrations at school and village, arranged dramatizations depicting life as it was before 1917, and recited revolutionary poems. Teachers, pupils, and the community together evaluated pupils' efforts.[62] One zealot, presumably a teacher, found a way to combine instruction, pupil activity, and community involvement. She wrote a play in which schoolchildren adopted the roles of themes, sub-themes, "subjects," and academic skills, demonstrating how the complex made undeniably good sense.[63]

Beginning in the fall of 1921, the Pedagogical Section championed the new method for both primary and secondary schools. In September, it called on themes to replace subjects, when teachers had the preparation to do so.[64] The following year, it recommended the method for elementary schools without any such reservation. In preparing its recommendation, the Section privately complained of an unacceptable reliance on subjects by local departments of education.[65] It was an indication of its impatience with the Narkompros apparatus that at least two of these departments had not endorsed subjects. The curriculum from the Moscow Department of Education for the 1921/22 academic year explicitly rejected an "artificial division of reality into subjects" for the first three grades.[66] The Viatka Department of Education denigrated subjects and rejected the separate study of grammar and history in the first three or four grades. It wanted instead a focus on "man in nature," life, conversational language, and popular culture.[67]

Bolder initiatives from Narkompros followed. The initial issue of *Na putiakh k novoi shkole* proclaimed the multiple virtues of the complex approach and subsequent issues applauded its successful applications. On February 21, 1923, Krupskaya presented to the Pedagogical Section a complex scheme for all nine grades. She proposed that eighth-graders concentrate on the human conquest of nature, the history of labor, and a "sociological review of the chief stages of human development."[68] Something considerably less sweeping followed on July 16, when the Narkompros Collegium approved a complex curriculum as an "obligatory orientation" for the first two grades of the elementary school.[69] It also recommended that all subjects in the fifth grade focus simultaneously on identical themes.[70] Later that month, a Narkompros circular and, in November, the Pedagogical Section's instructional letter on the complex method, suggested a rearrangement of subjects in the secondary grades to facilitate a unifying thematic approach. They recommended the designation of a single teacher for each of three cycles of natural sciences, physical sciences-mathematics, and social sciences-humanities.[71] Another advocate of the complex method, however, suggested not a reclassification of subjects but team teaching of individual subjects by specialists, each of whom would focus on the same interdisciplinary themes.[72] Whatever the approach, the Pedagogical Section made it clear that it preferred to "contrast 'complexes' to [separate] academic subjects."[73]

Two years later, the Section's curriculum for grades five through seven retreated from the cyclical approach. But it was no less committed in principle to the complex approach. It shied away from cycles because few teachers had the training to teach a variety of subjects, and because of the absence of special literature.[74] The Section continued to insist that subjects, which "do not exist as independent entities in their own right," relate to identical themes.[75] The teacher of mathematics, for example, was asked to build the course "to a significant degree [on] the content and basic ideas of complex themes."[76]

Other Progressive Methods

Narkompros suggested other methodological changes. It continued to scorn the use of tests. Success at school was to be determined by an assessment of an individual's performance in group discussions, collectively written assignments, preparation of exhibits, and socially useful activity. The Pedagogical Section urged that a pupil's own peers and the public assist teachers in this evaluation. Grades of "good," "satisfactory," and "unsatisfactory," or anything like them, were to be scrupulously avoided.[77] The whole evaluation process was promoted as a festival involving the school and local community. One of the Section's publications recommended one such example. At the end of the academic year, pupils and teachers of the third and fourth grades gathered in a workers club to display their drawings and notebooks, perform music and plays, and recite verses.[78] In one skit, the teacher wanted the pupils to study arithmetic. The children, quick learners in the ways of progressive education, knew better. They voted to convene a school assembly. The teacher submitted to the majority.[79]

Fascination with the complex method and relevancy meant disavowal of the standard textbook. Supporters of a progressive curriculum suggested instead a children's encyclopedia or workbooks designed for local use with themes or cycles of subjects in mind.[80] The First All-Russian Conference on Textbooks held in Moscow, May 9–13, 1926, repudiated the traditional text; the Narkompros Collegium rushed to agree.[81] A confusing situation followed in which new textual materials, when they existed at all, varied from school to school and year to year.

Narkompros counseled experimentation with another innovation, the Laboratory or Dalton Plan. Originally devised by Helen Parkhurst and applied in a high school in Dalton, Massachusetts, the method retained subjects but transformed the manner of their presentation. A subject consisted of contract assignments, each of which took about a month to complete and focused attention on an overall theme. Students completed assignments at their own pace, roving about rooms or laboratories, each designated for a particular subject irrespective of grade. Teachers responded as a friend when needed; more advanced students helped their younger or slower colleagues.[82] Soviet observers recommended one change—that contracts be assigned to groups rather than to individuals. The Moscow Department of Education warned that without such a modification, unacceptable individualism would result.[83] In 1925, a conference convened by the department recommended that at least 50 percent of the contracts go to groups.[84]

Revised to suit Soviet tastes, the laboratory plan had many of the same appealing features as the complex. In secondary grades especially, it could create the best of all possible worlds—subjects bound by unifying concepts and taught in a physical setting encouraging cooperation among pupils and teachers.

Curricula

The Pedagogical Section favored the complex method for its capacity to transform the content of instruction. Powered by the complex, the natural and physical sciences became vehicles for understanding local climate and soil, farming a school garden plot, or raising livestock. Mathematics, the 1924 curriculum declared, had value not as a self-contained subject but as a way to "understand and transform life. . . . Mathematics in and of itself has no educational value in the school; mathematics is important insofar as it helps to solve practical problems."[85] Russian language instruction was to acquaint pupils with colloquial speech and the style of newspapers.[86] The 1925 curriculum for grades five through seven suggested that pupils might learn mathematics by calculating the local rate of illiteracy, mortality or illness, or by comparing the work performed by a horse and tractor; chemistry could be learned through an examination of the composition of the soil; and physics by a study of housing, plumbing, and electricity.[87] Social sciences especially bore the brunt of the Commissariat's reforming zeal.

In 1921, the Pedagogical Section combined history, geography, law, political economy, and literature into a new discipline, social studies (obshchest-vovedenie). History in particular was affected.[88] Curricula of the early and mid-1920s reduced it to a source of information for recent developments in agriculture, industry, popular culture, and electrification.[89] The historian and Narkompros official, Pokrovsky, did not object. On the contrary, he welcomed a shift from empirical data, chronology, and political history toward the Marxist categories of labor, class struggle, and revolution.[90]

In addition to members of the Pedagogical Section, three educators, B. N. Zhavoronkov, S. P. Singalevich, and S. N. Dziubinsky, distinguished themselves as aggressive champions of social studies. Dziubinsky spoke for them all when he contrasted a teaching of "naked historical facts" with the learning of a "a Marxist world view."[91] History was only useful as a repository of information relevant to "Economics of Contemporary Russian Agriculture," "Class Ideology and Struggle," "Landholding in Tsarist Russia and the Soviet Republics," and, after Lenin's death in 1924, "Leninism."[92] Textbooks could not keep pace with current events. Schools should rely instead on newspapers, revolutionary songs, posters, literature, celebrations of revolutionary holidays, excerpts taken from speeches and decrees, interviews with workers and peasants, and excursions to a museum, monument, factory, and former landed estate. In this way, the school would foster friendship between teacher and pupil and between school and community. In the words of Singalevich, the school would be transformed into a "living organization, the center of mass work."[93]

It was not to be. We do not know whether the school requesting permission to use Lunacharsky's name measured up to Narkompros's standards. We know that many schools did not. Lunacharsky and his colleagues doggedly pursued both the teachers they hoped would create the new school, and the people—parents, pupils and local populace—they hoped to transform. It remained to be seen whether they would succeed or whether Narkompros and its policies might themselves undergo a transformation.

VI.

SLOW HISTORY

CLASSROOM PRACTICE

Despite the increasing specificity of its instructions, Narkompros's curriculum infrequently transcended the paper on which it was written. Narkompros might transform policy; it could not so readily control what transpired in the school. In primary and secondary schools throughout the Republic, teachers continued to teach and students continued to learn by means of the familiar cycle of dictation, memorization, and drill.

Traditional Methods

A variety of evidence proclaimed the failure of Narkompros policy—special investigations by Narkompros and its local departments; reports filed by inspectors; comments by teachers and officials at educational conferences; and observations following field trips by Shatsky, B. P. Esipov, member of the Pedagogical Section since 1923, and M. S. Epshtein, Deputy Commissar of Enlightenment and head of Glavsotsvos. All sources reinforced the conclusion that, despite the avalanche of instructions from above, teachers still taught the traditional curriculum in the usual way. One particular source of information repeatedly made this point. For several years following its establishment in October 1924, the newspaper *Uchitel'skaia gazeta,* published by the teachers union, reported reliably on the educators it claimed to represent. Relying extensively on letters from teachers and from its network of teacher-correspondents, *Uchitel'skaia gazeta* revealed that many instructors refused to implement the new curriculum, while others tried but failed.[1] The newspaper's editorial board had reason to boast in early 1926 that it had faithfully served its constituents with articles on problems associated with the new curriculum, especially with the complex method.[2]

The Pedagogical Section had only begun its effort, when, at a meeting of its presidium on November 20, 1923, it heard a series of reports on teachers' refusals to follow instructions.[3] Reports filed by inspectors that year and throughout the mid-1920s repeatedly revealed that little had changed in Nizhnii Novgorod, Yaroslavl', or Moscow.[4] A congress of inspectors for the Moscow Department of Education held in early 1925 spoke of progress, but found a considerable preoccupation with the standard academic (slovesnyi) approach.[5] Three years later the editorial board of *Uchitel'skaia gazeta* reached an identical conclusion.[6]

The more detailed the reports, the more apparent it was that little had changed. Teachers opted for a standard presentation of material from available pre-revolutionary textbooks.[7] They lectured, read from a prepared text, or asked pupils to read a story in turn. A question and answer session followed in which boys and girls attempted to regurgitate what they had just heard or read. To keep things moving, teachers impatiently prompted their pupils, mechanically corrected erroneous responses, or asked questions requiring an obvious or one-word response.[8] Consistent with these practices, the classroom retained its former appearance. Teachers stood apart from their charges, who sat in rows of desks, when desks were available, surrounded by an odd assortment of pictures, charts, and maps.[9] Few schools took their pupils on excursions, and fewer still got involved in community life.[10]

In violation of the spirit and the letter of Narkompros's directives, teachers assigned homework, measured each pupil's performance with tests, and issued grades.[11] Teachers everywhere assigned marks. The Moscow Department of Education in 1922 discovered attempts to resurrect the traditional (bal'naia) system of marks ranging from one to five.[12] Relying on information from inspectors, Narkompros unhappily concluded in 1923 that in the majority of provinces, that very system prevailed.[13] Another report compiled four years later observed that "old forms of evaluation (otsenka)" still held firm in the Moscow region,[14] a point repeated the following year concerning the Russian Republic by the editorial board of *Uchitel'skaia gazeta*.[15]

To maintain discipline, teachers issued marks for conduct.[16] Some resorted to physical punishment.[17] Schools restored the pre-revolutionary post of class tutor (klassnyi nastavnik), a person responsible for the behavior of a particular grade.[18] Teachers and principals avoided pupil self-government in the classroom and school, or converted it into an instrument to enforce discipline.[19] In 1923, only two of twenty-one provinces reporting to Glavsotsvos had mentioned pupil self-government.[20]

The situation did not change significantly in succeeding years.[21] Epshtein returned from a field trip in 1926 to tell the State Academic Council that he had found no evidence of pupil self-government.[22] At the same time, a Narkompros inspector reported that self-government was a sham.[23] Teachers criticized the Pioneer and Komsomol organizations for unduly interfering in the academic side of school life.[24] The retention of traditional forms of authority nevertheless failed to curb improper behavior. Teachers, parents, and members of the local community complained that children stole items (food, money, pencils, kerchiefs) from the school and from teachers, smoked, broke windows, and failed to return books.[25]

Narkompros had launched the new school without considering the possibility of academic failure. Well into the mid-1920s, it encouraged the promotion of large groups or an entire class. Narkompros's intent stood in stark contrast to practice. By assigning marks to individual pupils, teachers forced them to repeat a grade, and investigations of schools in the city and province of Moscow in 1920 and 1925 revealed that about one out of five pupils were doing so.[26] In the capital's elementary schools in 1924/25, almost 20 percent of those enrolled were repeating a grade; they made up more than half of some classes.[27] The Moscow Department of Education sought to control the problem by fiat. At the close of the academic year in 1926, it restricted repetition to fifteen percent of enrollment.[28] Other surveys found an even higher rate of failure during the mid-1920s in Nizhnii Novgorod, Yaroslavl', Ivanovo-Voznesensk, Tver, Briansk, and Leningrad.[29] Throughout the Russian Republic, about 16 percent of those enrolled in elementary grades in the 1925/26 and 1927/28 academic years were repeating a grade. Figures for urban and rural schools varied only slightly.[30]

Grade repeaters made up only one part of a large number of pupils who failed to meet expectations. Pupils dropped out for academic and other reasons during the middle of the year and did not return the following autumn. During the mid-1920s, those who dropped out of elementary schools ranged from a low of 8 percent in urban areas to over 20 percent in rural regions.[31] Adding those who flunked to those who dropped out reveals that 30 percent of all pupils in 1926/27 were not promoted.[32]

The Complex Method

Though launched with great fanfare, the complex method remained where it originated—in the minds of theoreticians. When given the opportunity, teachers and local administrators criticized the method and refused to use it. They did so in 1925 at the First All-Union Congress of Teachers (Moscow, January 11–19) and at the following First All-Russian Conference of Secondary Schools (Moscow, July 5–10).[33] Articles in *Uchitel'skaia gazeta* and in provincial periodical publications, Narkompros's own investigations, and inspectors' reports provided more evidence of the method's unpopularity.[34] Much to their disappointment, Esipov in 1924, and Epshtein and Shatsky two years later, found little evidence to the contrary while on field trips.[35]

Many of the schools claiming to implement the new method paid only lip service to it or used it to disguise a traditional curriculum. One teacher put it well in a letter to *Uchitel'skaia gazeta,* stating that pressure to use themes created a situation in which schools were analogous to the Emperor in the children's tale who ordered new clothes. Like the ruler's claim to the best finery, schools pretended to use the complex method when in fact everyone knew better.[36] Another teacher put it bluntly at a teachers conference in Perm' in 1926. Tired of lengthy and misleading lectures on the success of the new method, she sadly observed: "Sometimes it seems that between the former pre-revolutionary school and our complex school there is no difference."[37] Some schools made the complex theme a separate subject. Other schools treated labor, society, and nature as independent subjects. Still others, while ostensibly following the complex model, set aside periods for the study of subjects.[38] Based on inspectors' reports, the Nizhnii Novgorod Department of Education concluded that elementary schools spent 60 to 75 percent, and often 80 to 85 percent of class time, on instruction solely in academic skills.[39]

In 1925, the Workers and Peasants Inspectorate (Rabkrin) investigated educational practices in forty-two cantons *(volosti).* It reported its findings to a plenary session of the Pedagogical Section on December 10, 1925. The news was devastating. Rabkrin's detailed report confirmed what *Uchitel'skaia gazeta,* the provincial press, and many inspectors had already discovered. Teachers segregated the teaching of reading, writing, and arithmetic from thematic instruction, disposed of the complex theme in a single lesson (if that), and avoided involving the school in the life of the community. It concluded that the old academic school predominated almost everywhere.[40] After a tour of the provinces that included Tver, Yaroslavl', and Nizhnii Novgorod, Shatsky acknowledged the prevalence of "the subject-matter school."[41] The following year, he reported that some teachers made a mockery of the complex method by going beyond the three columns of labor, society, and nature to use twelve, sixteen, thirty-five, even sixty-one categories.

> Teachers have acquired the well-known skill of apportioning material on any theme by these columns. One says "a tack" and instantly they diagram the tack or cabbage etc. along sixty-one columns. I asked the teachers: "How do you work with these diagrams?" They answered frankly: "We don't work with them, we work as we did before. When the inspector comes and asks for a diagram, then we give it to him. He looks into space (na 'prostyniu') and says: 'This doesn't go there, and this should be put here.'"[42]

An "academic, scholastic and medieval approach" dominated the classroom.[43] Other observers found the number of columns ranging from twenty-two to seventy-one.[44]

Epshtein reached similar conclusions after visiting schools in southwestern Siberia, the southern Urals, and the Middle Volga. He presented his findings in early 1926 in a report to the State Academic Council and in an article "The School as It Is." His assessment went from bad to worse: only an "extremely small part of the school . . . actually, not schools, but only separate classes" had mastered the new programs, whereas instruction in typical subjects was a "mass phenomenon."[45] Several months before the public report, Lunacharsky knew of Epshtein's gloomy findings. He admitted that there were serious problems with the new curriculum and spoke of an "impending crisis, a crisis of the complex method."[46]

Laboratory Plan

A similar fate befell the laboratory plan. Narkompros did not require its use, but occasionally local educational organs did so, especially in secondary grades. It made little difference. Teachers continued to present lessons according to rigid class schedules to pupils organized strictly by grade.[47] Some teachers distorted the method by making pupils entirely responsible for their own progress. In one instance, contracts required fifth-graders to poll the local community with eighty-two questions about economic, political, and cultural life.[48]

Traditional Content

Familiar subjects dominated the classroom. Only classical languages and religion disappeared, while mathematics, the sciences, and Russian language continued to thrive, taught, as before, by dictation, memorization, and drill.[49] Instruction in reading, one inspector reported, amounted to pupils reading as rapidly as they could and then reciting everything they could remember. This procedure continued until a class had repeated a story in all of its detail.[50] Areas vital to the Pedagogical Section's plans for a new curriculum failed to materialize as wished. Neither nature study nor social studies received the prominent place assigned, since teachers were poorly acquainted with nature and the natural sciences.[51] In social studies, teachers continued to concentrate on the customary political events, wars, and historical personalities of the past, including those of ancient Greece and Rome.[52] Efforts to encourage greater use of non-academic fare likewise failed. Inspectors reported that schools reduced the hours the Pedagogical Section assigned to singing and drawing (risovanie).[53] In 1926, a Narkompros investigation of sixty secondary schools in fourteen provinces found that a majority virtually ignored socially useful labor, and many did not employ it at all.[54]

In 1927, Pistrak took a hard look at what was actually being taught in the schools. He followed with an article whose title betrayed the nature of his findings: "Impermissible Deviations in School Affairs."[55] Pistrak complained that schools, teachers, and even departments of education chose a traditional preoccupation with reading, writing, and arithmetic at the expense of natural sciences, social studies, physics, chemistry, physical education, art, and music. He observed a "tendency to return to the methods of the old academic school" and, somewhat illogically, the "dead hand of the classical gymnasium tenaciously grabbing hold of the Soviet school."[56]

Many schools never offered the newly anointed discipline of labor, so vital to Narkompros's plans for a transformationist curriculum. Local departments of education and teachers ignored instructions on the subject and reassigned funds allotted to it.[57] Epshtein confirmed this state of affairs in 1926.[58] Inspectors found that labor often amounted to sweeping the floor, dusting, stacking wood, taking care of a nature corner, or preparing an agricultural calendar.[59] Schools with tools, machines, and entire shops made no effort to use them; equipment remained in the very boxes in which it arrived.[60] Factories, collective farms, and government agencies responsible for practicums refused to cooperate. Factory managers found school excursions too troublesome, especially when pupils arrived at factory gates uninvited.[61]

Grand plans for school garden plots likewise had little in common with reality. Many schools lacked plots, while others failed to use them properly.[62] Schools with land needed instruments, animals, and seeds with which to cultivate it. Moreover, the soil was often of such poor quality, or the plot so far removed from the school, as to make instruction infeasible.[63] Some teachers and school administrators made the best of a difficult situation by renting plots to local peasants or allowing teachers to plant private gardens.[64] In one instance, a local official, over the objection of the school director, rented out the plot to the daughter of the former owner of the estate from whom the land had been purchased (or perhaps confiscated).[65] Another official went even further: he sold the plot.[66] A detailed study in 1926 of elementary schools in Nizhnii Novgorod province revealed the great extent to which plots were used for other than instructional purposes. Less than 10 percent of the schools put pupils to work on the land; about 10 percent allowed teachers to cultivate the property. The great majority of schools simply rented it out, allowed it to go uncultivated, or, perhaps under outside pressure, permitted government agencies and officials to work the land for a token fee.[67]

Type of School

It made little difference what kind of institution came under scrutiny. Careful surveys and impressionistic accounts agreed that primary and secondary schools ignored official policy. The most optimistic reports admitted that tradition held steadfast in elementary grades where Narkompros had hoped to begin its pedagogical revolution.[68]

For Narkompros the situation in secondary schools was little short of disaster. The Conference of Secondary School Teachers, organized by the Moscow Department of Education in January 1923, heard that these schools rarely used new methods and were little distinct from pre-revolutionary gymnasiums.[69] The school "remained isolated from life and from production."[70] At the end of the year, an inspector informed the Moscow Department of Education that the three secondary schools he had just examined relied primarily on "old methods reminiscent of former gymnasiums."[71] Other reports reached similar conclusions.[72] In mid-1925, the head of the Moscow Department of Education, M. Alekseev, informed the executive committee of Moscow's provincial soviet that few secondary schools managed to apply Narkompros's programs.[73]

Many schools under Narkompros's direct control performed no better. During the mid-1920s, the Commissariat supervised about thirty experimental or model schools, while local educational organs controlled altogether one hundred or more. While these institutions made a greater attempt at implementing the new curriculum than regular schools, many of them failed to employ correctly the complex method and laboratory plan.[74]

Teacher training institutions relied on a traditional curriculum. In early 1923, Krupskaya informed the Pedagogical Section's presidium of the seriousness of the problem and the enormity of its solution.[75] The presidium acknowledged that much remained to be done.[76] Little progress followed. The Second All-Russian Conference on Teachers Education (February 12–16, 1924), a Rabkrin investigation in 1926, and a Narkompros study that same year found that teacher education amounted to the usual fare: lectures, copying, memorization, and examinations testing content.[77] Institutions preparing primary schoolteachers, the pedagogical technicums, could not find instructors capable of teaching the complex method.[78] One model primary school complained that students sent to it for a practicum used old methods.[79] Higher educational institutions training teachers for secondary grades ignored shopwork and made little effort to correlate a study of production with other subjects.[80]

Narkompros's courses for retraining teachers reinforced old methods with boring lectures followed by examinations.[81] One course commenced with a four-hour presentation on the history of the complex method.[82] In 1928, a survey of repreparation seminars concluded that they avoided instruction in methods and offered little guidance for the teaching of labor.[83]

Labels and symbols, so important, as Richard Stites reminds us, to a revolution in the making, reflected more of the familiar old than the utopian new.[84] The Pedagogical Section campaigned for its new curriculum through its journal, optimistically titled "On the Paths to the New School." By the mid-1920s, Narkompros leaders chose less encouraging titles for their articles. Epshtein called his report "The School as It Is," and Pistrak labelled his "Impermissible Deviations in School Affairs." In mid-1925, some educational institutions in Moscow still displayed their pre-revolutionary signboards. Secondary schools presented themselves to a presumably emerging socialist society as gymnasiums, an accurate reflection, in many cases, of the actual content and methods of instruction offered inside.[85] Perhaps the offending boards were soon removed, but teachers continued to use other pre-revolutionary signs, in the form of the unreformed orthography. Epshtein was not amused when in 1928 he reported that eleven years after the revolution, many Soviet teachers were still using the old orthography.[86] Later that year, Narkompros issued a letter to all of its departments of education, complaining of "orthographic illiteracy" among the nation's instructors.[87]

The Commissariat of Enlightenment had created the myth of a new school with a polytechnical curriculum. Narkompros's failure stemmed from its inability to provide the means necessary for the building of a new school. Other factors, irrespective of material conditions, also played a role. Narkompros soon discovered that teachers and common Russians dismissed its vision and the policies that flowed from it.

VII.

TEACHERS

A PREFERENCE FOR THE CUSTOMARY

For many reasons, teachers failed to march forward under the Commissariat's banner. They adhered to a conventional curriculum because of impossible working conditions and their inadvertent ignorance of Narkompros's directives. They also rejected Narkompros's leadership because they had no intention of becoming teachers of a new curriculum and agents of a new culture.

The Poverty of Bureaucracy

Some teachers pursued a traditional course because they literally knew no better. Despite a bewildering array of instructional letters, directives, circulars, and journals from Narkompros, many teachers never saw nor heard of them.[1] They knew nothing of the proceedings of educational conferences, even those attended by their peers. Few of them read the Narkompros weekly *Ezhenedel'nik Narkomprosa RSFSR,* an uninspiring work to be sure, or the Pedagogical Section's livelier tribune, *Na putiakh k novoi shkole.*[2] Even the select group of teachers attending central and provincial repreparation courses in the summer of 1928 were not familiar with the Section's periodical.[3] In the city and province of Moscow, schools failed to receive the key publication of the Moscow Department of Education, *Biulleten' MONO.*[4] Such essential items as syllabi were not always available. Primary schools in the province of Yaroslavl', lacking their own copies, borrowed them from other schools in the region.[5]

Beyond a wealth of instructions, the Commissariat of Enlightenment provided little tangible support. Narkompros and its local organs had only limited funds at their disposal to provide teachers with instructional materials and the pay promised (a point discussed below). The bureaucracy was largely absent following extensive cost-cutting under the NEP. Cantonal departments of education were abolished in 1921 and 1922.[6] Over the persistent objections of Narkompros, soviets at higher levels consolidated departments of education with agencies responsible for health and welfare, slashing the number of personnel devoted to all of these functions.[7] Local governments reduced their

education staff by 60 percent in 1921 alone.[8] Narkompros's study, published
in early 1928, disclosed that the total number of officials responsible for
education throughout the state bureaucracy had been reduced by 30 to 50
percent.[9] Those who remained faced an imposing set of duties. A case in
point was Nikolai Iakovlevich Sikachev, the head of the educational department in Ranenberg from 1921 to 1927. In addition to his educational post,
Sikachev served as a member of the municipal soviet, helped organize the
campaign against adult illiteracy, chaired the district's civil defense council
(Aviakhim), served on the executive committee of the local soviet, and led
the local economic council.[10]

Where they existed, departments of education were unable to provide
leadership commensurate with Moscow's plans. In 1926, a study of provincial
departments disclosed that only 34 percent of their personnel had a higher
education; 60 percent could boast of a secondary education. Almost half
(46.6 percent) had no more than one year's experience in the post; only one-
fourth had more than two years' tenure.[11] An advanced degree and experience
would have helped officials understand and explain the rationale for the new
curriculum. Little wonder, then, that local authorities ignored their responsibilities. Some provincial departments of education refused to file reports
with Moscow. A frustrated Narkompros attempted to shame them into action
by publishing a list of offenders.[12] Perhaps they had nothing worth reporting,
as a result of understaffing and incompetence. In 1928, the Department of
Education for the Stalingrad Region submitted an annual evaluation to its
schools that contained over 200 questions with answers to be recorded under
912 columns.[13] It is unlikely that any useful responses were forthcoming.

Local departments of education found it impossible to provide schools
with textual materials. Each year, from February to June, Narkompros
bombarded its apparatus with circulars, telegrams, and letters demanding
immediate placement of orders with the State Publishing House. A number
of departments did not submit their requests until August, leaving their
schools without materials at the beginning of the academic year.[14] Such delays
were not entirely the fault of local authorities. Departments of education
lacked the personnel to move in a more timely fashion, and, moreover, had
to postpone decisions until local soviets approved the educational budget,
usually on the eve of the school year.[15]

The same assortment of problems derailed plans for a network of inspectors.[16] Consolidation of government agencies usually meant a sharp reduction
in their number and added responsibilities for health and welfare.[17] When
concerned with educational matters, inspectors had little time to visit schools.
They complained of a deluge of paperwork that precluded anything like the
desired norm of spending 50 percent of their time in the field.[18] Taking
advantage of the forum so many teachers had found useful, inspectors complained to *Uchitel'skaia gazeta* that they were expected to perform like other
officials in the local department of education, maintaining correspondence
and filing innumerable reports.[19] When they ventured out, local departments

of education refused to provide them with travel expenses,[20] and sometimes they arrived at a school quite hungry.[21] Meager salaries demoralized them further. Provincial inspectors received only forty or fifty rubles a month and their district colleagues were paid only thirty to forty, despite State guarantees of double those amounts.[22]

Although many inspectors in 1926 had several years of teaching experience, few had taught the new curriculum. As many as half had no more than one year's experience in their current position.[23] Narkompros complained of their ignorance of schools and the progressive curriculum,[24] and teachers observed that inspectors could not make the new program comprehensible.[25] Shatsky made the same point to the Pedagogical Section in December 1925.[26] Some inspectors preferred to wait for detailed instructions from the top telling them exactly how to proceed.[27] They might eventually opt to follow the example of one of their peers who paid little attention to how local agencies spent the few rubles allotted to education, and delegated the duties of inspection to three teachers from a single school.[28] No one should have been surprised when, following his trip in 1926, Epshtein concluded that inspection hardly existed.[29]

Working Conditions

The Pedagogical Section expected miracles. Successful implementation of its program depended on funds, materials, and human resources—all in short supply. A life of deprivation began at institutions training new teachers. Students went without adequate stipends (if they received them at all), rooms, clothing, and food. Unsanitary conditions in available dormitories made them sources of illness.[30] A 1926 investigation of pedagogical technicums by Rabkrin disclosed that the number of sick students on the average reached 57 percent.[31] Two years later, *Uchitel'skaia gazeta* printed a horrifying description of a dormitory in Tula under the headline "Dormitory or Morgue?"[32]

The Pedagogical Section could not expect innovation from elementary teachers responsible for more than one grade in an unspecified but large number of schools in rural areas.[33] For other instructors, a variety of ages and abilities in a single class, a product of late entry into the first grade and of grade repetition, created major difficulties.[34] Many pupils were not in school long enough to allow for effective instruction by even the most motivated teachers. Most schools in urban and rural regions did not function for the full academic year; some did not open until November or December.[35]

Teachers complained about the impracticality of the progressive curriculum at the Conference of Secondary School Teachers, December 15–16, 1923; at teacher repreparation courses visited by Esipov in the summer of 1924; and at a congress of school directors in the province of Nizhnii Novgorod in April 1925.[36] On the eve of the First All-Union Congress of Teachers (January 1925), N. N. Iordansky, head of Glavsotsvos from 1921 to May 1922 and professor of education at Moscow State University, issued a stern warning: delegates would have to address teachers' concerns about the absence of equipment, shops, and textbooks.[37] At the congress, several speakers questioned the wisdom of imposing a new curriculum on overworked teachers confronted with material shortages and a disemboweled academic year.[38] Krupskaya admitted that instructors did not know what to make of the new school.[39] At least one delegation, a group from Pskov, had met privately with her to complain about the complex method and poor textbooks.[40]

Some instructors presented their problems in verse form. Their words spoke forcefully of conditions hardly conducive to progressive methods. From one teacher in Tula came the determination to prevail despite it all.

> My school has no window glass
> And the building has no roof
> But with the complex system
> Proceeds my instruction.[41]

Other verses ended on a gloomier note:

> In the mornings the classroom is freezing,
> Little children there are shivering,
> Naked hands are like ice,
> It's impossible to write anything precise.[42]

> My back bends from tiredness,
> In the village all is darkness,
> From time to time doubt takes over,
> It's no use, wasted is my labor.[43]

Cause for Resentment

Inadequate Pay

Teachers were asked to perform miracles, but remained underpaid and overworked.[44] By the mid-1920s, guaranteed minimum salaries varied according to geographic region, urban or rural locale, school level (primary or secondary), training, ability, and length of service.[45] From 1924/25 through 1927/28, the average salary for primary teachers increased by about 75 percent (from about twenty-five to forty-four rubles a month), while the average income for teachers in the secondary grades doubled (increasing from about thirty-five to seventy rubles a month).[46] During the same period, the differential allowed between geographic locales and between urban and rural regions remained roughly the same. Instructors in the poorest paid (rural) regions, therefore, were to receive about 75 percent of the pay of their best paid colleagues who taught elsewhere, usually in major urban centers.[47] To redress the imbalance, rural teachers were supposed to receive fuel and apartments or an additional 10 percent in pay.[48] In an effort to reward the most experienced, in mid-1927 the Soviet government announced a schedule of supplementary pay ranging from 60 to 150 rubles a year depending on a teacher's training and the grade taught. These payments were to go first in 1927 to instructors with twenty or more years of experience, then in 1928 to those with fifteen to twenty years, and so forth until 1930, when those with five to ten years tenure would benefit.[49]

Even if teachers received every ruble promised, considerable cause for resentment remained. The differential in pay between primary and secondary teachers increased from 1924 to 1928, a situation that could not have pleased the overwhelming number who taught in elementary grades. The schedule of salary supplements widened the gap by granting secondary teachers twice the compensation promised to primary instructors.[50] For most secondary as well as primary teachers, however, supplements were of no immediate relevance. Payments were arranged so that in 1927, little more than 10 percent of the Russian Republic's teachers met the qualification of having twenty years of experience. Another 10 percent were eligible the following year, and perhaps an additional 15 percent the next.[51] Inflationary periods, such as those in the autumn of 1925 and summer and autumn of 1928, reduced the value of any salary increases. Moreover, minimum guarantees, when actually provided, failed to measure up to pre-revolutionary pay, a source of considerable embarrassment to Narkompros. Reporting to the All-Russian Central Executive Committee in 1926, Lunacharsky lamented that teachers received salaries equal only to about 47 percent of their pre-war pay;[52] the following April at the Thirteenth All-Russian Congress of Soviets, he put the figure at 44 percent.[53] A study in late 1928 concluded that primary teachers were officially paid salaries equal to only about 65 percent of their pre-war earnings and secondary teachers earned even less.[54] Teachers in and around Moscow fared no better. In 1928, primary school teachers in the city were provided only 54 percent of the pay set by pre-war schedules and those in the countryside were paid 70 percent.[55]

Teachers were promised considerably less than other professionals. The Soviet government guaranteed instructors in elementary schools about half the pay of rural doctors, veterinarians, and agronomists and about the same as rural medical orderlies (fel'dshers), midwives, and druggists. Although they were to receive about 25 percent more than nurses, primary school teachers were assigned an income no better than that of rural political agitators. Secondary school teachers were guaranteed 80 percent of the salary of rural doctors and agronomists.[56] In 1926, Lunacharsky observed that the average school teacher earned less than a Soviet textile worker, and far less than a printer.[57] Narkompros reported in late 1928 that even when disregarding overtime pay, the average industrial worker made more than the primary school teacher and about the same as instructors in secondary grades.[58]

Many teachers would have been happy with what was promised them.

The central government announced the guaranteed minimums and supplements, but required local governments to find the funds. Narkompros understood the problem this policy created for local soviets, but it could only hope to provide the most destitute with a special subsidy.[59] Many teachers were lucky to get anything, let alone the minimum. Teachers complained about payments made several months late and about refusals to provide the State guaranteed salary.[60] In May 1924, the Central Council of Trade Unions condemned a particularly creative way to cut costs: Local authorities fired teachers near or at the end of the academic year in order to avoid payments scheduled for the summer.[61] But the practice continued anyway, leaving some teachers to attend repreparation courses that summer without any funds.[62] In other instances, local governments stopped payment during the summer if a teacher died, leaving the family bereaved and destitute.[63]

Feeling compelled to do something, Lunacharsky called attention to the unfolding scandal in 1925 at the All-Union Congress of Teachers and the Soviet of People's Commissars.[64] His effort was for naught. A session of the All-Russian Central Executive Committee the following year heard that sometimes instructors were not paid.[65] Meanwhile, teachers desperately searched for the money owed them only to be told that peasants had no money, the cantonal executive committee had no funds, and the district executive committee could not help.[66] One teacher fired off telegrams and letters and embarked on several trips in an unsuccessful two-year effort to get either the district or regional government to pay. Everyone involved agreed that the money was due to her, but no agency would take responsibility.[67] In 1926, *Uchitel'skaia gazeta* reported that some teachers had waited for two to four years for back pay.[68] Some of the teachers in line for special supplements did not receive them.[69] Perhaps the worst abuses throughout the 1920s prevailed in the semi-private contract schools. Judging from the wealth of complaints submitted to Narkompros and *Uchitel'skaia gazeta,* their teachers found themselves at the mercy of organizations and parents unwilling to meet the guaranteed minimum or provide what they had agreed to pay.[70]

Most teachers could not work overtime or take any other kind of employment to supplement their meager income.[71] Total earnings rarely exceeded the average guaranteed minimum.[72] Teachers complained of hunger, a point acknowledged on June 12, 1924, by the Narkompros Collegium.[73] An extensive survey of the standard of living of teachers and their families in 1926/27 indicated that most of them were able to afford only the necessities of life. To improve their situation, other members of the family sought employment, and, in rural areas, the family raised its own food. Urban and rural teachers alike borrowed to make ends meet.[74]

Local Abuse

When local authorities did take an interest in teachers, it often meant a further deterioration of the situation. Teachers were arbitrarily transferred or dismissed, even in the middle of an academic year. The extent to which the Party's Central Committee, the All-Russian Central Executive Committee, and Narkompros condemned such practices revealed their widespread nature.[75] Teachers continued to be removed because of service in the tsarist armed forces, or for possession of a horse, cow, and chickens, or for being the "former wife of a servant of a religious cult."[76] Conditions worsened during the late 1920s when the envenomed nature of Party politics and the resurgence of a transformationist mentality encouraged abusive treatment of any group that seemed to consist of intellectuals.[77]

Teachers were victimized by distortions of Narkompros's noblest intentions to make the school a leader in the community. The Commissariat expected considerable civic activity from the nation's instructors as did *Pravda,* when it launched its campaign in 1923 to find the best teacher in the land.[78] Local agencies and officials abused the privilege by forcing teachers to gather wood for the school, manage the local reading hut, serve as secretary for the local soviet, Party, and cooperative organs (where they existed), collect statistical information on the harvest or on the number of illiterates in the region, read newspapers aloud to peasants, engage in campaigns against religion, buy and sell State bonds, and collect the agricultural tax.[79] Those who refused might well have been paid late (if at all), transferred, or dismissed. Complaints poured in and Narkompros and the All-Russian Central Executive Committee could do no more than protest the most grievous abuses.[80] A rural department of education found that teachers spent almost three hours a day in socio-political activities.[81] A careful survey of a typical teacher's week in 1926/27 revealed that elementary instructors in urban areas spent four to six hours in unpaid social work, and in rural areas they put in eight to ten hours. Teachers in the secondary grades contributed almost as much time—three to six hours in urban areas and five to eight in the countryside.[82] Following his field trip in 1926, Epshtein concluded that impossible demands made upon them at work and in the community had made teachers dispirited and passive.[83]

Female teachers had fewer civic obligations than males, spending two to three hours less a week performing such tasks. But they had their own problems. At home, they spent about twice the amount of time on domestic chores as men did.[84] At work, they were among the lowest paid in their profession, comprising 70 percent of elementary teachers and only 40 percent of the better-paid secondary staff.[85] They were removed for pregnancy shortly after their condition became evident or while on leave as a result.[86] Some women were expected to perform an especially denigrating form of socially useful labor during so-called official visits to their apartments.[87] In late 1928, a Samara court sentenced the former chairman of a local soviet and the secretary of the Party cell to two years' imprisonment for the harassment (izdevatel'stvo) and persecution of female instructors.[88] The problem remained significant enough to prompt a circular from the Republic's prosecutor, denouncing representatives of local soviets and Narkompros inspectors who forced teachers to provide room, board, and sexual favors.[89] Sometimes, however, women could benefit from abuse of authority if they knew the right male. One chairman of a soviet dismissed a teacher to make room on the school's staff for his wife,[90] and in 1927, *Uchitel'skaia gazeta* disclosed an intriguing alliance between a rural soviet and a group of teetotaling sectarians, the Molokane (milkdrinkers), to remove a teacher, making room for the wife of the soviet's secretary.[91]

Professional Concerns

Teachers responded negatively to the complex method because they did not understand it and because it had caught them by surprise.[92] Inspectors in Novgorod reported that the new programs frightened teachers.[93] The Commissariat's literature did not help when it reached the hands of the nation's teaching cadre; in his tour of repreparation courses in the summer of 1924, Esipov discovered that teachers could not understand the Pedagogical Section's forum, *Na putiakh k novoi shkole*. Their suggestions revealed their confusion—teachers recommended that the journal provide special dictionaries and explanatory footnotes to make its articles more intelligible.[94] Two years later, Epshtein found a more disturbing fact: teachers had stopped reading. In school after school he saw *Na putiakh k novoi shkole,* directives, and instructional letters lying about unread, their pages still uncut.[95] The same was true of books on education by Shatsky, Blonsky, and Krupskaya. An investigation of schools in Yaroslavl' province found identical conditions.[96]

Teachers preferred the familiar and the precise. Those who tried the complex method treated the themes and categories of labor, society, and nature as separate subjects. While paying lip service to the complex, they set aside time for traditional instruction. Mystified by the new learning, others waited for explicit instructions, asking *Uchitel'skaia gazeta* for specific guidelines on the application of the complex method.[97] Quite understandably, one teacher waited for instructions on how to employ it with the three classes and 100–120 pupils for which she was daily responsible. Without some remedial measures, she concluded, the result would be "not the complex but chaos."[98] A similarly frustrated instructor asked for "instructions and not phrases and demarcations into large general complexes."[99]

Bombarded with such requests, Pedagogical Section admitted that many instructors marked time waiting for a detailed "real program."[100] N. Ruberts, Academic Secretary of the Novgorod Department of Education, complained of a fetishism below for detailed instructions from above.[101] An investigation by the Moscow Soviet in early 1928 concluded that, in the matter of instructional methods, elementary teachers waited for detailed recipes to be handed to them.[102] Similarly, critics of textbooks conceded that most teachers preferred a traditional book that followed a predesigned program point by point.[103]

When teachers did take the initiative, they often rejected Narkompros's

Attempting the Impossible

"Daily Instruction by the Complex Method." A play on words—the complex
method makes teaching more complex. A harried instructor teaches three classes
at one time. The sign reads "Sit quietly and tell stories to each other." The legend
under the cartoon says "Three in One Incarnate."
SOURCE: *Uchitel'skaia gazeta,* no. 17 (92) (April 20, 1928), p. 4.

plans on professional grounds. For them, learning remained what it had
always been—the transmission of specific academic skills and knowledge
through systematic instruction in customary subjects. They refused to read
Narkompros directives and syllabi concerning labor instruction and contributed to the failure of some schools to use shop equipment when it was
available.[104] Elementary schoolteachers insisted on instruction in literacy and
numeracy.[105] They reported that children preferred it that way and that basic
skills were more easily learned when presented independently of broad
themes.[106] One inspector who shared teachers' concerns for correct writing
suggested that children first learn how to sit properly at their desks.[107]

Difficult conditions made the traditional seem even more reasonable. For
instructors committed to presenting the rudiments of literacy and numeracy,

the more curtailed the academic year was by a late start, early termination, or a high rate of absenteeism, the more important it was to focus on the basics and not on themes.[108]

Responsible for a particular subject, secondary schoolteachers contrasted the demands of their own discipline with the interests of progressive methods. They did so at the Moscow Conference of Secondary Schools, June 17–20, 1925, and at the First All-Russian Conference of Secondary Schools held two weeks later.[109] Their interest in particular subjects led to special meetings and journals devoted to geography, the natural sciences, social studies, and physics.[110] Teachers of the natural sciences gathered in Moscow in 1922 and then in Petrograd the following year; a number of them voiced doubts that the new methods could be applied to their specialty.[111] Their counterparts in Russian language became particularly active in 1928. At conferences and in a new journal, *Russkii iazyk v sovetskoi shkole* (Russian Language in the Soviet School), they insisted that the Narkompros curriculum had ignored the development of language skills. They wanted Narkompros to adopt vocabulary tables for each age group.[112] Teachers of foreign languages condemned the complex method and unapologetically insisted on the need for dictation, drill, and homework.[113]

When teachers involved pupils in the evaluation process, they found it something less than the festive occasion Narkompros had predicted. A sixth-grade student in a Moscow school wrote in 1926 of the difficulties involved.[114] Her teacher followed Narkompros guidelines relying on an oral question and answer session to be followed by a collective decision by the teacher and the class. All pupils were to receive a satisfactory or unsatisfactory mark based on their classroom responses, extracurricular activity, homework, and overall development. It did not go as expected. Pupils remained nervous and fearful lest they forget something deemed significant; some who received an unsatisfactory evaluation were reduced to tears. During the oral examination, individual pupils did not get a chance to answer a question before a babble of voices proclaimed the correct answer.

Training and Experience

Most teachers in the Russian Republic lacked the training that would predispose them to the new curriculum and help them in its implementation. Ben Eklof has shown that in the pre-revolutionary period, when little more was expected than instruction in the rudiments of reading, writing, and arithmetic, a high degree of training could be a hindrance.[115] If then, after 1917, the job had remained the same, the Russian Republic's teachers would have been ideally suited for the purpose. Narkompros, however, demanded much more, too much for teachers who were no more qualified than their rural counterparts had been before the revolution.[116] In the mid-1920s, about one-third of all elementary and secondary teachers had any kind of specialized education and considerably fewer, perhaps only 20 percent, had specialized pedagogical training. Slightly more than 10 percent had any higher education, while about the same percentage had no more than elementary schooling.[117] A large number, over 40 percent of the teachers surveyed in the mid-1920s, listed as their highest form of education attendance at such pre-revolutionary secondary institutions as gymnasiums, realschulen, and seminaries.[118] Among elementary teachers, less than 4 percent reported having attended institutions of higher education.[119] Teachers in the city of Moscow were better trained on the average, but in the surrounding rural areas, the situation was no better than in the Russian Republic at large.[120]

For some teachers, personal experience militated against the new methods. A large number of the Russian Republic's teachers had launched their careers before the 1917 revolution, and in 1925 and 1926, more than 40 percent of them had been teaching ten or more years.[121] About 30 percent of primary schoolteachers had ten years' or more experience.[122]

Narkompros responded with elaborate but impractical repreparation schemes. These efforts neither taught nor relied on progressive methods. When speakers at one conference in Vitebsk called for adoption of novel methods, teachers expressed their preference for something else. They applauded when the head of the local department of education cooled the ardor of the advocates of the new school.[123]

Repreparation often provided little effective instruction, progressive or otherwise, and aroused considerable resentment. Teachers angrily complained that courses were disorganized, underfunded, boring, highly politicized, and unjustified intrusions into an already overburdened schedule.[124] They had every right to be angry. Strapped for funds, Narkompros had withdrawn support of local attempts in late 1921 and 1922.[125] In 1923, it promised a small subsidy for summer programs, but suddenly reneged in late June.[126] Nor could Moscow supply guidelines and literature.[127] Many rural teachers found it impossible to attend local conferences because of a lack of roads, warm clothing, and footwear.[128] In one instance, teachers struggled to come to a regional two-week course only to discover that the authorities had abbreviated it to three days. Perhaps the sudden reduction was the teachers' good fortune, since available funds permitted a daily ration of hot water in the morning, and more water with a potato and a scrap of meat in the evening.[129]

Central courses, directly sponsored by Narkompros, fared little better. Narkompros promised to provide room and board, but local organs were required to cover transportation and incidental expenses. It was a formula for failure. Not all slots were filled because local departments of education could not afford to send their people,[130] and teachers who managed to get to Moscow sometimes found themselves stranded when local authorities refused to pay for transportation home.[131] On rare occasions when Narkompros itself agreed to cover travel, it had to petition the Commissariat of Transportation to set aside an appropriate number of train tickets. Narkompros begged for a prompt response because any delay in departure would leave teachers stranded in the capital without any means of support.[132]

Social Origins and Political Affiliation

There is considerable information available on the social origins and political affiliation of teachers.[133] Neither category, however, seems significant in determining acceptance or rejection of Narkompros's curriculum. Regardless of social origin, many teachers, like parents, favored the traditional approach. Peasant and proletarian parents believed education to be valuable only insofar as it provided fundamentals of literacy and numeracy and respect for authority. Salaried and white collar parents agreed, and demanded transmission of information as preparation for a higher education. Affiliation with the Party meant little when the Party itself harbored conflicting views on education and issued no definitive statement regarding the curriculum.

Almost everything important to teachers, from classroom conditions to their training, experience, and self-image, compelled a rejection of Narkompros's program. Any instructor who proceeded with the creation of the new school often aroused the hostility of parents and the local populace. Their distrust of novel educational methods and impact on instruction merit special attention.

VIII.

THE ABC'S BEYOND THE SCHOOL

In his study of utopian plans of the 1920s, Richard Stites finds that the lower and lower-middle classes opposed "the fantasies, the raucous debates, and the extravagant dreams of those intellectuals who had launched their schemes . . . [The] still uncultured masses may have genuinely preferred the familiar, the philistine, the vulgar, the safe, the old in culture and way-of-life to the unknown, the experimental, the exalted, the perilous, the risky, the novel."[1] So it was with the people Narkompros and its teachers came to serve. Common Russians preferred the traditional curriculum because they were accustomed to it and because they opposed any effort to transform school and community. Teachers who tried otherwise aroused public disapproval followed by rough treatment, a development not without its chilling effect on others contemplating taking up Moscow's summons.

Old Habits Die Slowly

Local authorities supported the public in resisting change. Teachers felt alone, without the support of the soviet, Party cell, and union local.[2] Although the report in *Uchitel'skaia gazeta* did not make it clear, the alliance between the secretary of a rural soviet and the Molokane to remove a teacher may have stemmed from the instructor's attacks on religion.[3] Chairmen of rural soviets aided efforts to convert the school into a church during the summer months and on religious holidays.[4] When a teacher refused to allow alcohol at a celebration marking the opening of a new school, peasants asked incredulously, "What's a holiday without vodka?" With the support of the soviet's chairman and the assistant inspector of the local department of education, drink was served. The teacher refused to participate and on the third day was fired as a person "not involved in social work."[5] Similar problems arose in Voronezh, where an instructor of fourteen years, a certain Riazanova, ordered the local custodian to wash the school's floors. The man refused and appealed successfully to the local soviet where his son and nephew worked. For Riazanova, the situation deteriorated further when the soviet and local Party secretary rallied the community against her, perhaps because of her activity on behalf of the literacy campaign, the census, and the Party's women's bureau (zhenotdel).[6]

In rural areas, teachers experienced difficulties with the communal gathering or village assembly (skhod), a meeting of heads of peasant households, and usually an all-male association. The gathering often emerged as the dominant governing body, deciding what and when to pay teachers with little regard for State law. In one case where a soviet did exist, it cooperated with the village assembly against a recalcitrant instructor. The soviet's chairman demanded that the teacher allow the communal assembly to meet in the schoolhouse. She protested. He convened it there anyway and entered her apartment to take her lamp and kerosene for the purpose. Undaunted, she complained to the soviet's executive committee, which rebuked its chairman and forced him to repay her for the kerosene. Equally as stubborn, he spread rumors that she was a poor teacher fit to be transferred. When she dismissed a pupil for poor behavior, the chairman successfully demanded the student's readmission. The teacher finally realized that discretion was the better part of valor and stopped her protests against improper use of school facilities.[7]

Other instructors were not so prudent and fortunate. Throughout the mid-1920s, *Pravda* and *Uchitel'skaia gazeta* referred to the persecution of activist teachers by "dark elements."[8] In 1922, *Pravda* reported on the case of school-teacher Nikolai Fedorovich Iovlev. Following the close of the Civil War, this Red Army veteran returned to his native village of Shileksha, located in a backward area along the Volga River. Iovlev joined the teaching staff and immediately became a controversial figure acting as agent for bringing the dubious benefits of the modern State to the region. Comrade Iovlev excoriated his colleagues for allowing deterioration of the school building and theft of the school's firewood. He mobilized them and other members of the village to collect the national tax from the peasantry, to seek better treatment of workers at several small sweatshops, and, perhaps most troublesome of all, to close down local moonshiners. His various campaigns, however, came to an abrupt end with his murder in November 1922.[9]

Three years later *Uchitel'skaia gazeta* featured a similar story. A teacher in a distant village, a certain Comrade Klimenko, struggled against a local bully, Ivan Shcherbin, who was characterized as a "thief, spendthrift, and moonshiner." It ended tragically for Klimenko, despite, if not because of, his efforts in the campaign against illiteracy, his editing of the local wall newspaper, and his role as a newspaper correspondent. On March 17 he was found dead, killed by Shcherbin with the support of some of the local citizenry.[10] In still another case reported in early 1928, kulaks, peasantry, and local police ganged up on a teacher, Ivan Kuz'mich Gur'ianov. Gur'ianov had angered kulaks by depriving them of their voting rights and had offended many other peasants by refusing them permission to cut down trees on school grounds. Rumors spread that Gur'ianov beat children and stole wood. Three drunks forcibly removed him from a parents meeting at school. The local Komsomol secretary added his voice to those who accused the teacher of child-beating. This account did end with Gur'ianov alive, although removed from his post.[11]

Blaming demon alcohol and petty bourgeois philistinism, these reports read suspiciously like contemporary Soviet fictional accounts of energetic young people bringing cultural and technological progress to the benighted village.[12] Whether or not these accounts were exaggerated, teachers who pursued cultural reform ran considerable risks without hope of support from the Soviet government. Narkompros could not even provide minimum salaries promised, nor could the teachers union help beyond offering its members such national forums for complaint as *Uchitel'skaia gazeta* and the monthly journal *Narodnyi uchitel'*. Most of their articles failed to mention a local branch of the union; the only reports given were about locals which had refused to help teachers or had participated in their arbitrary removal and transfer.[13] The union's composition and leadership further alienated it from the nation's instructors. Because the union consisted of everyone associated with education, only 37.6 percent of its total membership were primary school teachers, and only 7.2 percent taught in the secondary schools.[14] While only a small percentage of teachers belonged to Komsomol or the Party, Communists dominated the union's leadership.[15]

A Matter of Learning

Narkompros promoted learning as a medium for intellectual and social liberation; common Russians, as Jeffrey Brooks points out, valued it for its practical use in reading newspapers, agricultural almanacs, detective stories, tales of chivalry, and religious literature.[16] Teachers found themselves pressured from above by Narkompros and from below by parents. But if Narkompros was not in heaven, at least it was far away. Parents were another matter.

What Krupskaya found to be true during her trip down the Volga in 1919 was discovered by educators throughout the 1920s—that parents equated education with the acquisition of literacy and numeracy, after which the young were expected to work at home, in the fields, or in shops or factories. Peasants insisted on little else from their schools.[17] A survey of their opinions in late 1928 revealed disenchantment with the schools' failure to teach reading and writing. Some of those surveyed were more critical, asking, "Why does the teacher work only four hours a day?" and, "If all are taught, who will sow grain?"[18] In a small village in Moscow province, the local populace was not concerned that the school functioned in a working church. "Why do we need a school?" some asked.[19] In rural areas, attendance in the first and second grades dropped markedly when school schedules conflicted with harvest and planting seasons. Absenteeism in rural elementary schools followed the agricultural cycle—high in September and October (in those schools that attempted to open that early), and higher yet from March to May.[20]

Although not as pronounced, the same critical attitudes existed in urban areas. In 1925, the head of the Moscow Department of Education observed that parents everywhere judged the worth of a school by whether their children could read and write.[21] Many workers attending conferences on education in 1928 thought that secondary education was pointless.[22] Partly because the public did not share Narkompros's faith in education, pupils in the mid- and late 1920s received on the average only 2.8 years of schooling (a little less than four years in urban areas, and slightly higher than 2.6 years in rural regions).[23]

Given their limited objectives, parents needed little incentive to withdraw their children and support from schools. Sometimes they did so when fees, no matter how small, were imposed.[24] They skipped school meetings to avoid requests for firewood and money.[25] Parents and others in the community regarded school grounds and facilities as appropriate places for the removal of trees, the consumption of alcohol, communal gatherings, and church services. In one instance, negative attitudes toward the new school ceased only when it became useful by serving as a post office.[26]

The public saw little of value in the progressive curriculum. One inspector reported that parents, like teachers and local officials, did not understand the complex method or simply preferred the traditional approach.[27] Another inspector put it more bluntly: some peasants regarded the complex themes as "Bolshevik mumbo-jumbo."[28] Teachers who tried the progressive methods wrote to their union's periodicals that parents and local soviets jumped to the conclusion that there was little teaching in the schools. They regarded drawing and modeling as overindulgence of children, at best, and, more harshly, as absurd.[29] Excursions were met with the same skepticism. "There's nothing to do in the school so here you go off to the fields and meadows to step off or measure them with a rope; it's as if you want to make all of our children surveyors."[30] Teachers reported that parents preferred the traditional content and ambience—"lessons, bells, and books," and training in religion and in respect for elders.[31] For recalcitrant pupils, familiar remedies such as paddling and standing in a corner were suggested.[32]

An investigation of twenty-eight cantons in Penza province found considerable public hostility toward anything new in education. Angry because their children in the second grade did not know their letters, peasants blamed new instructional methods even when they were not used. "The 'compass',," they said, confusing "compass" with the "complex," "is only a form of amusement."[33] At school there is only "philosophizing and conniving and the object of this philosophizing is the children."[34] The same peasants wanted instruction in discipline, proper behavior, and religion. "We should teach children the fear of God or else they will grow up to become hooligans and thieves."[35] Teachers were distrusted as outsiders, as "dunces sent by Bolsheviks too ashamed to come themselves." While conducting an excursion, one instructor encountered the hostility of peasants who were certain that he was assessing property for the purpose of raising taxes.[36] The fact that so many teachers held a variety of official posts, even if compelled to do so, made the situation worse. Many peasants regarded them as representatives of an alien authority who had come "to collect taxes, arrest drunks, and compile a list of the belongings of each citizen."[37]

Confronted by this evidence, Narkompros acknowledged the unpopularity of its program. In 1925, the Pedagogical Section and the Moscow Department of Education admitted that the public equated progressive methods with an inadequate presentation of the "three R's."[38] Early the following year, Lunacharsky, while asserting that the complex method was gaining acceptance in urban areas, admitted that the peasantry opposed it because the "teacher teaches but children still do not know how to read, write, and count."[39]

More than anyone else, Shatsky exposed the widening gap between Narkompros and the public. Common Russians were stupefied by efforts to make the school a showcase of "cleanliness and beautiful flowers, a place for children to sing, play, and draw." They preferred old-fashioned instruction in the fundamentals of literacy.[40] After his field trip, Shatsky recalled a typical peasant response to progressive education.

> They [the pupils] sing, play, doodle, go out to look at frogs and don't study . . .
> That's not how they taught us. Let's say that they tell me to go to school
> and I don't want to go. Mother drags me there, I cry and go. Now that was
> a real school. But you only 'do da do' and that's what you're going to do
> for the whole time anyone's in school.[41]

School caretakers confided in Shatsky that pupils "only manage to sit or go out for a walk to look at frogs in the swamp."[42]

School graduates, their parents, and officials responsible for higher educational institutions joined common Russians in denouncing novel notions of learning. They demanded a curriculum congruent with requirements of higher educational institutions that had nothing to do with mastering complex themes. Narkompros's rhetoric aside, knowledge in the traditional disciplines had remained the best foundation for advanced instruction in Soviet Russia.

In 1923, the presidium of the Pedagogical Section admitted that its curriculum had failed those school graduates entering technical institutes and universities. Pupils taught according to progressive methods would have to memorize a great quantity of additional material. The presidium believed, however, that it could rectify the situation by persuading higher educational institutions to revise their expectations.[43] It was not to be. In 1926, they introduced oral and written entrance examinations in Russian language and mathematics, and oral sessions in social studies, literature, and physics. For the next few years, over half of the incoming class was chosen by competitive enrollment in which examination scores played a vital role.

Test results reinforced a preference among higher educational officials and secondary schoolteachers for systematic instruction. The first year of testing revealed that school graduates spelled poorly and were unacquainted with the classics of Russian literature (Pushkin, Tolstoy, Turgenev) and with contemporary Soviet literature. Many applicants failed the examinations in physics, and in some instances, over 60 percent flunked mathematics. They fared no better when questions shifted to the politically sensitive area of social studies. Many students knew little about the history of class struggle, Marxism, or the Soviet period. One respondent thought Komsomol was an "international organization of the homeless"; another, perhaps beguiled by visions of global revolution, asserted that Persia and China were entering the USSR.[44] The same distressing results occurred in 1927. Many students misspelled common words, misused foreign terms, rambled on aimlessly in written and oral responses, experienced problems with the division and multiplication of fractions, and could not use the metric system.[45] Nor had responses to questions on social studies improved. At the Herzen Pedagogical Institute in Leningrad, the Kazan Agricultural Institute, and Moscow State University, many applicants exhibited only limited knowledge about historical and recent developments essential to official ideology. They informed their examiners that the Chartist movement received its name from its leader, a Mr. Charter; that Bakunin was a French revolutionary who led the Chartist movement; and that imperialism was the best path to socialism.[46]

Independent testimony and other surveys reached the same conclusions. At the First All-Russian Conference of Secondary Schools, a delegate from Tula complained that school graduates knew little arithmetic and took fifteen minutes to read a page from Gogol.[47] The following December, a session on Russian language sponsored by the Moscow Department of Education spoke of the "scandalous illiteracy of our youth"; and a survey in Leningrad found what it called semi-literate pupils.[48] A confused seventh-grader wrote that with the abolition of serfdom, landlords in need of an occupation chose commerce, but because they were not acquainted with it, merchants took over.[49] A Narkompros investigation conducted in the spring of 1927 discovered that pupils in the third to seventh grades failed to distinguish between the 1905 and 1917 revolutions or between the February revolt of 1917 and the Bolshevik uprising eight months later.[50] One inspector claimed that pupils entering the fifth grade could memorize but not analyze material.[51] Reviewing these results, observers associated with Narkompros blamed teachers and students alike for ignoring its curricula and syllabi.[52] Other commentators critical of Narkompros's programs urged that more attention be paid to content, with periodic testing as reinforcement.[53]

Expert Opinion

The Soviet Union's first generation of Party historians joined the ranks of Narkompros's critics in demanding systematic instruction in history. In so doing, they refused to follow in the footsteps of their mentor, Pokrovsky, dean of the Marxist historical profession, member of the Pedagogical Section, and one of the authors of the new curriculum. They chose instead to pursue the interests of their discipline as they understood it. This independence of mind was most evident among members of the Methodology Section of the Society of Marxist Historians. L. P. Mamet, G. S. Fridliand, A. Z. Ioannisiani, and A. G. Slutsky, among others in the Section, condemned social studies and the complex method.[54] Failure to present historical information in chronological sequence had led to the memorization of sociological abstractions, slogans, and bits of unrelated information. As a result, students with seven and even nine years of education suffered from "historical illiteracy."[55] Students entering higher educational institutions understood neither capitalism, nor Party history, nor the historical method.[56]

These historians wanted structured syllabi and lesson plans, more attention to chronology, less preoccupation with themes, and improved instructional materials with more maps, illustrations, biographical information, and facts.[57] Ioannisiani spoke for his colleagues, demanding the study of history independent of any complex theme. What he called a "fetish for the complex" and the "complex for the sake of the complex" had contributed to "general educational illiteracy."[58] He stopped short, however, of calling for the complete abolition of the method, suggesting only that history be liberated from its influence.

Prominent Party members extolled the virtues of orderly instruction. Although they spoke primarily of political education, technical training, and higher specialized education, their comments contributed to an atmosphere increasingly inhospitable to Narkompros's school program. In the last years of his life, Lenin expressed his preference for a disciplined approach. These sentiments were echoed on the front page of *Pravda* in early 1921, by N. N. Baturin, historian and propagandist, who criticized Narkompros for its sloppy management of the school system and haphazard development of syllabi.[59] The Tenth Party Congress (March 1921) called for "systematic courses in the theory, history, and practice of Marxism."[60] On November 21, 1923, *Pravda* featured an article by students at the Party's Institute of Red Professors who rejected the application of the complex method to their curriculum. Although they conceded the method's possible usefulness for schoolchildren, they denounced it at their own level as a product of "super-revolutionary tendencies" and "super-contemporary platforms."[61] At the First All-Union Conference of Proletarian Students in April 1925, the Party's General Secretary, Joseph Stalin, complained that communist students fell behind their non-Party colleagues by wasting time on such political activities as debating world problems.[62] At the same time, the Party's Central Committee called upon Pioneer organizations to instill in their members better study habits and a respect for knowledge.[63]

Dropping Out

Some teachers remained determined to carry on as Narkompros wished. Their experiences demonstrated the difficult nature of the assignment and explained why so many of their colleagues avoided it. In an article in *Narodnyi uchitel'*, a teacher from Perm', K. Konovalova, recounted her despair at working against incalculable odds. She had had a particularly frustrating experience at a teachers' conference held during her December vacation, where she listened to boring and irrelevant speeches and complaints from colleagues. But on her way home late at night, Konovalova passed a brightly-lit school where children were spending the night preparing an exhibit. Revived by this sign of progress, Konovalova rededicated herself to her dual role as progressive instructor and cultural agent.[64] Another teacher kept going with the thought that history would vindicate the effort:

> We are Red Enlighteners
> And about us

> Some time historians will tell
> About how, when in those difficult days
> Hanging over the school,
> Hungry and stubbornly,
> Forward we marched.[65]

Most teachers, however, could not sustain any initial enthusiasm they may have felt for the Narkompros program. A captivating example appeared in the July 1926 issue of *Narodnyi uchitel'*. It included an article by E. Gaidovskaia, a young Muscovite who had been ordered to report to a school in a remote area, ninety miles from a town or a railroad.[66] She had first heard of the complex only two weeks beforehand. Now she ventured forth "with her instructions to report (naznachenie) in one hand and the Narkompros program in the other." Upon arrival, she found a dilapidated school with no books on the shelves, one blackboard for three classes, and, in her second grade classroom, one desk for every three pupils. Violating Narkompros's egalitarian spirit, she divided her class into strong and weak groups, the latter of which included pupils who had forgotten half of the alphabet. This device did not work, nor was help forthcoming from people associated with the school. When she pestered the director to help her draw up a plan for the complex method, he responded: "The complexes. On the table is the Narkompros program, on your shoulders a head. Think of something." Parents looked askance at anything new, including instruction in singing and drawing. They preferred harsh disciplinary measures; some withdrew their children from school. That first December, the inspector came and actually discouraged the use of the complex method. He created more difficulties by taking away the individual responsible for the local campaign against adult illiteracy, whose job then fell to an already overburdened Gaidovskaia. The result was predictable. Gaidovskaia, who had begun with so much enthusiasm, took her pedagogical library and the Narkompros program off the table and placed them under her bed, where both began, perhaps with Gaidovskaia herself, to hibernate for the winter.

By reporting to a remote village, Gaidovskaia demonstrated more dedication than some of her colleagues. She acceded to laws requiring that graduates of higher educational institutions be placed for a period equalling the number of years they received a stipend; graduates of technicums were required to accept an assignment for a period half that amount.[67] The law allowed students to avoid this obligation by reimbursing the amount of the stipend and the average cost of their education. However, few of those who refused their assignment ever made such reparations.

Many graduates promptly used their degree to find better paying and less hazardous jobs. In 1926, a conference of *Uchitel'skaia gazeta* correspondents concluded that a "significant number" of students completing pedagogical institutes avoided entering the profession.[68] The State Academic Council discovered that at best, 30 percent of students completing pedagogical institutes and technicums would become teachers.[69] In late 1927, the Party's

Central Committee complained that graduates refused to work in rural areas.[70] One Muscovite teacher thought that he and his colleagues could be induced to improve their behavior. He suggested that anyone sent out from a major city be guaranteed the right of return. To insure this possibility, he called for the construction of special dormitories in Moscow and in other urban centers.[71] Given the extent of the problem and the shortage of resources, the Soviet government was more inclined to consider tougher assignment procedures. By the early 1930s, if not earlier, it considered registering all persons with pedagogical training for possible reassignment.[72]

We do not know what became of Gaidovskaia. Perhaps she found another school with slightly better conditions—the flight of teachers from one school to another was a major problem throughout the 1920s.[73] Perhaps she retired from teaching. Many instructors entered another profession or joined the swollen ranks of the unemployed.[74] Some unemployment was unavoidable following dismissals, when neither teachers, Narkompros, nor local agencies could pay for transportation to another locale.[75] Some of the unemployed in Russian cities came from union and autonomous republics, where they had been removed from their posts upon adoption of the local language as the chief vehicle of instruction.[76] Many of the unemployed prolonged their status by refusing assignments to any area other than a major city. The First Conference of Secondary Schools heard of jobless teachers in "large cultural centers" who refused to go to rural areas where there was a "colossal shortage."[77] In 1927, a plenary session of the teachers union's central committee discovered the dimension of this problem. A survey of 6,000 unemployed teachers residing in Moscow revealed that only fifty-seven desired to take up positions in the countryside; of 5,000 in Leningrad, only three did so.[78]

Prospective teachers often quit before they had the opportunity to enter the profession. In the late 1920s, 12 percent of the enrollment in pedagogical technicums dropped out each year. Academic failure was not the primary reason in many cases;[79] an investigation in 1931 discovered that over half of the students quit because they did not want to become teachers after all.[80]

In sum, a variety of forces reinforced a preference among teachers to adhere to old ways. Pressed on all sides by Narkompros, specialists, parents, and local officials, and faced with difficult working conditions in the classroom, teachers had good reason to resent added responsibilities. For many, it was a major achievement to remain committed to the profession. For those who did take up Moscow's challenge to remake school and community, frustration and tragedy ensued. They inherited the worst of all possible worlds. One delegate at the 1925 First Congress of Teachers spoke for all his colleagues when he said that the government did not really trust its teaching cadre, while the peasantry regarded them as purveyors of Bolshevism and atheism.[81] Another instructor observed: "It's obvious that the peasantry and Narkompros sit on two stools, and we, the teachers, are in-between."[82]

When Narkompros tried to help, circumstances frequently went from bad to worse. Its teacher training institutions were dismal places, its repreparation courses horrendous displays of insensitive and bad management, and its publications and instructions, when available, incomprehensible. Its efforts to raise the minimum salary allowed for a widening differential between secondary and primary teachers, to the detriment of the latter, and it watched helplessly as local authorities arbitrarily set the amount and date of payments. Laws designed to protect teachers were honored in the breach, sometimes with the complicity of the very organs empowered to enforce them.

For many reasons, then, teachers rejected the new curriculum. By their imagination and excellence, and by the absence of such qualities, they undermined Narkompros policy. It seemed heroics enough to cling to their jobs and provide the basics of literacy and numeracy. The most bold and articulate of their number, however, expressed their opposition vigorously at conferences and in the press. Narkompros had no choice but to acknowledge widespread passive and active resistance. Would Narkompros follow with changes in policy? Would it budge?

Part Three.

Compromise, 1925-1928

I doubt very much whether the communists
are the ones who are leading . . . . To tell
the truth, they are the ones who are
being led.
>—Lenin at the 1922 Eleventh
>Party Congress

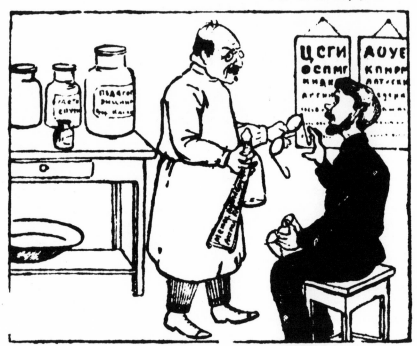

У глазного врача.

Школы работают по стабилизированным программам.

Рис. С. Я. Барсукова.

ДОКТОР: Вот вам новые очки другого размера. Они будут сидеть отлично. А это — примочка для глаз, употребляйте чаще...

Narkompros Compromises with Teachers

"At the Eye Doctor's. Schools work with stabilized syllabi." Cartoon by S. Ia. Barsukov. Lunacharsky, posing as the doctor, tells his patient, a teacher, "Here are new eyeglasses in a different size. They will fit you perfectly. And here is some eyewash. Use it more often . . . " Lunacharsky is prescribing the new 1927 curriculum, more suitable to classroom conditions than previous curricula. On the large label attached to the bottle of eyewash is written "a methods guidebook." The large jar on the table reads "the Pedagogical Encyclopedia of Prof. Kalashnikov," referring to the initial volume of a three-volume work published from 1927 to 1930 and written by A. G. Kalashnikov and others associated with Narkompros.

SOURCE: *Uchitel'skaia gazeta,* no. 4 (179) (January 20, 1928), p. 3.

IX.

POLICY RUNNING
AFTER PRACTICE

While Narkompros acknowledged that its program created hardships for everyone involved with schooling, it insisted that pupils, teachers, and public conform to its expectations of them. Stubbornly maintaining its opinions, the Pedagogical Section increased the number of obligatory features in its curriculum. Narkompros intended to remake more than just the classroom; it could not allow anything to impede the march of progress.

In late 1925, a different attitude began to emerge in the Pedagogical Section, State Academic Council, and Narkompros Collegium. Major concessions toward traditional instruction in both primary and secondary schools followed over the next two years. The primary stimulus for these changes came from below. Responding to pressure from teachers, parents, and the lower echelons of its own apparatus, Narkompros began to rewrite policy in the image of classroom practice. By the fall of 1927, policy and practice had entered into an intriguing courtship, fraught with many happy possibilities for all concerned.

Arrogance of Scruples, 1921–1925

The Pedagogical Section's new curriculum immediately encountered popular resistance. It was an ugly truth, challenging reigning pedagogical and ideological scruples at the Commissariat. Narkompros first responded by disingenuously pleading ignorance of developments below.[1] Certainly the flow of information within the Narkompros apparatus, from the top down and the bottom up, was not what it should have been. But inspectors' reports, periodical literature (especially *Uchitel'skaia gazeta*), conferences, field trips by officials, and reports from Rabkrin amply demonstrated the actual state of affairs. Much of this information came directly to the Pedagogical Section and the State Academic Council.[2]

Another tactic was therefore in order. Narkompros chose to blame recalcitrant teachers. It was an intriguing twist for a body that had begun with such optimistic faith in people. But perhaps it could do little else. It had little hope for additional funding that might make a difference, and it did not want to condemn policies to which it remained committed. In addition, as Margaret Stolee demonstrates, the very organization of Narkompros encouraged a stubbornness of purpose. The State Academic Council and its Pedagogical Section had so many subsections, committees, commissions and subcommissions, all staffed by the same people, that their members had little opportunity to get out from under the ideological and intellectual baggage with which they arrived.[3] A plenary session of the Pedagogical Section held on September 8, 1925, declared that the Section's work was dysfunctional because so many organs existed within it.[4] At the next session, Krupskaya raised the issue again with a complaint about disorganization and duplication of effort.[5]

Little was done to correct the problem. Archival records reveal that leading figures in the Pedagogical Section were kept running hither and yon, from one policy-making body to the next. In addition to his responsibilities at the First Experimental Station, Shatsky attended meetings of the Section's presidium and plenum as well as of its departments (subsections) for methods and for management. Blonsky attended sessions of the Section's presidium and plenum, chaired the presidium's department on methods, and served as a member of the department on pedagogical education. O. L. Bem, head of the State Academic Council in 1924, sat on the Pedagogical Section and served in the department for the protection of juveniles, in the department for children's literature and textbooks, and on the commission for developing a textbook for social studies. Krupskaya was active in the Pedagogical Section and Political Section of the State Academic Council, and also headed Glavpolitprosvet. Despite this overlapping of personnel, organs within the State Academic Council and Pedagogical Section failed to exchange information and worked at cross purposes.[6] Years later, an incestuous relationship among agencies, each duplicating the impractical efforts of the other, was given as one of the major reasons for an extensive purge and reorganization of Narkompros.[7]

Lacking the inclination and organization to do otherwise, Narkompros stayed the course, with the Pedagogical Section leading the way. In early 1923, it rejected restoration of the pre-revolutionary class tutor (nastavnik).[8] The State Academic Council followed with a stern denunciation of the practice in a circular to all of its provincial departments.[9] Later that year, when higher educational institutions criticized the new curriculum for neglecting the needs of advanced instruction, the Pedagogical Section assumed that higher education would change its expectations of school graduates.[10] Narkompros scolded its local departments of education for complaints about the lack of instructions from Moscow. It informed them that all such items were published in the Commissariat's *Biulleten' ofitsial'nykh rasporiazhenii i soobshchenii* (Bulletin of Official Orders and Reports), of which three copies were sent to each provincial department of education and one to each district department.[11] In so doing, Narkompros ignored the fact that its intentions in the way of publication and distribution hardly matched performance. Similarly officious remarks were made the following year. A teacher requesting advice on methods was told that local pedagogical institutions and method bureaus could provide such information.[12] The State Academic Council asked instructors to pay more attention to penmanship, while at the same time prohibiting special lessons in the subject.[13]

In 1925, the Pedagogical Section adopted what appeared to be a more helpful approach. It published two editions of *Programmy GUS'a i massovaia shkola* (GUS Syllabi and the School), a manual for the new curriculum.[14] The following year, Narkompros prepared a similar work specifically for elementary schoolteachers.[15] None of these projects was printed in sufficient quantity to make a difference. The two editions of the 1925 manual were printed in runs of 7,200 and 16,000 copies, while the volume that followed numbered 8,000. Teachers who received one of the three may have regretted it. The Section used the publications to remind rebellious instructors that learning was not the transmission of content, but a process leading to a scientific-materialistic understanding of the world.[16] It declared the complex method to be a Marxist device and blamed teachers for its dismal record. Such teachers were purportedly politically backward, inert, uncreative, and disorganized. In a burst of convoluted thinking, the Section condemned the "reactionary tendencies of the passive element among the teaching cadre."[17]

Addressing the gap between policy and practice, the Pedagogical Section resolved to force the adoption of the complex method by issuing precise instructions for its implementation. Teachers were given detailed advice on how to overcome all difficulties by a display of energy and willpower. Drawing from developments in industry, the Section proposed adoption of the so-called scientific organization of labor (nauchnaia organizatsiia truda or NOT, as it was often abbreviated).[18] To compensate for a shortage of materials and equipment, it recommended that teachers devise a production plan.[19] To overcome parental resistance, it urged teachers to become propagandists in the local community.[20] One member of the Pedagogical Section, A. S. Tolstov, went to great lengths to explain how a teacher responsible for three classes might employ the complex method.[21]

Architects of the new curriculum rushed to its defense. In 1924, Blonsky disapproved of more precise instructions, hoping that schools would move spontaneously in the preferred direction.[22] Bem, however, defended the Commissariat's initiative. Putting it in Manichean terms, he spoke of a need for a "class school which must be . . . at the communist front to conduct an uncompromising struggle with the old world." Bem regarded the Narkompros program as the basis for the creation of such a class school.[23] Krupskaya boasted in *Pravda* in mid-1926 that the new curriculum had won global prestige for the Soviet Union.[24] While addressing the All-Russian Central Executive Committee that year, Krupskaya charged that many teachers deviously picked on the complex method because they found the Narkompros program new and its content revolutionary.[25]

Efficiency Through Order

"NOT [The Scientific Organization of Labor] in the year 2027. Motto: NOT."
The sign under the clock reads "Advanced laboratory." A sign behind the teacher
says "Hot breakfasts." The dials on the lectern are labeled "Unconditioned
reflexes" and "Conditioned reflexes." The sign above the door says "Schedule."
In the caption under the cartoon the teacher, a practitioner of NOT, tells his
class: "Well, Comrade mechanisms, attention! Gather up your reflexes. One and
a half seconds—one, two, three."
SOURCE: *Uchitel'skaia gazeta*, no. 46 (169) (November 11, 1927), p. 5.

Esipov opposed any concessions. After graduating from Petrograd University in 1918, Esipov taught history in a secondary school before joining
Narkompros and the Pedagogical Section in 1923.[26] His experience as a
teacher did not make him sympathetic to the plight of his former colleagues.
In articles and in major addresses at educational conferences, Esipov insisted
that teachers stop grumbling, work harder, and adopt new curricula devised
with current difficult conditions in mind.[27] Esipov had a ready answer for
every conceivable problem. When informed that instructors lacked adequate
knowledge of the complex method, he told them to read *Na putiakh k novoi
shkole* and the Pedagogical Section's instructional letter on the subject.[28]

Apprised of the absence of equipment and instructional materials, he observed that the new methods required fewer of these items.[29]

Esipov was no less demanding and curt with teachers during his tour of repreparation courses in the summer of 1924. Told of excessive socially useful labor, he responded that schooling and community service were interrelated functions.[30] When informed of parents' antagonism toward new methods, he ordered teachers to march out and persuade them to think otherwise.[31] Although Esipov encouraged the adaptation of Moscow's syllabi to local conditions, he denounced the result. He was not pleased when local departments of education repositioned complex themes from one part of the year to the next, or when individual teachers permitted more attention to instruction in specific skills. Esipov adamantly opposed widespread efforts to focus attention on subjects in the secondary grades to the detriment of a thematic approach.[32] He believed that Narkompros's 1923 syllabus for the fifth grade suffered from "an insufficient adherence to the complex principle."[33] While acknowledging the importance of factual knowledge as a prerequisite for higher education, Esipov insisted that higher educational institutions alter their curricula to accommodate the progressive school program. He referred to negotiations underway in 1924, which would lead to the alterations desired.[34] Two years later, however, higher educational institutions and technicums moved in the opposite direction by introducing competitive entrance examinations.

Provincial Departments of Education

Provincial departments of education proved more accommodating than Narkompros of the desires and practices of teachers. Their behavior put more pressure on the Commissariat of Enlightenment to compromise. While not all provincial organs issued curricula that departed significantly from central instructions, many demanded presentation of knowledge and skills arrranged by subjects.[35] At the elementary level this meant a preoccupation with literacy and numeracy, with approximately 25 percent or more of instructional time devoted to reading and writing and about 20 percent to arithmetic.[36] Like teachers, some departments proceeded cautiously, manipulating the complex method to allow for familiar disciplines. In 1923, the Petrograd Department of Education limited its suggestions for innovation to recommending wood, iron, and fire as common foci for subjects in the primary grades.[37] The following year, the Urals Regional Department of Education specified the knowledge and skills to be taught in each subject, while proposing broad overarching themes for primary and secondary grades.[38] Two years later, the Ivanovo-Voznesensk Department of Education proceeded to do the same for the third and fourth grades. Upset by the high rate of failure in grades four and five and by the illiteracy of elementary school graduates, it demanded special attention to reading, writing, and arithmetic. Sixty percent of instruction in language and mathematics was to be devoted to the inculcation of skills rather than to the study of themes or the performance of socially useful activity.[39]

Departments of education used their own curricula to censure Narkompros. Their objections echoed complaints of the Republic's instructors: Narkompros failed to provide sufficiently detailed curricula and tailored its program to the ideal rather than the real world.[40] In 1922, the Vladimir Department of Education condemned Narkompros for "fruitless attempts to build grand structures on sand."[41] One year later, the Samara Department of Education criticized Narkompros for devising programs for the nonexistent new school, new teacher, and new text.[42] Even two friendly departments registered mild demurrals in 1925. The Northern Dvinsk Department of Education remarked that teachers found the complex method difficult to implement;[43] the Komi regional department observed that teachers adhered to subjects "covered by the sauce" of the complex method.[44]

It was the Moscow Department of Education (MONO), however, that emerged as the Commissariat's toughest critic and rival. Comparing their own department with the Commissariat, MONO's leaders proudly pointed to its greater concern for the needs of teachers. From the point of view of the nation's instructors, the Moscow Department had reason to strut. While Narkompros recommended less formality in judging a pupil's progress, MONO urged periodic oral and written evaluations of small groups and individuals.[45] Its Central Pedagogical Laboratory followed with standards for measuring skills in reading, writing, and arithmetic.[46] Every Monday and Tuesday, the department's methods section met with local inspectors, school directors, and teachers; about half of each meeting was devoted to a critical evaluation of Narkompros curricula. Officials and teachers alike questioned the feasibility of the complex method and emphasized the importance of content.[47] The following year, MONO's representative to the Pedagogical Section, N. M. Shul'man, took the department's art of communication with teachers as justification for a didactic message. At the Section's session of September 24, he reported that the department's methods section had maintained contact with instructors through a special laboratory. He suggested that the Pedagogical Section and State Academic Council do the same for "only then will our work be adapted to life."[48]

In its own curricula, the Moscow Department made good on its promise of independence. It started cautiously in 1921 with programs little distinct from what Narkompros proposed.[49] This compliance was short-lived. In 1923, MONO's program emphasized subjects for primary as well as secondary grades, an approach that provoked criticism from the Commissariat's Pedagogical Section.[50] P. N. Shimbirev, a teacher since 1904 and now an instructor at a Moscow pedagogical technicum, responded in kind. The Section's curriculum lacked substance; it was especially unfortunate that it neglected literacy and numeracy.[51] That fall, the Moscow Department's agency responsible for primary and secondary schooling, the Council of the Administration for Social Training, gave the new Narkompros curriculum only tepid support and that only after stern criticism of it. Blonsky came to defend the complex method; council members denounced it for preventing the logical development of a pupil's knowledge from year to year. The Council recommended that only those schools that believed they could manage somehow should adopt the new method.[52] One year later, the same organ approved another of the Commissariat's programs, after insisting that not all subjects respond to a single theme and that separate hours be set aside for the learning of a body of knowledge.[53] MONO's own curricula for 1925 reflected its escalating concern for content, including support for separate lessons in arithmetic in the primary grades.[54]

The following year, the Moscow Department took bolder steps. Its letter on methods for the elementary grades released in January 1926 declared that the complex method precluded acquisition of knowledge. The Department recommended lessons free of complex themes, especially in reading, writing, and arithmetic. To reinforce its point, it listed by grade the skills it thought all pupils should learn in language and arithmetic, and approved systematic instruction by subject in grades five through seven.[55]

Later that year, MONO challenged Narkompros programs with two manuals for elementary teachers. Written by teachers at the Department's School No. 14, the volumes recommended that more attention be paid to instruction in reading, writing, and arithmetic. The introduction to each manual called special attention to articles by A. Tikhomirova, who stressed the need for special exercises and lessons independent of complex themes.[56] Tikhomirova complained that adherence to Narkompros programs had produced inarticulate and illiterate pupils who could not perform basic arithmetical calculations.[57] Many complex themes, such as those dealing with revolutionary holidays or the seasons, contained little or no material to rectify the situation. She demanded detailed lessons and not "hit and miss exercises."[58]

The new curriculum released by the Moscow Department that year reflected these concerns. Its program for primary grades in rural schools, although pledging loyalty to the complex method, demanded systematic instruction in traditional subjects.[59] The curriculum for grades five through seven moved dramatically in this direction. It began with the assertion that schools should not lose sight of their "eternal mission" to teach reading, writing, and arithmetic.[60] While concerned with themes, the curriculum arranged information by subject—geography, natural sciences, physics, chemistry, mathematics, Russian, German, and social studies.

In December of 1926 the Moscow Department of Education took one more step toward traditional education. It agreed with those teachers who relied on tests to check the academic progress of pupils.[61] Several months later, MONO declared that homework was useful for the transmission of information and necessary where material and human shortages reduced the amount of classtime.[62]

State and Party Organizations

The Moscow branch joined other provincial departments of education in stressing the importance of literacy and numeracy for the vast majority of pupils enrolled in primary schools. A few departments proposed curricular changes with the loftier goal of preparing students for higher education.[63] Elements within the technical lobby favored a traditional curriculum in the secondary grades as a prerequisite for the training of specialists.

A concern for a knowledgeable and useful product rather than for a "new person" dominated the thinking of the highest State organ in the Russian Republic, the Soviet of Peoples Commissars. On July 23, 1926, it complained of "inadequate leadership of secondary education by central and local educational organs" and of the absence of firm syllabi and texts. It wanted curricula and textbooks relevant to the needs of industry.[64] The same considerations were evident in a decree by the Party's Central Committee on social studies, January 18, 1927. Narkompros had not compiled sufficiently detailed syllabi or textbooks and had not taken into consideration the admission requirements of higher educational institutions. The Party demanded that Narkompros, together with the Central Committee's Agitation and Propaganda Department (Agitprop), quickly correct the problem.[65]

A Change in Attitude

Teachers, provincial departments of education, the technical lobby, and government and Party organs all brought pressure upon Narkompros to change its ways. Faced with criticism from above and rebellion in the classroom below, Narkompros cast aside some of its arrogance. It began with a modest reassessment of the curriculum in the early 1920s that turned into an extensive reappraisal in the mid-1920s. This process was well under way before Sovnarkom and the Central Committee required new syllabi and texts for the secondary school. When Narkompros and the Pedagogical Section issued new curricula in 1926 and 1927, they sought primarily a compromise with the forces below—provincial departments of education, teachers, and parents.

Of the architects of the new school, Krupskaya was one of the first to propose closing the gap between central pretense and classroom reality. Concerned for the substance as well as the methods of instruction, she urged that textbooks be made available to provide information and direction to pupils and teachers. She reported that where schools lacked textbooks, "peasants simply stopped sending their children because they considered it to mean the absence of serious lessons."[66] In comments to the State Academic Council and Pedagogical Section, she appealed for careful instruction in the basics. Krupskaya still opposed lessons which were not based on complex themes, but she did favor the preparation of an instructional letter on inculcating language and arithmetical skills within the context of the complex method.[67] At the Pedagogical Section's session of September 24, 1925, Krupskaya demanded the preparation of detailed syllabi that specified the knowledge and skills to be learned in elementary and secondary grades.[68] As a point of departure for future deliberations, she asked the Section to pay more attention to everyday problems encountered by the school.

By the mid-1920s, other key figures in the Pedagogical Section had expressed a willingness to compromise. In 1925, Pistrak commented that the new Narkompros curriculum for grades five through seven accommodated teachers by preserving separate subjects. Although themes remained important, the secondary school teacher was not required to relate each subject each day to a particular theme.[69] Blonsky modified his position. At the Pedagogical Section's session of September 24, 1925, he agreed with Krupskaya that future policy should allow for classroom practice.[70] That same year, a less prominent but active member of the Pedagogical Section, A. Radchenko, sympathetically acknowledged difficulties experienced by teachers and promised to pay more attention to instruction in reading, writing, and arithmetic.[71] The complex method should not be a fetish, he insisted, and should not stand in the way of instruction in skills.[72]

In 1924 and 1925, the Pedagogical Section acknowledged that more attention should be given to a presentation of knowledge by discipline. When its School Commission met on March 27, 1925, teachers came to urge it in this direction. In particular, they insisted that Russian language and mathematics be taught apart from complex themes. Parents demanded a traditional approach and teachers complied. But the Section was reluctant to stray too far from the thematic approach. Krupskaya feared concessions would doom any hope for the eventual implementation of the complex method. A majority agreed.[73]

It took a devastating report by Rabkrin, presented to the Section on December 10, 1925, to elicit a stonger response. Based on an investigation of schools in forty-two cantons during the first half of the year, Rabkrin found a distorted application, at best, of the complex method amidst traditional instruction in literacy and numeracy. It demanded that the Section consider conditions confronting schools and the real and desired practices of teachers. While Rabkrin avoided suggesting an abolition of the complex method, it favored fewer themes, with those that remained being suitable for teaching content.[74]

Promises to do better followed, one tripping over the other. Gone was the former stubbornness when confronted with complaints and objectionable practices of teachers. At the December 10 session, Shatsky, Krupskaya, and Epshtein agreed that future programs should be more practical. Shatsky put it simply: "Our programs are too complicated for the teacher."[75] The Section created a commission to devise curricular changes to match "real life conditions."[76] Exactly one week later, under the prodding of Epshtein, the

Pedagogical Section proposed to help the effort with a standardized list of instructional materials. It called upon a special commission to compile a list of manuals, reference works, laboratory instruments, drawings, and toys to facilitate systematic instruction.[77]

Concern for content led the Section to reassess socially useful work. On March 11, 1926, V. N. Shul'gin, director of the School Methods Institute, defended community activity as an integral part of education.[78] The Section's membership was skeptical. Led by Shatsky, they proposed careful regulation of socially useful activity to ensure that it had pedagogical value. Even Esipov agreed with this altered emphasis.[79] An author of one of the articles appearing in the first issue of *Na putiakh k novoi shkole*, G. O. Gordon, declared: "The teacher must be a real teacher and only then a social worker (obshchest-vennik)."[80] Krupskaya followed with the axiom, "better less, but better."[81] One of the Section's less prominent but active members, I. L. Tsvetkov, captured the spirit and promise of this day: "We systematically are mistaken with our campaigns [that] confuse the most active teachers (aktiv) for the mass of teachers . . . In 1926, we should talk not about launching campaigns but about consolidating our work."[82]

More than any other figure in the Pedagogical Section, Shatsky urged a compromise with teachers. By the mid-1920s, he had concluded that the Section could march in advance of teachers, but not by much. Otherwise, teachers would lack any sense of achieving change in concert with Narkompros. They would oppose "administrative pressure and old author-itarian ways."[83] M. N. Skatkin, a teacher at Shatsky's Experimental Station from 1920 to 1930, later recalled that Shatsky returned from the Section's sessions convinced that new syllabi should consider the "real situation and the needs of the average teacher."[84] In the Section's *Na putiakh k novoi shkole* and in Narkompros's monthly, *Narodnoe prosveshchenie*, Shatsky admitted that the Commissariat's curricula and its "pile of letters on methods" had asked far too much of teachers, who were coping with shortages and public hostility. He insisted that future curricula and syllabi must be more realistic, and should include lessons in reading, writing, arithmetic, and other subject areas apart from complex themes.[85] Current syllabi were not the "gospel or a Talmud"; instruction in silent vowels need not be connected with the theme "cow." Shatsky's dictum became: "If old methods achieve your aims, use them."[86]

The first to follow his own advice, Shatsky attempted to spend less time in Moscow and more in the practical work of his Experimental Station. In 1926 he confided in a letter to Krupskaya his fear of becoming a damnable bureaucrat (chinovnik).[87] Two years later, Shatsky approached the heretical at a gathering of educational theoreticians with the declaration: "We give ourselves too much significance."[88]

Yet Shatsky hoped to retain many of the progressive elements. His letter to Krupskaya referred to this "very dangerous moment in the transition of our school to a path too sensible (zdravye rel'sy)."[89] He urged Narkompros to preserve complex themes, socially useful labor, and activity methods by encouraging their intelligent use.[90]

Social Studies

The reappraisal of Narkompros's curricula included a lively discussion of social studies and history. The First All-Russian Conference of Secondary Schools, held in Moscow July 5–10, 1925, declared that history "does not have significance in and of itself" in the junior division of the secondary school.[91] But the matter became more complex when Porovsky took the floor to speak about the senior division. He seemed a changed man, ready to promote instruction in history. Perhaps educators had angered him with their attacks on history, declaring it an incurably bourgeois, scholastic, and bankrupt discipline. Whatever the cause, Pokrovsky instructed educators in the virtues of historical scholarship. Marx and Lenin loved history and recognized its importance for an understanding of the contemporary period; relevance should not preclude knowledge of chronology, feudalism, or capitalism.[92] But after this rhetorical flourish, Pokrovsky stopped short of calling for substantial changes in the curriculum. When pressed by questions from the floor, he allowed only the addition of an unspecified amount of historical material.[93]

Some delegates were satisfied that Pokrovsky had avoided making concrete suggestions. Others feared that any concession would lead to a preoccupation with the past to the detriment of relevance.[94] For a majority of delegates, social studies remained a course focusing on the local area and contemporary period, allowing for no more than an episodic treatment of the history of labor, production, classes, and revolution.[95]

Eight months later, Pokrovsky seemed to shift his position at a conference on "Historicism as Applied to Social Studies in the Secondary Schools," organized by the Pedagogical Section. Krupskaya delivered the major address, recommending that the social studies curriculum permit some study of the past apart from contemporaneity.[96] Her proposal stirred up a hornet's nest. Zhavoronkov and Dziubinsky declared that history instruction would burden pupils with a difficult subject and would obstruct implementation of the complex method.[97] Pokrovsky agreed, adding that Krupskaya's suggestions would allow a quasi-bourgeois concentration on national and political history. He asked sarcastically whether memorization of the names of all the Roman emperors should be required.[98] Krupskaya responded that she had not proposed a separate course in history, but only something consisting of more than hit-and-miss excursions into the past. In her estimation, a more systematic approach to the past that relied on detailed directions and a textbook would guarantee relevant instruction along Marxist lines.[99]

Following his quarrel with Krupskaya, Pokrovsky returned to a more moderate view in speeches and articles in 1926 and 1927.[100] School curricula had not provided a sufficient study of history, he admitted, and had unduly focused on the local region. He endorsed the suggestions of the Methodology Section of the Society of Marxist Historians for improved instructional materials to facilitate an understanding of past and present.[101] Yet Pokrovsky remained committed to social studies as the proper context for history.[102] Without the medium of social studies, inexperienced and untrustworthy teachers might become fascinated with chronological tables, political reforms, state decrees, and the activity of tsars and government ministers.[103] To insure the preservation of "Marxist social studies," Pokrovsky required that future history texts be submitted to politicians who could "filter [them] from the Marxist dialectical point of view."[104]

Turning Point: The Curricula of 1926 and 1927

Pokrovsky was justified in believing that major changes were in the offing. On March 31, 1925, the State Academic Council sanctioned instruction in language and arithmetic independently of the complex method in elementary schools.[105] The following year, on January 29 and May 19, the Pedagogical Section discussed draft curricula with similar proposals.[106] The curriculum for the elementary grades diverted attention away from themes and toward instruction in literacy and numeracy. It explicitly allowed separate lessons in language and arithmetic. The draft for grades five through seven emphasized subjects and proposed instruction in history separate from contemporaneity. These major concessions to the Section's critics went a long way toward matching desired and actual practices of teachers. The Pedagogical Section understood the significance of what it had done. Some of its members thought the retreat too extensive; others warned against any further concessions.

Blonsky expressed serious reservations. He complained that the new curricula isolated complex themes from instruction in the elementary and secondary school.[107] Bem remained hostile, opposed to any revision of the complex method in the secondary grades.[108] Others objected to the disappearance of their pet themes.[109] B. V. Vsesviatsky, a former teacher of biology and head of the Timiriazev Agro-Biological Station for Young Naturalists, grumbled that programs should be compiled "not with the present level of teacher in mind, but based on the teacher's growth; otherwise we will return to old programs."[110] Esipov was surprisingly quiet at these two sessions,[111] but he insisted on the importance of complex themes at the Section's sessions later in the year and in articles published in 1927.[112]

Even Krupskaya expressed some concern. Although the Pedagogical Section had mistakenly attempted to force its will on schools, it was no time to panic. The draft curriculum for the primary grades had gone too far toward the traditional. Reading instruction amounted to recitation and retelling stories. The language program smacked of a fondness for memorization and the syllabus for natural sciences was preoccupied with facts. Fearing that the complex method might be abandoned in the primary school, Krupskaya opposed the preparation of syllabi until improved model complexes could be devised.[113] Shatsky, Epshtein, and Shul'man, however, found the new curricula to be an effective compromise between the complex method and content-oriented instruction.[114]

On May 6 and 7, as the draft curricula were being returned to the Section's commissions for refinement, Epshtein reported to the State Academic Council on his recent field trip. Concluding that the new school did not exist, he recommended syllabi that stressed content. The new school could be no less serious about literacy than the old.[115] The State Academic Council agreed, if only to prevent a loss of control over the Republic's teachers:

> Reactionaries do not yet have influence over teachers, but they will acquire it if the center does not consider the needs of teachers. It is time to become realists, it is time to lower our demands of teachers and arm them with the necessary knowledge and skills.[116]

Finding Epshtein's experience worthy of emulation, the Council suggested that its members spend three months annually in the field, working with teachers and schools.[117]

A rewriting of policy to match practice ruled the day. A few months after Epshtein's report, Narkompros released new curricula for the first two elementary grades in rural areas and for grades five through seven everywhere which were similar to earlier drafts presented to the Pedagogical Section. The program for elementary grades allowed lessons in reading, writing, and arithmetic which were not based on complex themes.[118] For the secondary grades, the curriculum feebly tied instruction in mathematics, chemistry, physics, and literature to such broad annual themes as "The City as a Center of Production" or "Our Tasks in the Countryside." Narkompros recommended that almost 30 percent of instructional time in grades five through seven be devoted to mathematics, physics, and chemistry; 12 percent to language and literature; and 9 percent to foreign language.[119] Social studies separated history and contemporaneity and directed more attention to the past.[120] Subsequent instructional notes urged more instruction in history, even in the elementary school.[121]

On November 15, 1926, a Glavsotsvos conference on methods endorsed the new direction in official policy. After acknowledging the importance of the complex method and of modifications to meet local needs, it demanded content-oriented instruction that would vary little from place to place. Relating instruction to a theme was of secondary importance to a larger objective of providing academic skills, especially in literacy and numeracy.[122] At the same time, Glavsotsvos required teachers to test each pupil's knowledge through conversation and written work.[123]

More changes followed in the spring and summer of 1927. On March 3, the Narkompros Collegium demanded a new secondary school curriculum

more detailed in its content, applicable for many years to come, and obligatory. Local departments of education might implement their own variants
only after confirmation by Narkompros.[124] The Collegium suggested a law
requiring a minimum number of hours for the study of each individual
discipline in each grade throughout the Republic.[125]

That summer, the Pedagogical Section issued detailed curricula and syllabi
for elementary and secondary grades.[126] The Section still employed a progressive vocabulary of community involvement, labor, and activity methods.
Full reliance on the complex method remained the ultimate goal.[127] For the
first time, the secondary school curriculum offered labor as a separate subject
to which over 8 percent of the total instructional time was to be devoted.[128]
The syllabus for social studies, released later that year, moved only cautiously
toward a greater focus on the past.[129] These concessions to progressive education aside, in every other respect the Section's curricula emphasized content
arranged by traditional subjects. The elementary school offered reading,
writing, and arithmetic as "one of the most important tasks of the school."[130]
"The new school values academic skills in native language no less than the
old."[131] The section allowed up to 50 percent of classtime in the first four
grades for instruction in linguistic and arithmetical skills outside the study
of any theme.[132] For the first three grades of the secondary school, it proposed
that foreign language, chemistry, literature, natural science, and contemporaneity be taught independent of complex themes.[133]

The Section suggested a table similar to that of the secondary curriculum
of the previous year: 28 percent of the classtime would be devoted to mathematics, chemistry and physics; 13 percent to language and literature; and
8 percent to a foreign language.[134] Although labor instruction would occupy
8 percent of total classtime, academic subjects would receive more attention
than before because of an expanded school week. In 1926, Narkompros had
suggested 32, 34, and 35 hours per week of instruction in grades five through
seven respectively, whereas in 1927 it required 35, 36, and 36. Moreover,
Narkompros prohibited using hours assigned to academic subjects for the
preparation of holiday celebrations or campaigns.[135] Like the Moscow Department of Education a year earlier, Narkompros accepted homework as a
necessity, limiting it to no more than five hours per week for fifth graders
and six hours for sixth and seventh graders.[136]

Narkompros offered these changes chiefly as adjustments toward classroom
practice.[137] Sure of its efforts to accommodate the Republic's teachers, the
Pedagogical Section made the 1927 curriculum obligatory and predicted that
it would remain in force for at least four years.[138] With stable and obligatory
programs in place, the Commissariat of Enlightenment planned textbooks
to match. It reduced the number of titles on its approved list from 600 in
1925 to 87 in 1927/28, with more reductions planned.[139] The Nizhnii
Novgorod Department of Education followed suit with a commission whose
task was to compile a list of textbooks good for the next three to four years.[140]

Formerly rebellious departments of education now found the 1927 curriculum much to their liking.[141] However, the Moscow Department of Edu-

cation remained troublesome, pressing forward with its own program for the fifth through the seventh grades.[142] MONO chose not to set aside any hours for labor instruction because of a lack of equipment in its schools.[143] It favored more systematic instruction, especially in language skills (reading, writing, and speaking).[144]

Teachers responded favorably to concessions from above. The journal of the Nizhnii Novgorod department of education enthusiastically reported that instructors could make sense of the new programs.[145] Epshtein found that relations had greatly improved among Narkompros, teachers, and the public.[146] He predicted better times ahead as Narkompros strengthened its concern for subjects, skills, and textbooks. For one critic, however, the new relationship between Narkompros and teachers succeeded all too well. M. N. Krupenina, a member of Shul'gin's School Methods Institute and of the Pedagogical Section, who had little to say in the Section's discussions of 1925 and 1926, now said a great deal. She complained that under pressure from Soviet society and government, "schools have proceeded for the last two years under the standard of drill, drill, drill (ucheba)."[147] Teachers in the classroom, allied with Narkompros and its new curricula, had shoved aside the complex method, socially useful labor, and a concern for collectivity, and reasserted the importance of content, examinations, and individual marks. Confirming her worst fears of a resurrection of the old school, Krupenina found a segregated classroom with boys and girls at different benches and teachers distancing themselves from their pupils.

The 1927 curriculum, given a life expectancy of four years, did not last more than one. Political and ideological forces associated with the cultural revolution would obliterate the compromise so stubbornly fought for by teachers and so carefully crafted by Narkompros. Before this dramatic turn of events, however, institutional critics and a social dimension ignored by Narkompros and teachers undermined prospects for a mutually supportive relationship among government, teachers, and parents.

X.

KOMSOMOL AND THE TECHNICAL LOBBY

From 1918 to 1921, Narkompros had responded to criticism from the technical lobby and Komsomol with tactical maneuvers and a promise to convert the senior division of secondary schools into technicums. After 1925, it made substantive concessions to teachers, parents, and departments of education. It remained to be seen whether it could deal as effectively with a technical lobby demanding more vocational training and a League calling for expanded opportunities for children of workers and peasants.

Komsomol and the lobby made a strong case for vocational education as a way to address the shortage of semi-skilled and skilled workers. Most adolescents holding jobs—5 to 6 percent of the total work force in the 1920s— could not attend regular schools, and if they did, found the curriculum irrelevant to their work.[1] Children of workers and peasants rarely advanced beyond the third or fourth grade. Narkompros's acceptance of a more traditional curriculum strengthened what critics insisted was an elitist academic bias in its policy.

Komsomol: Schools for Everybody

Komsomol continued its earlier efforts to transform secondary education. Its fourth, fifth, and sixth congresses held in 1921, 1922, and 1924 insisted that the secondary school's student body, teaching cadre, and curriculum had remained unchanged from the pre-revolutionary period. The nation's secondary schools prepared non-proletarian elements for a higher education. The rhetoric matched the damning nature of the indictment. At the Fourth Komsomol Congress, Treivas, a delegate from Moscow, upon noting an absence of working class youth in secondary schools, turned to Lunacharsky and asked: "Really, is this permissible in a workers' state?"[2] Ryvkin, the Commissariat's chief critic at the Second Congress two years earlier, hastened to calm passions by commenting that his comrade's speech seemed "contradictory to the serious tone of our congress."[3] He was mistaken, since Treivas's manner corresponded to the mood of delegates, who punctuated his remarks with applause. The following year Treivas returned to the Fifth Congress as a member of the League's Central Committee and made the unforgiving remark that the secondary school did little more than prepare the children of the petty bourgeoisie for admission into a higher educational institution.[4] This time no one emerged to repair the damage. A. P. Shokhin, Komsomol official since 1920, declared that the secondary school was preparing "old musty rubbish."[5] Another speaker spoke of training "sickly *intelligents*".[6] The congress obliged these remarks with resolutions calling for the destruction (unichtozhenie) of the secondary school.[7]

Demand for the secondary school's destruction distorted the substance of Komsomol's position. At the Sixth Congress, Nikolai Chaplin, First Secretary of the Komsomol's Central Committee, put it more accurately when he called for a reorganization of the secondary school.[8] The Congress agreed. It proposed first that pupils in grades five through seven receive more labor training and production practice. Second, upon completion of the seventh grade, pupils should proceed either to a Factory Apprenticeship School or begin vocational training in the eighth and ninth grades, which were to become the junior division of technicums. Third, a limited number of pupils could proceed to a higher educational institution (or its rabfak) after a period of employment.[9]

The Young Communist League looked with special favor on the Factory Apprenticeship School as an institution capable of combining general education, technical instruction and production practice. The League agreed with Narkompros on the principle that the school should accept only pupils fifteen to seventeen years of age who had completed seven years of general education. But in practice, it realized that most pupils of the appropriate age had considerably less schooling, and that this situation would continue for years to come.[10] New rules for admission in 1923 stipulated four years of education as the norm, and even less in exceptional cases.[11]

In the mid-1920s, the League challenged the united labor school with two additional types of schools, one designed for rural pupils and the other for urban youth. First, it proposed a School for Peasant Youth (Shkola krest'ianskoi molodezhi or ShKM) made up of grades five through seven, which would combine a general education with special instruction relevant to rural life. Komsomol's chief advocate of this new school, Shokhin, presented his proposals to the Pedagogical Section on July 31, 1923, and then in considerable detail to the Sixth Komsomol Congress.[12] The proposals were sweeping in their intent and scope. For Shokhin, the peasant school would assault the petty bourgeoisie and its instincts of private property with a curriculum designed in part by the local Party cell, soviet, and state farm (sovkhoz).

Perhaps aware of the absence of Party and State organs in the countryside, delegates adopted resolutions more reserved than those put forward by Shokhin. They wanted schools to be involved in community activities: assisting the work of rural cooperatives, cleaning seeds, participating in the campaign against pests, and conducting political agitation.[13] Following approval by the Pedagogical Section and Narkompros Collegium, about 200 Schools for Peasant Youth with a total enrollment of 20,000 pupils appeared in 1924.[14]

Second, Komsomol proposed the Factory Seven-Year School (Fabrichno-zavodskaia semiletka or FZS), which would combine a general education with industrial training. It would begin with manual exercises in grades one through four and technical instruction, preferably in a school shop, in the senior grades. The effort on behalf of this new school climaxed in 1925 at the First All-Russian Conference of Secondary Schools with a presentation by P. V. Rudnev, representative of Komsomol's Central Committee, Narkompros official in charge of the Schools for Peasant Youth, and member of the Pedagogical Section. He advanced the Factory Seven-Year School as a way to keep adolescents of working class families in school beyond the elementary grades, to make education relevant to an industrial economy,

and to prepare pupils for more specialized training in a Factory Apprenticeship School.[15]

Occupational Training

Throughout the 1920s, leading Party and State organs called for the
expansion of the Factory Apprenticeship School, the School for Peasant
Youth, and the Factory Seven-Year School. It was thought that these schools
and the senior division of the secondary school could produce the cadre
required by both industry and agriculture.[16] They grew at an impressive
rate. By the mid-1920s, approximately one thousand senior divisions with
a total enrollment of 100,000 pupils—about 70 percent of the total enrollment
in the eighth and ninth grades—claimed to offer some form of specialized
training.[17] Factory Apprenticeship Schools were established at an increasingly
rapid pace, their number reaching about 500 with 50,000 pupils in 1925
and 600 with 60,000 the following year.[18] As expected, its students were
predominantly male (about 80 percent), Komsomol members, and children
of workers.[19] The number of Schools for Peasant Youth in the Russian
Republic similarly increased to 767 with 73,000 students in 1927.[20] The
majority of its pupils were male (75 percent) and almost exclusively children
of the peasantry.[21] The Factory Seven-Year Schools developed less impressively. During the 1927/28 academic year, they numbered about 100 with
over 60 percent affiliated with either steel or textile plants.[22]

For the technical lobby, however, the nature of the curriculum mattered
as much as the number of schools and pupils. In need of individuals trained
in a particular skill or for a specific job, industrial managers demanded a
narrow vocational course of study. On this issue, they clashed with a Commissariat of Enlightenment still determined to preserve a general polytechnical program.

Narkompros Maneuvers and Compromises

Narkompros acquitted itself surprisingly well before a demanding technical
lobby and Komsomol. It did so by reaching tactical compromises, begrudgingly implemented, and by finding common interests with the Young Communist League. Until the end of the NEP period, the leadership at
Narkompros could give itself high marks for protecting its programs against
its institutional foes.

Lunacharsky responded to criticism with his usual eloquent defense of
Narkompros's governing vision and ideology. In a less obvious but substantive
way, he preempted successful attacks with his willingness to compromise.
In 1921, he conceded that Narkompros should devote special efforts to the
creation of schools for working youth. He put it elegantly, making a con-

cession into an apparent victory. The Commissariat had for a long time called the proletarian Mohammed to the school mountain, but now it was necessary to move the mountain in the direction of factory youth.[23] Similarly, Lunacharsky accepted the need for Factory Apprenticeship Schools, Schools for Peasant Youth, and professional instruction in the eighth and ninth grades of the united labor school. But he did so on condition that these institutions offer a minimum of general subjects and acknowledge the ultimate goal of nine years of polytechnical instruction for all youth eight to seventeen years of age.[24]

The Commissariat of Enlightenment followed Lunacharsky's lead. It conceded some points while defending its overall program at the Third Conference of Commissariats of Education, December 1–3, 1923; at a meeting of the Narkompros Collegium on July 7, 1924; at the Conference of Secondary Schools, July 5–10, 1925; and at the All-Russian Congress of Commissariats of Enlightenment in 1926.[25] In every case, spokespersons for the Commissariat and the resolutions that followed cautiously accepted the Factory Apprenticeship School, the School for Peasant Youth, and some vocational instruction in the senior division of the united labor school. Krupskaya spoke for Narkompros and for a majority of delegates at the conference in late 1923, when she declared that the Factory Apprenticeship School and School for Peasant Youth were permissible only if they avoided a narrowly specialized curriculum.[26] For the eighth and ninth grades, she allowed a limited focus on a branch of industry, not on a particular vocation, and only as part of a general education.[27]

In giving up a little, Narkompros preserved a lot. It embraced the Factory Seven-Year School and then devised for it a standard academic curriculum.[28] Narkompros allowed modifications only when it was necessary to acquaint pupils with industrial life and, perhaps in the final grades, with a particular kind of production.[29] The curriculum issued in 1927 differed little from that for regular schools, suggesting that study of industrial technology be incorporated into lessons in natural science, physics, and chemistry, and also into extracurricular activities.[30]

Narkompros also insisted that the School for Peasant Youth make special agricultural training no more than a supplemental part of the regular curriculum. In late 1923, Narkompros warned against specialization and insisted on a reliance on complex themes.[31] Subsequent statements, including a 1924 statute, reinforced this effort by limiting special training to the selection and cleaning of seeds for planting, acquaintance with basic machinery, and the eradication of vermin and weeds.[32] Anxious over these restrictions, Shokhin complained at the Sixth Komsomol Congress that under Narkompros's tutelage, the School for Peasant Youth might become only an improved secondary school.[33] However, Narkompros continued to issue standard curricula featuring complex themes.[34] Difficult conditions supported Narkompros's argument. The backward state of peasant agriculture made instruction in advanced machinery and farming techniques largely irrelevant.

Narkompros's tenacity and conditions combined to make general education important in the Factory Apprenticeship School. While most of its students were between fourteen and eighteen years of age, only a small minority had completed seven years of education.[35] So few potential students met the requirement that the Petrograd Department of Professional Education reduced entrance requirements in 1922 to the ability to read, write, and count.[36] In the 1925/26 academic year, only 6 percent of the students entering Factory Apprenticeship Schools had more than four years of education. Two years later the situation had improved somewhat, yet only 14 percent had completed the seventh grade.[37] To make matters worse, many of these students had dropped out years before, in the interim forgetting much of what they had learned.

Normally victimized by such a state of affairs, Narkompros turned it to its own advantage by insisting that these students required a general education. It proposed preparatory classes, and in the regular curriculum, an accent on Russian language, social studies, political economy, and mathematics.[38] Curricula released in 1926 and 1927 assigned about 25 to 30 percent of classtime to Russian language and social studies.[39]

The Commissariat of Enlightenment opposed curricular changes in the eighth and ninth grades. In 1921, both the First Party Conference on Education and, more significantly, Lenin and the Central Committee, had demanded that these grades offer vocational training. Early that same year, the Narkompros Collegium obliged with a plan for converting the junior division into technicums. The Commissariat's real intentions were clearly otherwise. On February 15, 1923, the Pedagogical Section demanded that Glavprofobr cease requiring professional education in these grades.[40] One year later, on June 7, the Narkompros Collegium again spoke of compromise while it reaffirmed its major positions. It admitted that secondary schools had ignored production. At the same time, Narkompros insisted on the need for a single school offering nine years of polytechnical instruction for all children.[41] The Collegium accepted the School for Peasant Youth and the Factory Apprenticeship School as temporary expedients if they followed Narkompros directives on instruction in general subjects to the letter.[42]

The Collegium then turned to the primary issue, the senior division of the united labor schoool. As in 1921, it allowed specialized instruction, but only as a temporary concession to the country's "economic and cultural backwardness."[43] It proposed a curriculum designed not for particular occupations, but rather for broad categories of those professions for which a general education might prove most useful. The reorganized senior division would train employees for producers', consumers', and credit cooperatives; for administrative and financial organs (bookkeepers, tax inspectors and statisticians); and for cultural and educational institutions (primary schoolteachers, librarians, and instructors for nurseries, kindergartens, and the liquidation of adult illiteracy).[44] The Collegium added two final conditions. It made adoption of a specialized curriculum contingent upon the presence of a genuine need for trained workers and on the availability of technical instructors and equipment.[45]

Narkompros meant to keep its secondary school intact. Shortly after these concessions in 1924, it condemned local authorities who in order to save funds, shut the doors of secondary schools altogether.[46] Narkompros clearly had a right to respond in this fashion. It was on much shakier ground in its continuing campaign to restrict specialized training in the eighth and ninth grades. Krupskaya, Lunacharsky, the Pedagogical Section, Glavsotsvos, and the Narkompros Collegium openly opposed conversion of the senior division into technicums.[47] Sometimes they did so on principle; on other occasions, they referred to an absence of personnel and equipment.

A department of education which introduced vocational training in the senior grades ran the risk of incurring Narkompros's wrath. The Moscow Department of Education did just this when it too readily embraced what Narkompros had endorsed in July 1924.[48] The following July at the Conference of Secondary Schools, Narkompros condemned Moscow's attempts to provide "narrow professional training" in the eighth and ninth grades.[49] General subjects were deemed important for the development of a "cultured element" and for preparation for higher educational institutions.[50] The conference agreed, suggesting that only 40 percent of classtime be devoted to technical instruction and practice.[51] Six months later the Moscow Department of Education was again singled out for allowing excessive specialization in these grades.[52]

Narkompros had itself to blame for the behavior of its Moscow department. It did not release a curriculum for the senior grades until 1927, and then with many restrictions in deference to the polytechnical principle.[53] Preparatory training for bookkeepers, officials for a cooperative or soviet, primary schoolteachers, or political agitators could take no more than 24 percent of the total instructional time in the eighth grade and 34 percent in the ninth.[54] It would not even bow, Narkompros said, to pressure from higher educational institutions to alter the balance among traditional subjects. The Commissariat announced that it had not emphasized mathematics to the extent hoped for by higher education.[55]

Critics Know Best: Counterproposals

Addressing the All-Russian Executive Committee on October 16, 1927, Lunacharsky observed that the Factory Apprenticeship School possessed two masters—economists and Narkompros.[56] He was well aware that from the perspective of the technical lobby, the Commissariat sought to be the master with the greatest authority. Required by law to support these schools, the State's economic bureaucracy, individual enterprises, and organized labor concluded that they received little in return. The Commissariat of Agriculture opposed the School for Peasant Youth.[57] The Supreme Economic

Council publicly questioned the value of the Factory Apprenticeship School. V. Shmidt, Commissar of Labor, denounced it as worthless, capable of producing good Komsomol activists but bad production workers.[58] His Commissariat agreed, and proposed to reduce the wages of working adolescents.[59] Junior organs and officials felt the same way. Shortly after the inception of the Factory Apprenticeship School, industrial administrators reached the conclusion that during classtime pupils did little more than smoke cigarettes, discuss Komsomol activities, and swap tales about their latest encounters with girls.[60] In 1927, the Supreme Economic Council, probably against its better judgment, had to goad agencies and industrial enterprises under its control to fulfill their obligations to the Factory Apprenticeship School. The Commissariat of Agriculture had to coax its subordinate organs to do the same for the School for Peasant Youth.[61]

Industrial management found alternatives to Narkompros's apprenticeship schools. Enterprises created special courses designed to provide narrowly focused training over a few months' time. Varying widely from place to place and year to year, these courses amounted to on-the-job training— inexpensive, and suited to fill immediate needs. Beginning in 1920, the All-Union Council of Labor Unions sponsored courses designed to train individuals for specific jobs over a period of three to six months. This program was administered by the Central Institute of Labor headed by A. K. Gastev.

The son of a schoolteacher, Gastev followed in his father's footsteps until his expulsion from a teachers institute. He became a metal worker and turned to writing poems with a romanticized vision of factory life and a mechanized view of man.[62] Planning to translate this hope into reality, Gastev devised a training program which was anathema to Narkompros's way of thinking. Enamored with recent proposals for the rationalization and discipline of industrial labor (Taylorism), Gastev designed short courses to teach the value of work and standard physical movements deemed essential to mechanized plants of the present and future.[63] On at least two occasions, February 19, 1923, and December 3, 1925, Gastev went before the Pedagogical Section to argue for such training in secondary schools and Factory Apprenticeship Schools.[64] At the latter session, he charged that the Factory Apprenticeship School taught handicraft skills but not the uniform movements he believed industry required of workers. Gastev admitted that a female textile worker, expert at repetitive action on the job, was "more progressive, more cultured than any kind of female member of the intelligentsia." She was even more advanced than metal workers who, though undeniably skilled, were anything but efficient as they the workers, not machines, controlled the pace of work.[65] The Section's response was surprisingly subdued. Epshtein charged that Gastev failed to differentiate between a human being and a machine; Shatsky noted that the speaker had ignored the intellectual aspects of training.[66] The remainder of the Section's members resorted to a familiar maneuver to dismiss annoying proposals—

they demanded more specificity and recommended that its own Subsection on Labor study them further.[67]

The Supreme Economic Council and individual enterprises adopted a more direct way of achieving specialized training of youth. They sought to remove vocational schools from Narkompros's control as a preliminary step toward a wholesale revision of their curricula. Narkompros responded in defiance. At the 1925 Conference of Secondary Schools, its representatives insisted, and most delegates agreed, that the senior division remain under the administrative control of the Commissariat of Enlightenment.[68] The following year, the All-Russian Congress of Commissariats of Enlightenment and the Narkompros Collegium demanded that Narkompros retain control over the Factory Apprenticeship School to insure something other than narrowly specialized training.[69] Such militant reaffirmations of Narkompros's program did not end the dispute. In September 1927, the Supreme Economic Council's First All-Union Conference on Professional-Technical Education proposed to limit the Commissariat of Enlightenment's authority over vocational schools to the area of instructional methods.[70]

Common Ground

In its effort to promote a polytechnical curriculum, the Commissariat of Enlightenment found that a trenchant critic, the Young Communist League, could also be a vocal defender. These two organizations, each responsible in its own way for the education and training of the nation's youth, had reason to cooperate. Because of its concern for socio-political training, Komsomol shared the Commissariat's misgivings about early vocational training. Once Narkompros accepted the need to provide educational opportunities for the working class and peasant youth through the Factory Apprenticeship School, the Factory Seven-Year School, and the School for Peasant Youth, the way was cleared for a loose alliance against the technical lobby. The Fourth Komsomol Congress censured factory administrators who favored specialized curricula for the Factory Apprenticeship School.[71] At the following two Komsomol congresses, delegates (including Shokhin) objected to attempts by factories to limit the schooling of their working youth to short courses or on-the-job training.[72]

At the Seventh Komsomol Congress, March 11–22, 1926, Narkompros escaped without criticism. It was a representative of the Supreme Economic Council that was on the defensive. He had come to argue the need for short courses and for industry's jurisdiction over Factory Apprenticeship Schools.[73] In response, Ol'ga Anikst, long associated with Glavprofobr, announced to applause that the League and Narkompros together defended the Factory Apprenticeship School.[74] Tarasov declared that the Commissariat of Enlightenment and Komsomol were partners in a "united front."[75] The congress conceded that more attention might be paid to preparing pupils for production, and in a somewhat shorter period of time. But it would not surrender its support of general education for all youth and of Narkompros's control over the Factory Apprenticeship School.[76]

During the mid-1920s, Narkompros had moved decisively to accommodate the wishes of teachers and parents. When dealing with its institutional critics, however, Narkompros consistently followed another tactic. It made modest concessions to the Young Communist League and technical lobby, while preserving intact the principle of a general polytechnical education for all youth. In this effort, Lunacharsky and his colleagues proved to be far abler opponents than expected, capable of bureaucratic infighting and deft maneuvering. By the late 1920s, however, Narkompros had reason to be worried about the future. Its recent embrace of elements of a traditional curriculum collided with Komsomol's hostility for the "bourgeois school." Nor could the Commissariat of Enlightenment make limp concessions followed by their incomplete implementation, no matter how artfully done, when dealing with the technical lobby. With different objectives than Narkompros, agencies responsible for economic development wanted a quick and cheap way to train the youth—never mind Narkompros's humane vision of a school present and society future.

Although still in a position to make educational policy, Narkompros was in no better position than before to control practice. Some industrial enterprises actually got their way with Factory Apprenticeship Schools. Factories that funded the school used their financial stranglehold to force narrow vocational instruction or on-the-job training.[77] In other instances, efforts to make the school self-supporting meant that production of marketable products replaced classroom instruction.[78] Narkompros condemned these practices, but it received little support from its local departments and inspectors who regarded the apprenticeship school as an unwanted and insignificant part of the education system.[79] Glavprofobr complained in 1925 that the failure of local departments of education to provide it with information made it difficult to counter "numerous attacks from various organizations attempting to belittle the Factory Apprenticeship School."[80]

Narkompros's policies had failed to match their promise. When friend or foe alike examined the school system in its broad social context, as Narkompros had always insisted it should be viewed, an ugly truth emerged. During the first decade of Soviet power, the school system had not contributed to a transformation of traditional Russia.

XI.

A THREAT OF FAILURE

For Bolsheviks impatient with the pace of change, Narkompros's schools perpetuated the old ways of life. The persistence of a traditional curriculum was only part of the reason. By the late 1920s, few youths advanced beyond the third grade; illiteracy among the young was increasing; students continued to express religious and petty-bourgeois sentiments; a high percentage of pupils failed; and the children of socio-occupational groups the Party claimed to represent were precisely those not attending school or were the first to fail or drop out when they did enroll. The school system could claim its greatest success with children of the bourgeoisie, hardly an achievement to be trumpeted given Soviet ideology and Narkompros's promises.

Universal Compulsory Education

The 1918 Statute for the United Labor School mandated compulsory school attendance for all children eight to seventeen years of age.[1] Reality rudely intervened. More modestly, on August 31, 1925, Sovnarkom of the Russian Republic spoke of achieving attendance by almost all children of elementary school age by the tenth anniversary of the October revolution and universal compulsory instruction by the 1933/34 academic year.[2] When the jubilee year of 1927 arrived, however, Sovnarkom adjusted its expectations downward. Now it hoped that all children eight years of age would attend school over the next four years.[3] Even that would have been no small achievement. The partial census of December 1926 revealed that in the European portion of the Russian Republic, the number of children eligible for elementary school would rise by 30 percent from 1927 to 1932.[4] There also remained the dismal reality that far more children suffered from hunger and homelessness than received a secondary education. In 1926 the Fifth Congress of Commissariats of Enlightenment and the Narkompros Collegium put the number of hungry and dying children, exclusive of the Ukraine, at 7.5 million.[5] It was only a guess. These children remained outside of school and beyond the reach of statistics on school attendance, which were depressing enough without their numbers.

The lack of progress among those who did enter the first grade was discouraging. A survey published in 1925 disclosed that the average length of time spent in school amounted to 2.4 years—2.3 for girls and 2.5 for boys. In urban areas, only 3.1 years of schooling was the norm.[6] Put another way, in rural regions, only 22.8 percent of the boys and 15 percent of the girls who entered the first grade were still in school four years later.[7] Urban areas, with a much smaller number of pupils, boasted of much higher figures—54.5 and 51.9 percent for girls and boys respectively.[8] The appearance of this survey in the Narkompros monthly, *Narodnoe prosveshchenie*, provoked a comment that the situation had recently improved because of escalating public interest in education.[9] Not so, the editorial board grimly responded. Conditions remained much the same, and had even deteriorated in Smolensk province where fewer pupils than before advanced to the fourth grade.[10]

Over the next few years additional surveys found improvement in urban locales, but only modest progress in the countryside. From 1923 to 1926, less than 40 percent of pupils enrolling in the first grade remained in school.[11] More detailed figures for the four year period beginning in 1924 reached the same conclusion. Although urban schools retained almost nine out of ten pupils, their rural counterparts could keep less than one in three. Almost half the number of rural people entering the first grade in 1924 failed to advance to the third grade.[12] By 1926, pupils entering the first grade spent only 2.77 years in school.[13] Lack of advancement also occurred in the secondary grades. From 1925 to 1928 in the Russian Republic, more than one in three fifth-graders did not enter the seventh grade.[14]

These figures concealed worse problems. A statistical year spent in school did not necessarily mean that a pupil completed the course or advanced to the following grade. Many youths did not attend anything remotely resembling a full academic year. A yawning chasm separated what Narkompros wanted and what it got in this respect. In 1926, Narkompros set the academic year at 200 days for urban schools and 176 days for their rural counterparts.[15] The following year, it increased the norms for elementary and secondary grades to 205 and 215 days in urban areas and to 190 and 200 days in rural regions.[16] Narkompros boasted that schools managed to achieve 90 percent of the norm.[17] It knew better, for Moscow received a steady flow of information to the contrary. Some schools, especially in rural areas, did not open their doors until October or as late as December.[18] Many schools did not function during the fall harvest or the spring sowing season. A 1923 survey of schools in Orlov province found that while urban elementary schools operated 188 days a year, their counterparts in the countryside managed only 102.[19] The situation was little better in many other areas three years later: only 30.6 percent of the schools in Vologda province offered instruction for more than 175 days; in Leningrad province the total reached 38.9 percent, but in Kursk it plummeted to 15.2 percent.[20]

Nor did a usual school day or week measure up to Narkompros's standards. Shortages of human and material resources compelled schools, even in Moscow, to abbreviate their schedule to twenty-four or twenty-five hours of instruction per week instead of the thirty or more recommended by Narkompros.[21] Poor attendance added to the problem. Pupils in elementary grades missed about twenty-five days a year in rural areas and somewhat less than twenty in urban regions.[22] Truancy in urban schools tended to occur at an unvaried rate from month to month. In those rural schools that chose to compete with the growing season, absenteeism peaked in the fall and spring, when parents required their children to work or stay home to look after younger family members.[23]

Careful analysis of attendance revealed more problems. Many pupils who for statistical purposes had received several years of schooling, achieved less because of grade repetition. The percentage of all students repeating a grade varied from 15 to 20 percent from the early 1920s through the 1927/28 academic year, occurring slightly more often in elementary grades and in urban areas.[24] Available information does not allow for an estimation of the number who were lost in an endless cycle of repeating the same grade. Frequent repetition combined with delayed entry into the first grade meant that a high percentage of pupils in a particular grade were older than the official norm. In the mid-1920s, 34.5 percent of the pupils in urban elementary schools and 26.4 percent in the countryside were above twelve years of age.[25]

Academic failure was commonplace. About one in five pupils failed a grade at the close of the 1926/27 school year. Figures for specific grades and for rural and urban areas varied little. Only children in the first grade and those few students who managed to reach the senior division passed at a rate markedly better than the average.[26] Pupils who failed were more tenacious than those who dropped out in mid-year. A 1924 study of a rural district in Nizhnii Novgorod found that 26 to 29 percent of the pupils enrolled at the beginning of the school year had not managed to make it to the end.[27] A survey conducted in the Russian Republic in 1926/27 reached a better but yet disturbing conclusion—well over 10 percent of those initially enrolled were no longer attending at the end of the year. Unlike figures for failure, the number of dropouts fluctuated depending on grade level and location. The highest percentage of dropouts occurred, as expected, in elementary grades and rural localities. Over 20 percent of students enrolled in rural elementary schools did not finish the year.[28] Added together, the dropout and failure rate exposed an educational system in crisis. In 1926/27, about 30 percent of all pupils in elementary grades and 20 percent in grades five through seven either dropped out or flunked. In rural elementary schools alone, an astounding number—more than one out of every three pupils— fell into this category.[29]

To cushion criticism and for the sake of accuracy, Narkompros insisted on the misleading nature of many statistics. The horrible promotion rate overall concealed the number of pupils who dropped out but returned at a later time, or who transferred at some point to a vocational school. The atrocious retention rate of rural elementary schools failed to take into consideration pupils who transferred to urban schools. Yet in every instance, revision of figures in favor of one category came at the expense of another. Movement of pupils from rural to urban institutions made the retention rate in the latter less impressive. Reentry by older pupils after a year or more out of school exerted a negative as well as a positive impact on the retention rate of specific grades. Whatever the count, it produced the same distressing result. The nation's schools provided youth with little more than the rudiments of an education.

Narkompros hastened to point out that at least the censuses of December 1926 and December 1927 seemed to reveal a rather high percentage of school-age youth attending elementary school. For every ten children eligible to attend (aged eight through eleven), more than eight were actually enrolled. Rural localities boasted a figure only slightly less than that.[30] But these statistics overlooked the large number of pupils who were repeating a grade or who were overaged according to official norms. Almost half of the pupils in the fourth grade in 1926 were not eleven or twelve, as might have been expected, but thirteen or older. In the first grade, 44 percent were not eight or nine, but ten years of age or more.[31] The varied ages and diverse skills represented in a single class added to the many burdens already heaped on teachers. It also meant that a careful comparison of attendance and population turned what appeared to be an arithmetical success into a failure.

In late 1923 Krupskaya lamented that only 50 percent of all children eligible for an elementary education were in school.[32] Perhaps she exaggerated for effect, but not by much. When making adjustments for grade repeaters but not overaged children, the censuses of 1926 and 1927 found that more than 30 percent of children aged eight to eleven did not attend school, a number that declined to only 25 percent in the Republic exclusive of its autonomous republics.[33] A more accurate assessment, which did not count those over eleven years of age, concluded that as late as the 1927/28 academic year only one out of every two children in that youngest category attended elementary school.[34]

Certainly these censuses somewhat exaggerated the problem. They did not adjust for absenteeism on the day of the census, nor could they calculate the unknown but large number of children aged eight to eleven who had once attended school, but had temporarily or permanently withdrawn.[35] Neither could they account for youngsters who would begin the first grade several years hence. Finally, census figures disregarded pupils who did not enroll because the local school did not offer anything beyond the second or third grade or provide enough vacancies to meet demand for the grades it did have. In late 1927 Lunacharsky complained that elementary schools turned away 25 percent of the children seeking admission and secondary schools 20 percent.[36] Whatever the extenuating circumstances and however

Narkompros and its friends might shuffle the data, one conclusion persistently emerged: Soviet youth did not go to school.

On April 7, 1928, in *Pravda*, Krupskaya discussed the problem in an article titled "The Stabilization of Illiteracy." The socialist state was not winning its war against illiteracy; for every adult taught to read and write, a young citizen was growing up illiterate.[37] One month later at the Eighth Komsomol Congress, Krupskaya declared that half of the school-age children were illiterate.[38] Her gloomy appraisal was no exaggeration; the census of December 1926 classified over half of the children eight to eleven years of age as illiterate. In urban areas almost eight out of ten could read and write; in the countryside, where the overwhelming majority of children lived, almost 60 percent could not.[39] Narkompros could claim that the youngest of school-age children were traditionally highly illiterate because they postponed entering school until the age of eleven or older.[40] Yet it had promised to break this cycle and would have to do so if it were to achieve a polytechnical education for all children.

Social Composition

On June 8, 1887, the tsarist Minister of Education, I. Delianov, provoked a torrent of abuse with the so-called Cook's Circular. His directive proposed discriminatory admissions policies to "free the gymnasiums from children of coachmen, menials, cooks, washerwomen, small shopkeepers, and the like."[41] Thirty-one years later, the constitution for the new Russian Republic reversed the order of priority by calling for a "full, comprehensive and free education for workers and the poorest peasants."[42] People who thought otherwise and conditions annulled both pronouncements. After 1887, children of those socio-occupational groups derogated in Delianov's circular penetrated the gymnasiums as well as other educational institutions in increasing numbers.[43] In revolutionary Russia, it was primarily the children of workers and peasants who never attended school in the first place, or when they did so, either failed or withdrew never to return. Children of parents classified as intelligentsia, white-collar salaried personnel (sluzhashchie), or members of the independent professions (doctors, lawyers, writers) completed the full elementary and secondary course. Reports from the provinces of Orlov, Ul'ianovsk, and Nizhnii Novgorod provided supporting evidence.[44] The school census of December 1926 revealed the dimensions of the problem throughout the Russian Republic. Although many children of workers and peasants entered the first grade, a rapidly descending number remained, and few made it beyond the fourth grade. In contrast, children in all other categories continued, and by virtue of their numbers dominated the secondary schools. Put another way, for every ten children of workers enrolled

Social Composition by Grade, 1926/27[45]

Grade	Workers	Peasantry	White Collar (sluzhashchie)	Other
1	11.2%	79.2%	4.8%	4.8%
2	12.4	75.2	6.4	6.0
3	14.9	67.5	9.9	7.7
4	19.9	52.5	17.4	10.2
5	28.0	25.8	31.6	14.6
6	23.5	23.2	37.5	15.8
7	21.5	21.5	40.5	16.5
8	16.0	18.3	46.2	19.5
9	15.0	19.6	45.9	19.5

Social Composition by Grade
Municipality of Moscow, December 1926[46]

Grade	Workers	White Collar (sluzhashchie)	Independent Artisans	Peasants	Other
1	47.72%	33.29%	7.73%	1.98%	9.20%
2	47.39	33.48	7.34	2.04	9.75
3	47.36	35.57	6.77	2.10	8.10
4	44.36	39.23	6.49	2.12	7.76
5	39.33	43.80	6.35	2.40	8.08
6	33.19	50.45	6.20	2.14	7.02
7	27.15	56.81	6.09	1.75	8.20
8	17.50	68.54	4.48	2.46	7.02
9	18.61	68.02	4.47	2.54	6.36

in elementary school, only two managed to attend secondary school; out of ten peasant children, only one went on to the higher grades.[47]

Working-class children did not fare well even in the proletarian capital of the world. In Moscow in 1926, children of the socio-occupational groups regarded as bourgeois or petty-bourgeois dominated the classroom in the fourth through the ninth grades. In Sverdlovsk, children of workers comprised 13.9 percent of seventh grade enrollment, while children of white-collar personnel made up 67 percent.[48]

To friend and foe of Narkompros, it seemed a cruel joke of history that something on the order of the Cook's Circular was alive and well in Soviet Russia. The situation was so dismal that Narkompros found plausible a letter accusing teachers of conspiring to prevent working class children from taking examinations for promotion to the next grade.[49]

Fortunately for a beleaguered Narkompros, such accusations were rare, for there were difficulties enough. From the official point of view, social composition of schools had deteriorated during the mid-1920s.[50] Figures for other educational institutions provided no comfort. Special efforts by higher educational institutions to recruit workers and peasants and the presence of many students so classified by virtue of bogus documents allowed each of these groups to reach about 25 percent of the total enrollment in 1927/28.[51]

Schools for children of workers failed to live up to expectations. In Factory Seven-Year Schools their percentage declined from 80 or 90 percent in elementary grades to only 45 or 50 percent in secondary grades.[52] Factory Apprenticeship Schools experienced a decline in enrollment of working class children from 1925 to 1927 (from 79 to 75 percent) and a rise in children of salaried personnel (from 10 to 13 percent).[53] Although this shift was small, it alarmed Narkompros officials.[54] Schools for Peasant Youth experienced similar difficulties. From 1924 to 1926, the percentage of admittants classified as children of the poorest peasantry declined, while the portion represented by the middle peasantry significantly increased to almost 50 percent of the total.[55] A concerned Glavsotvos alerted all provincial departments of education in 1926 that the Schools for Peasant Youth were squeezing out the poorest elements of the population and becoming the haven of the well-to-do.[56]

Gender

Statistics on gender troubled Soviet officials and Narkompros. The number of females enrolled in schools declined from the early to the mid-1920s. In 1925 they constituted 36 percent of the total enrollment in all elementary schools, 33 percent in rural elementary schools alone.[57] Girls in urban schools, however, tended to stay in school longer than boys. They may have been more highly motivated than their male counterparts, and may not have experienced the same pressures for employment. Of all Soviet youths entering the first grade in urban locales in the early 1920s, female pupils received on the average 3.1 years of education while the boys received 3.0.[58] Because of this greater retention rate, girls made up almost 50 percent of the enrollment in urban elementary grades in 1925.[59] In this respect, as in other statistical categories, urban areas were not typical of the country as a whole. Addressing a conference of women in October 1927, Lunacharsky expressed his dismay over low female enrollment overall.[60] If the figures had already been available for that year, Lunacharsky would have been even more disappointed. In 1927/28, females accounted for 39 percent of enrollment in all elementary schools, 37 percent in rural elementary schools alone.[61]

Narkompros Responds

Confronted with a failed school, Narkompros reacted predictably with a reaffirmation of its ideology and program. Lunacharsky did so in November 1926 at a session of the All-Russian Central Executive Committee. Ia. Iakovlev, Deputy Commissar of Rabkrin, suggested that Narkompros adopt a more realistic goal of three years of universal education, rather than four.[62] In response, Lunacharsky admitted to a battery of problems, from a disemboweled academic year to a failure to provide instruction to working-class and peasant children. He could do no other. But the Commissar would not be bullied by rhetoric or facts. He denied any responsibility for the terrible material conditions under which schools operated, defended vigor-ously the Commissariat's educational record, and rejected any retreat from the proposed four years of universal elementary education, a goal substan-tially less than the original standard of nine years.[63]

At the same session, Lunacharsky placed the educational crisis in a social and political context. Narkompros needed funds from the State to build more schools, purchase materials, and pay teachers. Larger appropriations and support from economic, social, and cultural organizations would allow schools to attract and retain children of the poor by providing, free of charge, shoes, clothes, hot meals, and school supplies.[64] Narkompros suggested stipends for needy schoolchildren, free transportation to and from school in rural areas, and, for pupils living at a great distance, free room and board in dormitories. Sovnarkom of the Russian Republic made these proposals its own on June 28 and again on July 23, 1927.[65] As an additional social measure, Narkompros reaffirmed its ban on entrance and promotion examinations.[66]

Studies continued to reveal that poverty and distance from home to school contributed to difficulties experienced by pupils. Narkompros, the Moscow Department of Education, other local departments of education, and indi-vidual schools ascertained that illness and the absence of a coat and other wearing apparel had an effect upon a child's enrollment, attendance, and academic performance.[67] In Moscow's working class Bauman district, the number of children with clear signs of tuberculosis increased from 17 to 26.3 percent from 1923 to 1925.[68] The Moscow Health Department responded with an amply illustrated fourteen-page pamphlet designed for classroom use. It warned of the dangers of tuberculosis and urged strict measures of personal hygiene and physical fitness.[69] A 1925 survey revealed that as many as 44 percent of the pupils attending Schools for Peasant Youth lived over ten kilometers away, and that these schools could not provide the necessary overnight sleeping quarters.[70]

Once again the Soviet government studied a problem better than it could cope with it. In early 1927, the Small Sovnarkom (Maly Sovnarkom) assigned 1.25 million rubles so that pupils could be provided with footwear, clothes, and academic materials. This modest sum proved too much for the Com-missariat of Finance, which shuffled the matter off to Sovnarkom for a final decision.[71] Narkompros and the Soviet government had little at their disposal to make good on this or any other promise. Every directive and decree mandating free food and wearing apparel called upon mutual aid societies, local soviets, labor unions, cooperatives, Komsomol, and the Red Cross to make good on Moscow's intentions. Only a small amount of aid to a small number of pupils was provided in 1928.[72] One school in Moscow reported that its hot breakfast amounted to the consumption of tea. The school pro-vided the hot water, and the children brought their own tea, sugar, and glasses.[73] Another school in the city charged a fee for meals, forcing the poorer students to bring sack lunches.[74]

Migration, shortage of space at home, parents unwilling or unable to help with homework, and parental drunkenness contributed to truancy and poor academic performance.[75] Some pupils who joined the Pioneers or Young Communist League experienced more difficulties than usual because they had less time for homework and relaxation.[76] Many children did not enroll or attend regularly because their parents expected them to work in fields and factories or at home. The rather vague but important category "responsibilities at home" was responsible for half of the dropouts in Moscow province and half of the truants in elementary schools in the mid-1920s.[77] Girls who combined their studies with chores at home experienced persistent fatigue and headaches.[78]

Impoverished conditions from peasant hut to Narkompros treasury threatened the Commissariat's plans to end socio-economic inequities with non-compulsory measures. Discriminatory proposals were not long in coming. The Young Communist League had long insisted on funding and admissions policies favoring working class and peasant children. A sharp decline in central funding, the closure of many schools, and privatization of others strengthened Komsomol's case. Cautiously, in measured steps, Narkompros began to give ground. During the early and mid-1920s, it adopted admissions procedures that favored the children of industrial workers, poor and middle peasantry, military personnel, and teachers.[79]

Conditions and Narkompros reservations limited the impact of these discriminatory policies. The Commissariat of Enlightenment insisted that discrimination occur only as a result of a shortage of vacancies and not as an end in itself. It condemned purges of students by higher educational institutions in 1924, and by schools that same year and later.[80] Narkompros hoped to limit discrimination even in schools designed for children of the working class. In 1926, it permitted removal of non-working class pupils from the Factory Seven-Year School only if they constituted 25 to 30 percent of total enrollment and if another school nearby could take them.[81] In practice, prospective pupils were most often turned away in rural areas where a limited number of schools could not meet demand, especially for the first and second grades.[82] No information on the socio-economic status of their parents was published or, perhaps, available.

Limited data on urban schools, however, reveals only a mild form of discrimination. In the fall of 1924, Moscow's schools rejected less than 1 percent of all applications from children of salaried personnel, independent artisans, and the free professions. They denied access to one of every four applicants from a very small group classified as children of private traders, functionaries of religious organizations, and private employers of hired labor.[83]

Modest attempts at discrimination sometimes produced a contradictory effect. Anxious parents registered their children in many schools with the expectation that acceptance would be forthcoming in at least one. This effort contributed significantly to a number of "dead souls" on school lists at the beginning of the year. Administrators suddenly discovered not a shortage of vacancies, but a deficiency of pupils.[84] Whether applying to one or more schools, working class parents resented the interviews and paperwork required to verify their socio-occupational status.[85]

Success into Failure

Even its achievements discredited Narkompros. Success turned into failure when graduates of the school system took entrance examinations introduced by higher educational institutions in 1926. These and other evaluations of pupils found considerable ignorance in all grades in reading, writing, mathematics, science, and social studies. Moreover, pupils exhibited petty bourgeois prejudices that Narkompros had hoped to eliminate. The Commissariat's supporters and critics were less disturbed by reports of disorderly conduct than by the persistence of religious sentiment in and out of the classroom. Surveys by Narkompros, its inspectors, the League of the Godless, and Komsomol concluded that religion thrived among school children of all ages. Narkompros claimed in its defense that a 1926 study failed to show any significant connection between absenteeism and the observance of religious holidays.[86] But many local administrators closed their schools on holy days. When educators confronted religious conviction, they lost. Narkompros admitted as much in 1926, when it demanded that local departments of education end "massive absenteeism on religious holidays."[87] Subsequent reports disclosed that 50 to 70 percent of pupils avoided school on religious holidays.[88] Many children practiced religion; one school began the year with a prayer.[89]

Schools had some success in inculcating a respect for Lenin or, more precisely, for Lenin as a cult figure.[90] Surveys in 1927 of student attitudes toward the Soviet State and Party revealed positive feelings, but it was difficult to distinguish between sincere statements and memorized slogans. Pupils wanted less red tape in Soviet institutions and more creature comforts.[91] When seventh-graders in a Moscow school were asked in the spring of 1928 to list the most important recent events in the capital, they disappointed their surveyors. Almost as one they responded: "Amanulla has come," referring to the reforming Afghan monarch who was passing through Moscow on his Grand Tour. Few pupils mentioned the Eighth Komsomol Congress and no one knew who Bukharin was.[92]

Membership patterns in the Pioneers and Young Communist League, initially a source of great hope, became a cause for concern. Membership in the Pioneer organization grew impressively, representing almost 15 percent of enrollment in elementary schools and over 20 percent in other types of schools in 1925/26. It declined the following year by four or five percentage points.[93] Over the same period, membership in the Young Communist League peaked at 9 to 10 percent of all secondary school students and then declined slightly.[94] From 1925 to 1926 in Nizhnii Novgorod's secondary schools and schools with a seven-year course, Komsomol membership declined from 13.2 to 9.6 percent of total enrollment and in the Pioneers from 27.3 to 22.8 percent.[95]

Failure of Vocational Training

The Factory Apprenticeship School, School for Peasant Youth, and Factory Seven-Year School, all creatures of compromise, struggled for recognition. Organized labor, economic agencies, and individual enterprises failed to provide equipment, technical instructors, and opportunities for practicums. Many Factory Seven-Year Schools lacked shops. Perhaps 30 percent of the Schools for Peasant Youth lacked a garden plot; others had no equipment with which to work it. Of the 116 Factory Apprenticeship Schools serving the steel industry in 1925, only 81 possessed their own shops.[96] Teachers at Schools for Peasant Youth and Factory Apprenticeship Schools lacked experience and anything beyond a secondary education.[97]

Better teaching might have created more difficulties. Schools for Peasant Youth enrolled pupils who had less than four years of instruction; Factory Apprenticeship Schools had many pupils who did not meet the norm of seven years.[98] Suggestions to raise academic standards provoked instant opposition because of the social implications. Narkompros and the Young Communist League condemned entrance examinations for Schools for Peasant Youth as measures excluding children of poor peasantry.[99] Narkompros stipulated that an effort to raise standards in Factory Apprenticeship Schools should not lower the enrollment of children of the proletariat.[100] As expected, the rates of absenteeism, failure, and withdrawal in these institutions matched those of regular schools.[101]

Apparent success proved to be yet another failure when graduates of Schools for Peasant Youth, Factory Apprenticeship Schools, and senior divisions of secondary schools refused to join the ranks of the peasantry and proletariat. They sought instead administrative positions or entry into a technicum or higher educational institution.[102] Students completing the Factory Seven-Year School made similar career choices, avoiding enrollment in the Factory Apprenticeship School for which they were trained.[103] Those graduates who did seek employment appropriate to their specialty often found no such jobs available.

Despite the efforts of Narkompros and the Supreme Economic Council to maintain some uniformity, Factory Apprenticeship Schools and senior divisions offered a general course of instruction, while others provided narrowly focused technical traning. The end result was either too few or too many specialists. One senior division in a small city graduated forty dental technicians in one year.[104] Responding to the interests of pupils and industry, other schools tried to offer five or six specializations.[105]

One of Lunacharsky's recent biographers concludes that perhaps it is better to judge him "not by his accomplishments but by his aspirations, goals, and vision."[106] Maybe so, but friend, foe, and Lunacharsky himself expected more. By the late 1920s, teachers, parents, students, Komsomol officials, and the technical lobby expressed their dissatisfaction in an increasingly effective way. Teachers, parents, and local departments of education had made considerable headway with Narkompros; other critics had been less successful.

The Commissariat of Enlightenment felt victimized by inadequate appropriations and by rivals seeking narrow economic, social, and political gain. There was little that Lunacharsky, Krupskaya, and Epshtein could do but complain about the absence of funds, make concessions when necessary, and draw upon their vision of a rosy future. By the late 1920s, Narkompros's line had worn thin, and its authors knew it. Narkompros had hoped for something more for the Revolution's tenth anniversary than a minimal amount of schooling for most pupils, a secondary school dominated by the middle classes, and pupils possessing a little knowledge and a lot of petty-bourgeois sentiments.

Narkompros knew it had a crisis on its hands. In May 1926, Epshtein informed the State Academic Council of dirty, disorganized, ill-equipped, and poorly heated schools with short children seated at big desks and walls covered with illiterate posters and announcements. Teachers knew little or nothing of progressive education and some had ceased to read. Many instructors refused to implement new programs, even when they were acquainted with them. Schools arbitrarily abbreviated the school year, and senior divisions which supposedly offered a specialization did not arrange practicums. Other reports to the Council reinforced Epshtein's observations.[107] Rabkrin's presentation to the All-Russian Central Executive Committee in November 1926 and the censuses of 1926 and 1927 dismembered any remaining illusions. This kind of information had a devastating cumulative effect on Narkompros as an institution and on the people who worked there. An anguished response born of frustration came in the form of a hand-written note by someone at the Commissariat, perhaps V. N. Iakovleva, Deputy Commissar since 1922. Responding to another one of Rabkrin's brutal (but correct) reports, the author complained that Rabkrin gave Narkompros no peace.[108]

A candid assessment of problems could not keep pace with a deteriorating situation. In April 1928, the Sixth Congress of Commissariats of Enlightenment declared: "We stand before the danger not only of a growth of illiteracy among children, but also of a return to pre-revolutionary indices."[109] Illiteracy among children had in fact surpassed the point of danger. In many respects, a "return to pre-revolutionary indices" would have been a major step forward in 1928.

Narkompros's concessions concerning curriculum, types of schools, and admissions had not secured a stable future. Its compromise with teachers and parents required time to bear fruit, but it came at a time when patience had joined the list of deficit commodities. Meanwhile, the technical lobby sought narrow specialized preparation, and toward that end, administrative control over Factory Apprenticeship Schools. The Young Communist League demanded discriminatory policies in support of working class youth.

Narkompros never had the means to implement policy. As a result, in 1928 it possessed little more than its original vision and ideology. It had fought well, but it was no longer enough to convince critics that the educational system should continue without major modifications and that an unreformed Narkompros should remain the preeminent policy-making body.

Part Four.

Cultural Revolution, 1928–1931

Men make their own history, but they do
not make it just as they please; they do not
make it under circumstances chosen by
themselves; but under circumstances
directly found, given, and transmitted from
the past.
—Karl Marx, *The Eighteenth Brumaire of
Louis Bonaparte*

Рисунок худ. Паровицкого

Предпасхальная чистка

Cultural Revolution in the Schools

"Pre-Easter housecleaning." Cartoon by Parvitskii. A teacher leads his pupils in an assault on religion and alcohol. The signs, from top to bottom, read "School. Down with drunkenness. Down with religious rotgut."
SOURCE: *Uchitel'skaia gazeta,* no. 52 (279) (May 4, 1929), p. 4.

XII.

COMPROMISE BETRAYED

Lunacharsky and his colleagues had long insisted that the school change society by changing people's hearts and minds. Their vision of the school's role in forging the future did not include its participation in political confrontation and class warfare. It had been their good fortune that the New Economic Policy provided an environment conducive to this philosophy and the policies that proceeded from it. Far different circumstances followed in a period characterized by cultural revolution, forced collectivization, and rapid industrialization.

From 1928 to 1931, the educational issues remained the same. Narkompros, the technical lobby, and the Young Communist League continued to fight over the proper combination of academic study, production training, socially useful activity, and political relevance, and also over the merit of discriminatory policies in favor of children of peasants and workers. Narkompros discovered that it had become considerably more difficult to defend its program. Its relationships with the Young Communist League and with teachers and parents collapsed. The technical lobby, and not Narkompros, benefited from a mad dash for modernization. By 1931, Narkompros had lost more than its ability to successfully defend cardinal tenets of its program; it had surrendered much of the vision imparted by Lunacharsky and had forfeited the prerogative to make policy as it saw fit.

Cultural Revolution

The cultural revolution affected almost all fields of intellectual endeavor. Writers, historians, economists, and educators were pummeled by the chief features of the period: apocalyptic and millenial thinking; strident anti-intellectualism; efforts to find a single "Marxist" or "proletarian" line; discourse reduced to formulas and slogans; a preoccupation with relevance, defined in narrow economic and political terms; mobilization of man and machine to transform nature and society; and base meanness.

Reflecting this diversity, the cultural revolution affected different areas in a variety of ways, amply demonstrated by the rich historiography on the subject. In some fields it ended discussion among contending groups; in others it provoked debate, often of a shrill nature.[1] Much of the impetus for the revolution came from intellectuals seeking the right to speak for the Party.[2]

Official statements for science, scholarship, and culture were often ambiguous, a result of the Party's own contradictory needs. The Party's leadership jealously guarded its prerogative to make cultural policy and felt ill at ease with the iconoclasm of many of the advocates of cultural revolution. Yet it benefited from cooperation with radicals opposed to Trotsky and Bukharin, two Party leaders who were less inclined to subject intellectual pursuits to shock treatment. At any rate, the Party's leadership issued mixed signals. It encouraged radicals by its own transformationist policies and rhetoric of class war, while it withheld official endorsement of any one group.[3] Education was no different than other fields in this respect.

The Party's Educational Policy

"It is necessary to master science (nauka)," Stalin declared to the Eighth Komsomol Congress on May 16, 1928, and to do so "it is necessary . . . to study, study, study in the most stubborn of ways."[4] Concerned with the need for the preparation of specialists, he cautioned his audience to dispense with "barbaric attitudes toward science and toward cultured people." In present conditions of peaceful development, "a cavalry charge can only do harm."[5] In the same speech, Stalin proceeded to go against his own advice by approving of confiscations of grain and the recent arrest of over fifty mining engineers and technicians in the Shakhty area of the Donbass. His listeners were to launch a "merciless struggle with bureaucratism," to "beat the enemy," and to "take the fortress of science come what may."[6]

Stalin's primary interest in advanced education paralleled recent initiatives from the Party's Central Committee. Its resolution, "On the Improvement of Preparation of New Specialists," adopted July 12, 1928, and a follow-up decree on November 16, 1929, ordered the transfer of most higher technical institutes, technicums, Factory Apprenticeship Schools, and senior grades of the secondary school to the jurisdiction of economic agencies.[7] Any mention of schools was limited to a call for revising the secondary school curriculum to improve preparation of graduates for higher education.[8]

The Party refrained from indicating just what revisions it preferred. By intent or by default, it left the field open to individuals and groups advancing their own notions. Nor did it effectively intervene when Narkompros continued to obstruct the conversion of senior grades to a more specialized curriculum. A purge of Narkompros in late 1929 and early 1930 followed no pattern, leaving many of the old guard to pursue familiar policies.

A Second Party Conference on Education made little difference, reflecting a diversity of opinion on many critical issues. Conflicting points of view may have accounted for the conference's tardy convocation. At the end of

1928, the educational press announced that the conference would open the following February in Moscow.[9] It was a false signal. In mid-year, things finally seemed to be coming to a head when *Uchitel'skaia gazeta* featured a series of articles by antagonists jockeying for position.[10] The conference did not take place until April 1930. Like the first, ten years earlier, it ended with resolutions that fueled debate.[11]

The School, the Foxtrot, and the "Collectivization of Life"

And a heated debate it was, devoid of a civility of tone and a willingness to compromise. It began at the Eighth Congress of the Young Communist League, May 5–16, 1928, with the sharpest exchange yet between Komsomol and Narkompros. Only a hint of their recent cooperation remained. Komsomol and Narkompros still agreed on the danger posed by Gastev and his Central Institute of Labor, but that hardly compensated, in Komsomol's view, for the failure of Narkompros in every other respect to provide proper leadership.[12] The League's General Secretary, Chaplin, set the tone with an unforgiving appraisal of an educational system that catered to the children of kulaks and Nepmen and failed to counter pornography and the foxtrot. Such criticism came as no surprise to the Commissariat of Enlightenment, but what followed may have. Chaplin introduced a threatening note: "We must send our best workers to the Narkompros apparat to shake it up for new work."[13]

On the fourth day, May 8, Lunacharsky boldly responded. He suggested not nine, but ten years of non-specialized instruction as the desired norm for all Soviet youth. He reminded his audience that limited resources prevented a better performance by the Commissariat and its schools.[14] Krupskaya seconded Lunacharsky's remarks. Adopting the tone of a school-marm, she instructed her pupils to avoid "anarchistic criticism that disrupts work . . . or supervision (kontrol') of the carping or destructive sort."[15]

Krupskaya's advice went unheeded. Shortages of funds were no longer relevant; enthusiasm and storming could accomplish all. "He cried here," Chaplin said, belittling Lunacharsky, "more than he called us to feats at the front of the cultural revolution."[16] Chaplin then expanded his assault to include the entire Commissariat. Narkompros must not be an "old driveling woman but a militant headquarters of the cultural revolution."[17] Once again, Chaplin called for personnel changes at the Commissariat. The "Narkompros ship," under its captain, Comrade Lunacharsky, could go forward under full sail only with the help of "entire detachments of brave selfless Komsomol sailors."[18]

Similar criticism came from Shul'gin's sharp tongue and acerbic pen.[19] Lunacharsky knew him well. In 1918, Shul'gin had supported a version of the Statute for the United Labor School that called for the creation of a school-commune which would function all year, seven days a week, and merge academic study with everyday labor tasks.[20] The Statute's final version did not conform to Shul'gin's vision of life and schooling as one, but he refused to pass from the scene. He continued to present his case from within Narkompros as deputy head of the Department of the United Labor School from 1918 to 1922 and member of the Pedagogical Section, and from without as Director of the School Methods Institute from the time of its creation in 1922. He championed a captivating utopia free of distinctions between school and life, teachers and the taught, mental and physical labor, State and society, and urban and rural areas. Any institution such as State or school that existed apart from life (byt) would (taking a cue from Marx) wither away, as would the idiocy of rural life.

Throughout most of the 1920s, Shul'gin's was a loud but isolated voice. At the Pedagogical Section, on January 29, 1926, he unsuccessfully opposed the separation of contemporaneity and history in the secondary school curriculum.[21] More failure followed on March 11, when he presented socially useful labor as the key ingredient in education, while a majority preferred more academic instruction.[22] Angrily, he turned to *Narodnyi uchitel'* with an article titled "Once More and Once More Again on Social Work."[23] The First Five-Year Plan and the cultural revolution provided a more hospitable environment. Now emboldened, Shul'gin verbally assaulted anyone with the temerity to disagree with his effort to push Soviet Russia "by the collectivization of life" toward a utopia of self-governing communes.[24]

Narkompros Fights Back

Not to be outdone, the leadership at Narkompros matched harsh criticism with a stubborn defense of its program. It came from all sections of the beleaguered agency: Lunacharsky, its Commissar; Iakovleva, the Deputy Commissar; Krupskaya, the chair of the Pedagogical Section; Epshtein, head of Glavsotsvos; and Pistrak, his deputy. They were supported by Pokrovsky; M. Aleksinsky, head of the Moscow Department of Education since February, 1928; and S. Gaisinovich, head of the Department for Workers Education in Glavprofobr.

Lunacharsky led the way with familiar arguments. In 1928, he carried his message anywhere he thought he might make a difference: to the Sixth Congress of Heads of Departments of Education in April; the Eighth Komsomol Congress in May; the Conference of Teachers of Social Studies in June; and the Academy of Communist Training in October.[25] As before, the Commissar tried to shame Party and State into greater efforts on behalf of an educational system that was underfunded in comparison with tsarist times. He even found a way to turn the Shakhty trial to his own advantage. Lunacharsky told the Eighth Komsomol Congress that sabotage by engineers proved that "serious economic construction requires simultaneously massive cultural construction."[26] Lunacharsky then questioned whether the noise associated with the emerging cultural revolution could lead to much without the full development of the polytechnical school.[27]

Lunacharsky's understanding of enlightenment clashed sharply with Shul'gin's version of cultural revolution. The Commissar credited Shul'gin with alerting Narkompros to the dangers of old teachers who refused to change their ways, but went no further toward accommodating his outspoken critic. At an open session of the Narkompros Collegium on December 3, 1928, and then at a course for heads of regional departments of education the following month, Lunacharsky instructed his listeners and Shul'gin in the necessity of the school. He invoked the authority of the founders of Marxism-Leninism. Marx and Engels understood the possibility that consciousness, of the sort that schooling might provide, could influence events. Lenin stressed the school's importance to learning bourgeois culture.[28] Lunacharsky then resorted to harsh words of his own. He charged that Shul'gin's negation of the school amounted to a "most harmful deviation" and to "desertion," his manner something in the nature of an Indian on the warpath, and his tone one of "polemical shrillness."[29]

Krupskaya spoke almost as boldly. Like Lunacharsky, she regarded the cultural revolution as something of a shouting match.[30] In two remarkable articles printed in 1929, she condemned the practice of purging children from school.[31] She was reacting to what in some areas had become a wholesale removal of children of the middle peasantry and self-employed artisans.[32] Purging was a "bureaucratic approach toward children that resurrects the Middle Ages." Past heroes such as Chernyshevsky, Marx, and Engels (she did not mention Lenin) would have lacked the credentials to save them from such rude treatment. "There is class struggle and then there is class struggle"; to deny the young an opportunity for an education "is not class struggle."[33]

Meanwhile, in preparation for the Second Party Conference on Education, Pokrovsky drafted theses reaffirming the traditional Narkompros program.[34] Approved by the Narkompros Collegium on May 18, the theses insisted on the temporary nature of professional training in senior grades, Factory Apprenticeship Schools, and Schools for Peasant Youth. With their adoption, the Collegium increased the desirable norm for polytechnical education from nine to ten years.

Friend and foe alike should not have been surprised. Lunacharsky, Krupskaya, and Pokrovsky had aggressively responded to difficult conditions before. The notion of an extra year culminated at least a year's campaign. At the Eighth Komsomol Congress, Lunacharsky had raised the possibility of a tenth year. Several months later, Aleksinsky and Gaisinovich spoke for the addition of an extra year (fifth) to the elementary school to entice working-class children to stay in school longer.[35] That December, Epshtein presented the case for a tenth year to Sovnarkom,[36] and at the end of the month, Krupskaya told the Conference of Teachers of Secondary Schools that the Narkompros Collegium had approved the idea.[37] She expressed, however, a fear that another year might strengthen the case of those who wanted to convert the senior division into a technicum.[38]

Pokrovsky and the Collegium moved forward despite Krupskaya's anxiety. Pokrovsky, Lunacharsky, Epshtein, and Iakovleva marched out to present and defend the theses. Their campaign began in February with Pokrovsky's appearance before the Conference of Heads of Regional Departments of Education, continued through the deliberation of the State Academic Council on May 8 and of the Narkompros Collegium ten days later, and included presentations before local departments of education and Party organs.[39] At the same time, the Narkompros Collegium denounced purging. Angered by dozens of daily reports, it condemned a "large wave of dismissals" from secondary and primary schools. In partial compensation for its stubbornness in this matter, Narkompros restated its objection to homework in the hope that lower academic standards would help children of peasants and workers make the grade.[40]

In mid-June, Lunacharsky brought the theses to the plenary session of the central committee of the teachers union. Shokhin spoke for the Young Communist League. Predictably, they crossed swords, as one cartoonist for *Uchitel'skaia gazeta* represented it. More stirring combat occurred between V.

Narkompros versus Komsomol

The legend under the cartoon reads "A 'duel' between Comrade Lunacharsky and Comrade Shokhin over the public education system." Lunacharsky's shield defends the polytechnical "ten-year school." Shokhin's lances are "For the seven-year school" and "Professional-technical school."
SOURCE: *Uchitel'skaia gazeta*, no. 72 (299) (June 22, 1929), p. 2.

Panfilov, head of the Planning Department of the Organizational and Planning Administration of the Commissariat of Enlightenment, and A. I. Berdnikov, the representative of the State Planning Agency (Gosplan). Berdnikov came flushed with the latest fever of gigantomania at Gosplan, now purged of its more realistic members. He insisted that the success of the First Five-Year Plan depended less on the presence of material resources than on the enthusiasm of the people.[41] He ended as he had begun, stressing the need to "overcome dilatory attitudes with bold campaigns."[42]

Deliberately at first, and then with bursts of sarcasm, Panfilov spoke at great length for the offended Narkompros. After a formal bow to the importance of enthusiasm, he countered with demands for more funding for education. Like Lunacharsky, Panfilov pointed out how the pre-revolutionary government had spent more than its Soviet successor on teachers and on elementary education.[43] Flirting with heresy, he condemned efforts to launch grand campaigns with little more than "large billboards and much pomp," and questioned proposals for electrification.[44] By ignoring harsh realities, Berdnikov had engaged in "most harmful bureaucratic tomfoolery."[45] Speakers who followed, some of them teachers and inspectors, agreed and pointed to shortages of desks, pencils, and paper.[46] Unmoved by the facts, Berdnikov charged Panfilov with a "liquidationist, dilatory position."[47] He could have extended the charge to the entire plenum. While it approved Gosplan's ambitious plans, it demanded more funding for education.[48]

Defeat

Gosplan got its way. The Commissariat of Enlightenment, schools, and teachers were asked to make do with little material support. Through no fault of its own, Narkompros could not devise a consistent policy for support. It again encouraged a reliance on self-taxation, an effort clearly needed to save some schools, while it asked schools to limit fees because they discouraged attendance by poorer pupils.[49]

The overall situation deteriorated before shrinking sources of support. Local governments had to increase their share of funding for enlightenment from 65 to 70 percent during the 1920s to 75 to 80 percent from 1928 to 1932.[50] Of these funds, the percentage set aside for education declined steadily from 70 percent in 1927/28 to less than 60 percent in 1931. Only half that amount was designated for primary and secondary schools.[51] An 89 percent increase in the total number of rubles assigned to schools from 1928 through 1931 was more than offset by an inflationary rate of at least 40 to 50 percent, a 66 percent increase in enrollment (69 percent in the primary grades), and a 50 percent increase in the number of teachers.[52]

The old guard at Narkompros also had to stand by and watch the collapse of its relations with teachers and parents. Even as Lunacharsky and his colleagues campaigned against radical proposals for curricular change, programs issued by Narkompros and by its provincial organs began to reflect remarks by Chaplin and Shul'gin.

This development occurred with surprising speed. By the fall of 1928, everyone associated with schools was told to join campaigns to provide Soviet Russia with a uniform secular culture and transform it into a mighty colossus of machines, black smoke, and waves of grain. The educational press, from Saratov's *Nizhe-Volzhskii prosveshchenets,* Nizhnii Novgorod's *Shkola i zhizn',* and Yaroslavl's *Nash trud,* to *Na putiakh k novoi shkole* and *Ezhenedel'nik Narkomprosa* emphasized the importance of the school's participation in the election of soviets, attacks on alcoholism and religion, celebrations of Lenin and the October revolution, and the planting and harvesting of grain. In a rush toward relevance, the Commissariat's press organs devoted less and less attention to academic matters and everyday problems of teachers. Perhaps the change contributed to an unexpected fall in subscriptions to *Shkola i zhizn'.*[53] The shift in content was most noticeable in the publications of the teachers union, *Narodnyi uchitel'* and *Uchitel'skaia gazeta.* In keeping with its new approach, in 1928 the newspaper featured cartoons urging teachers into battle with the many evils of home and society—vodka, religion, eroticism, wifebeating, and uncultured speech.

At the provincial level, purges accompanied changes in each journal's content. In Yaroslavl', a reorganization at *Nash trud* occurred in the fall of 1927.[54] In Nizhnii Novgorod, the editor of *Shkola i zhizn'* since 1926, A. Akun'kov, was replaced in early 1928. His successor immediately published an article, "Our Achievements," announcing that this and subsequent issues would stress the positive.[55] Akun'kov dutifully contributed a masterpiece of self-criticism and panegyric to the cultural revolution.[56] In the capital, a purge of the Moscow Department of Education began in late 1927 and continued until the fall of 1929. During this period, the number of organs in the Moscow Department declined from seventeen to nine, and personnel from 243 to 148.[57] In the middle of this process, the department's journal, *Vestnik prosveshcheniia,* announced a new politicized format. It dispensed with such useful sections as "Program-Method Issues" and "Pedagogical Practice," replacing them with new features such as "Socialist Society and Cultural Construction," "Mass Work in the Countryside" and "Linking the School with Production."[58] That same issue announced the department's intent to require that its schools pay more attention to socially useful activity.[59]

New curricula and instructions from Narkompros reflected these altered concerns. The Commissariat terminated its compromise with teachers by demanding that they and their schools become agents for transformation of society. The 1928 curriculum for the School for Peasant Youth directed teachers to adhere to complex themes focusing on livestock, agricultural machinery, fertilizers, construction, planting, and harvesting.[60] That same year, Narkompros responded to the threat of war with a manual demonstrating how subjects could incorporate military instruction—social studies might provide a history of the Red Army; natural sciences could inform pupils on measures to counter poison gas.[61] The following year, Narkompros's Collegium emphasized the obligation of all teachers and pupils to merge education with harvesting, grain procurement, and anti-religious campaigns.[62] It proposed socialist competition among departments of education, schools, and groups of pupils to improve funding, social composition, academic performance, and community service.[63]

In the summer of 1929, Narkompros and the Moscow Department of Education jointly published drafts of new curricula for the elementary school.[64] Acknowledging that the 1927 curricula were meant to last four years, both agencies justified their effort with the slogan "a program is not a dogma."[65] Programs followed with complex themes on class struggle, industrialization, collectivization, and anti-religious activity. For the moment, Narkompros refrained from releasing similar instructions for secondary schools. The reformed Moscow Department was not so timid. That October, it tied instruction in primary and secondary grades to a study of the First Five-Year Plan.[66]

Not every department of education was swept up by politicized relevance. In the fall of 1929, the Leningrad Department of Education released a weighty manual for rural elementary schools which was openly critical of Narkompros syllabi.[67] Although not disavowing the importance of themes, the manual called attention to the importance of systematic instruction, especially in such areas as grammar, spelling, and arithmetic. Its concern for academic content was, however, exceptional.

Narkompros's theses embodying the vision and program of the Commissariat of Enlightenment came at a time when Lunacharsky and his lieutenants were suffering a diminution of their authority. Narkompros now appeared indecisive. Responding to the desperate needs of its schools, the Commissariat encouraged the levying of fees, while at the same time it tried to limit the practice. Concerned about academic standards, it nevertheless ordered the abolition of homework. While Lunacharsky and Krupskaya complained of the noise associated with the cultural revolution, local departments of education and Narkompros demanded participation in its campaigns. Within a year of the compromise of 1927, Narkompros once again sought to use teachers and pupils as means for reshaping society. It remained to be seen how far Narkompros would go toward a full embrace of the cultural revolution and the extent to which teachers, parents, and pupils would follow.

XIII.

PURGES AND PROJECTS, 1929–1930

The Presidium of the All-Russian Central
Executive Committee resolves to release
Comrade Lunacharsky from his duties as
People's Commissar of Enlightenment of
the RSFSR in accordance with his personal
request.[1]

In such unsentimental terms, *Izvestiia* announced Lunacharsky's removal. It was a long time in coming.

Since early 1928, Lunacharsky had proved especially troublesome. He had used the Shakhty Affair to advance his own concepts about education; had questioned the wisdom of the cultural revolution, coming close to dismissing it as a noisy affair; and had expressed grave doubts about the transformationist assumptions behind the First Five-Year Plan, almost calling it a waste of effort and funds. Sometimes he did play the role expected of a Commissar in revolutionary times. In November 1928, he called upon overworked teachers to participate in the campaign to reelect soviets. Shortly thereafter, he went before the First All-Russian Musical Conference in Leningrad to denounce jazz. Sounding like his Komsomol antagonist Chaplin, Lunacharsky damned the music and the foxtrot as forms of human degradation.[2] When the Academy of Sciences rejected three Marxist nominees for membership in January 1929, Lunacharsky labelled the academicians "supercilious mandarins of science."[3] Yet that same month, at the Conference of Natural Scientists in Leningrad, he distinguished between science and contemporary politics. Although his comments were met with applause, they quickly provoked the criticism he must have known would follow.[4]

That February, Lunacharsky took a bolder step. In a letter to Stalin, he objected to the practice of purging students from schools and higher educational institutions. His tone was sarcastic, his message familiar—such policies violated common sense and provoked the "hate and counterrevolutionary activity of a certain part of the youth, who, once in our educational institutions, perhaps might grow anew in our spirit."[5] It was one of the last times that Lunacharsky would invoke his vision of a new school for a new society.

Sheila Fitzpatrick surmises that shortly after writing this letter, Lunacharsky submitted his resignation, as did Krupskaya, Pokrovsky, Iakovleva, and Epshtein.[6] They had cause to do so. That spring, while the old guard promoted the Narkompros theses, events passed it by. Pupils continued to be dismissed, and the spirit of class strife permeated educational literature and curricula. Forces imperiling the conventional wisdom at Narkompros became apparent at its own Conference of Heads of Regional Departments of Education, February 15–20, 1929. Lunacharsky and Pokrovsky seemed to dominate with their defense of the Commissariat's program and recent theses.[7] The conference nevertheless adopted resolutions in keeping with the cultural revolution. It demanded that the Narkompros Collegium be expanded to include representatives from workers groups, the Central Committee's Agitprop, and the Young Communist League's Central Committee. Some time prior to the end of March, the Narkompros Collegium approved these resolutions.[8]

It is not known whether major changes followed in the Collegium's membership.[9] Things seemed much the same when on May 18, the Collegium approved the theses, and in mid-June when Lunacharsky and Panfilov defended them at the plenary session of the central committee of the teachers union. However, ominous changes were already in the making. In early 1929, a special commission formed by the Party's Central Committee suggested a purge and reorganization of the Commissariat. The Narkompros Collegium dutifully placed the matter on its agenda.[10] Then, on July 16, the Collegium embraced class war and occupational training. Its circular, "To All Departments of Education," commanded that the educational apparatus become a "center of the cultural revolution" and an "organ of the class struggle of the proletariat."[11] Moreover, it rejected the principle of a single unified labor school by endorsing the Factory Apprenticeship School, the Factory Seven-Year School, and the School of Peasant Youth as "institutions closest to meeting the needs of workers and poor peasantry."[12] Finally, the Collegium proposed to include in its number workers from the bench; representatives from Agitprop, Komsomol, the Central Council of Trade Unions, and local departments of education; and a peasant or former peasant (a rural vydvizhenets).[13] The announcement of Lunacharsky's dismissal soon followed.[14]

Lunacharsky's replacement, A. S. Bubnov, was a political appointee with limited experience in the field of education. He had earlier served as an administrator of the Party's propaganda machine, first as head of Agitprop and then as chief of the Red Army's Political Administration. While Lunacharsky had attempted to put some distance between the Commissariat and cultural revolution, Bubnov encouraged active involvement. He called upon schools to participate in the class war at the ideological front, against religion, kulaks, and illiteracy.[15] Under his guidance, Narkompros fell victim to a purge.

Purge

On August 5, 1929, the Party's Central Committee adopted a decree, "On the Leading Cadres of Education," demanding the removal from Narkompros of "alien elements who distort the proletarian class line." It required the appointment of factory workers and Komsomolites to positions in the educational apparatus.[16] Curiously, the decree was not published until three months later. In a process that began before then, the Narkompros Collegium removed about 10 percent of the Commissariat's central personnel.[17] At the same time, the purge of the Moscow Department of Education continued; its journal *Vestnik prosveshcheniia,* as well as Yaroslavl's *Nash trud,* ceased publication. With its tenth issue in 1929, *Narodnyi uchitel'* presented an entirely new editorial board, and in September *Ezhenedel'nik Narkomprosa* came under new editorial direction.[18]

In December, Rabkrin created a Commission for the Purge of Narkompros. Narkompros's headquarters came alive with daily meetings, walls were adorned with posters, and suggestion boxes were placed in corridors.[19] The Commission made certain of society's wider involvement by recruiting 350 factory workers and 80 representatives of various organizations to help with the investigation.[20] Intended to last two and one-half months, the entire process appears to have spanned almost twice that amount of time.[21] As a result, the commission dismissed an additional 14 percent of Narkompros's personnel. It also suggested that Glavprofobr and Glavsotsvos be replaced by a Methods Sector to devise curricula, and by a Sector for Mass Measures to promote participation in campaigns associated with the cultural revolution and First Five-Year Plan.[22]

Rhetoric preceding the purge promised a wholesale removal of the old guard.[23] Shul'gin and Shokhin gleefully observed that Narkompros was receiving its due.[24] Lunacharsky's removal and the purge that followed were major events, but they did not signal the departure of the entire Commissariat leadership, or a new direction of policy. In two published reports, Ia. Bauer, the chairman of the Purge Commission, identified his effort as a streamlining of the Commissariat's administrative structure, geared toward the removal of superfluous theoreticians, the illiterate, and those individuals best suited to work on collective farms.[25] The point was not without some substance. As early as the mid-1920s, the State Academic Council had become a labyrinth of departments, commissions, and subcommissions which often duplicated and obstructed one another's work. In 1926 and 1927, Rabkrin complained that the Council's Pedagogical Section had fourteen commissions and its Political Section fifteen.[26] Despite a plan to reduce personnel, by April 1929 the Pedagogical Section included a presidium of 40 members and a plenum of 300.[27] Reasons publicly given for dismissal of individuals ranged from service in the Provisional Government or in one of the White Armies during the Civil War, to incompetence.[28]

Sometimes the purge rewarded the inept. A corresponding appointment of workers from the bench and of Komsomol activists meant the placement of the disinterested, unqualified, and semi-literate.[29] A Narkompros report ruefully observed that it took more than class feeling for an individual to function successfully.[30] Krupskaya complained that she had been sent workers who had no desire to be at Narkompros.[31] A Komsomol member, L. N. Martirosian, later recalled that he had opposed his assignment to Narkompros. He had preferred instead a post in industrial administration so that he might qualify for admission into a higher technical institute.[32]

Changes at Narkompros promoted individuals favoring policies associated with the cultural revolution and left key members of the old guard untouched. The Commissariat's unyielding Komsomol critic, Shokhin, became head of the Sector for Mass Measures, a member of the Narkompros Collegium, and an editor of *Narodnoe prosveshchenie*. At the Methods Sector, Shatsky temporarily headed the group for elementary education, Shokhin the group for secondary education, and Shul'gin the group for teachers training.[33] A Komsomol representative in the Commissariat since 1923, Rudnev, joined the Methods Sector to lead its Brigade for Schools of Peasant Youth. He then replaced Shatsky as head of the Elementary School Group.[34] Epshtein stayed on as a Deputy Commissar, as did Krupskaya. She continued to edit *Na putiakh k novoi shkole*, and Epshtein headed *Narodnoe prosveshchenie* until its last issue in September 1930. Both of them remained on the editorial board of *Uchitel'skaia gazeta*, which was renamed *Za kommunisticheskoe prosveshchenie* in April 1930. For Aleksinsky and for Panfilov, nothing changed as they moved from their posts of head and assistant head respectively of the now defunct Planning Department to the same posts in the new Sector of Cadres.

Some institutions also survived to oppose the cultural revolution in schooling. Glavsotsvos continued to function until 1930, and the State Academic Council and its Pedagogical Section even longer. Krupskaya, Epshtein, and Shatsky remained active in the State Academic Council, resisting the efforts of the Methods Sector and the Sector for Mass Measures.

Occupational Training

In early 1930, the Narkompros Collegium reaffirmed its support of specialized training in the School for Peasant Youth (now called the School for Collective Farm Youth), and the Factory Seven-Year School.[35] It projected a rapidly expanding number of schools for collective farm youth which would train a cadre of tractor drivers, combine operators, dairy farmers, and mechanics necessary for the success of collectivized agriculture.[36] The Factory Seven-Year School would enroll half of the working youth at the beginning of the next academic year, and soon thereafter comprise at least half of all secondary schools in industrial districts.[37]

On April 26, 1930, the long-awaited Second Party Conference on Education convened, much later and in an entirely different fashion than originally intended. Bubnov, not Lunacharsky, took the floor. He presented not the theses of 1929, now thoroughly discredited, but rather resolutions "On the Secondary School," approved days before by the Narkompros Collegium, Komsomol Central Committee, and central committee of the teachers union.[38] Adopted by the Conference, this document intended to end the united labor school. Only the elementary school remained to offer a standard general education. The former secondary school would disappear. Its junior division would provide occupational training as part of a Factory Seven-Year School, a School for Collective Farm Youth, or a new institution, a School for Communal Services.[39] The senior division was to be immediately reorganized into technicums under the jurisdiction of economic agencies.[40] Several months later, the Party's Central Committee and Sovnarkom of the Russian Republic approved the resolutions.[41]

In mid-August, Narkompros organized the First All-Russian Polytechnical Congress in Moscow to celebrate the apparent unanimity of institutional opinion favoring specialized training in the secondary school.[42] The Commissariat had initially expected 222 delegates representing labor, education, industry, agriculture, transportation, and the Young Communist League,[43] but on the eve of the congress Narkompros was besieged by hundreds of requests. In the end, the congress consisted of enough delegates for a very loud celebration. Under the prodding of Rudnev and Shokhin, the 679 voting and 472 non-voting delegates and 100 guests condemned Narkompros for its past errors and endorsed vocational training in grades five through seven. It demanded that all urban secondary schools form an association with a factory or some other enterprise by September 15, and all rural schools with a collective farm by October 1.[44]

Faced with a hostile array of individuals, institutions, and conferences, the advocates of a general polytechnical education resisted as best they could. Perhaps privately, Krupskaya, Epshtein, Aleksinsky, and others acted vigorously. When addressing the Second Party Conference, Bubnov referred to stiff resistance to the resolutions he brought for approval, and mentioned specifically objections to conversion of the senior division into a technicum.[45] But the public effort at this time was not so bold. Lunacharsky was gone and with him his eloquence. Aleksinsky demanded that Narkompros become the headquarters of cultural revolution, even as he warned of the dangers of overspecialization.[46] Krupskaya chose to redraw the line of defense at seven years of polytechnical instruction, condemned Gastev as usual, and criticized industry for its failure to support education.[47] Epshtein did what he could by carefully avoiding a full endorsement of new policies. At the polytechnical congress, he praised the teaching of production skills, but defended general polytechnical education. Epshtein's behavior was duly noted when a delegate from the Lower Volga region demanded not "defensive speeches" from the Deputy Commissar, but thoroughgoing self-criticism.[48] A delegate from the central committee of the teachers union followed with a damning indictment of Epshtein, Lunacharsky, and the former leadership at Narkompros.[49] For the moment, Krupskaya remained beyond reproach.[50]

The 1930 Curriculum

The Second Party Conference and the Polytechnical Congress focused on a need for occupational training, neglecting other important aspects of schooling.[51] The task of curricular development for all grades remained with Narkompros and subject to controversy among competing groups. In 1930, conflict erupted over the merit of a radical device, the project method.

Years earlier, Western educators had responded to Dewey's call to relate school and life by replacing subject-matter fare with projects. A group of pupils, a class, or an entire school, sometimes joined by parents and other members of the local community, worked together to mend clothes, repair the school building, make rabbit traps, or organize a school choir or community orchestra.[52] At Narkompros, interest in community activities and learning through doing made the new device of official interest. During the 1920s, however, the Pedagogical Section emphasized complex themes while paying only formal homage to projects.[53]

Until the late 1920s, the method's most avid supporters were confined to Shul'gin's School Methods Institute and units in Narkompros charged with overseeing the School for Peasant Youth. Efforts to impose anything of this sort on teachers, such as Shul'gin's presentation on behalf of socially useful activity at the Pedagogical Section in early 1926, were met with defeat. The cultural revolution changed this situation. Narkompros's 1929 curricula used projects to involve pupils and teachers in campaigns relevant to the cultural revolution, collectivization, and industrialization.

Doubts and doubters persisted. At a Methods Conference sponsored by the State Academic Council in late December 1929, Epshtein and Shatsky referred favorably to the method, but made no suggestions for its implementation.[54] Pistrak reminded delegates that years earlier, the Commissariat's curricula had outstripped the desires and abilities of schoolteachers.[55] Early the following year, on February 20, the Glavsotsvos Collegium considered a proposal for the exclusive use of the project method. The Collegium rejected it in favor of a variant combining projects with a traditional form of instruction.[56]

Ignoring such an apparently definitive statement from the Commissariat's leadership, Rudnev's group at the Methods Sector, with an assist from Shokhin's Sector for Mass Measures, devised curricula with the project method as their central feature. In late April, Rudnev presented these curricula to bodies outside Narkompros, first to an All-Russian Conference on

Schools for Collective Farm Youth and then to a Conference on the Factory Seven-Year Schools.[57] In May, Shul'gin's Institute assisted the effort with a conference devoted to the method. According to one report, most of the 296 delegates, many of them teachers, approved of the radical device. Shul'gin and Esipov came to praise the method as a means for uniting theory with practice and for compelling production training.[58] Esipov favored such projects as "Help Fulfill the Industrial-Financial Plan" and "Help Collectivization," designed for several grades or the entire school. He would allow only occasional lessons for the development of particular academic skills.[59] Not everyone agreed. On July 20, the Commissariat's weekly publication, *Biulleten' Narkomprosa,* indicated continued disenchantment with proposals tying instruction too closely with projects.[60]

Meanwhile, Krupskaya attempted to find middle ground between radical methods and a concern for content. She began at a session of the Society of Marxist Pedagogues on March 4, by scolding Shul'gin and his School Methods Institute, without naming them, for fantasies of abolishing the school. She sharply disagreed with the notion that children could learn everything they needed to know through work at a factory. A factory was not a pedagogical institution and would tend to require narrow professional training.[61] Two months later at Shul'gin's conference, Krupskaya praised the project method, while warning against its precipitous introduction into Narkompros curricula.[62]

In mid-year, Krupskaya concluded that her advice for caution had been ignored. In notes sent to the Methods Section and to Shatsky and Shokhin, she angrily assessed draft curricula and syllabi then under consideration,[63] claiming that their projects were more interested in sloganeering and production than with logical presentation of information. Without major surgery, the new curricula and syllabi would produce little more than "braggarts and loudmouths." Krupskaya contemptuously dismissed projects such as "The Struggle for the Industrial-Financial Plan," appeals for the organization of parents into shock brigades, and demonstrations protesting absenteeism at a factory. In her opinion, the programs suffered from Great Russian chauvinism, were criminally negligent of historical perspective, and paid insufficient attention to reading and writing.

Krupskaya's complaint came to nothing. On July 21, the Methods Sector approved new curricula with only the slightest concern for content.[64] It recommended reorganizing grades into links or shock brigades, each consisting of pupils from several grades and the occasional parent.[65] The curriculum for the year-round School for Collective Farm Youth required that less than 30 percent of class time be devoted to literature, mathematics, and science and that these subjects should be subordinate to projects.[66] Almost 19 percent of instructional time in the Factory Seven-Year School was set aside for labor, while remaining subjects fueled projects and associated campaigns. Social studies and literature focused on class struggle and the fight against religion; music instruction culminated in a presentation at a factory to raise production; and natural sciences centered on the use of fertilizers, building materials, and machines.[67] The authors of this new program arrogantly dismissed its predecessors in 1923, 1925, and 1927 as irrelevant.[68] Only when discussing native language and foreign languages did the new curriculum show concern for the potentially harmful effects of the project method.

New textual materials in support of projects and contemporaneity were not long in coming. In early 1930, pressure mounted for the publication of looseleaf workbooks, which could be easily adapted to meet local conditions, while staying abreast of current events.[69] Teacher and pupil could remove old pages and insert new ones as needed. When on March 28 the Narkompros Collegium rejected for only the "present time" a standard list of textbooks, critics declared its hesitancy to be a political error.[70] The matter was settled in May, when the Second All-Russian Conference on Textbooks endorsed journal-textbooks.[71] Narkompros followed with the publication of these items, sporting such martial titles as *Shkol'naia brigada* (The School Brigade) in Moscow, *Malen'kie udarniki* (Young Shock Workers) in Leningrad, and *Malen'kie stroiteli* (Young Builders) in Samara and Smolensk. They presented an adult message geared toward children. Featuring large print, ample illustrations, and short snappy stories, the latest in reading asked pupils to attack social evils, including the custom of Christmas trees.[72] *Shkol'naia brigada* challenged first- and second-graders with a fold-up page which revealed the caricature of a kulak as the enemy of the First Five-Year Plan.[73] Bem and Esipov, opponents of an earlier compromise with traditional forms of instruction, now found their views in the ascendant as editors of *Shkol'naia brigada.*[74] The talented author of children's tales, Kornei Chukovsky, was not so enamored with the adult campaigns, and suffered heavy-handed criticism because of the alleged irrelevance of his work.[75]

As in an earlier period, policy was no guarantee of practice. Proposals for occupational training in secondary schools depended on the cooperation of economic administrators and factory managers heretofore unwilling to help. Representatives from the Supreme Economic Council, Commissariat of Agriculture, and Central Council of Trade Unions came to the Polytechnical Congress to promise better behavior in the future.[76] But no provisions were made to compensate organizations, if and when they assigned their scarce human and material resources to schools. For industry and agriculture, short-term and on-the-job training remained far cheaper and faster ways of preparing a new cadre of workers.

Factory managers were not the only ones who were skeptical of the value of recent changes in educational policy. Departments of education and school administrators, jealous of their own authority, had reason to obstruct the administrative transfer of senior grades. Short of funds, local governments would remain unable to support schools. Most important of all, teachers would again resist becoming agents of cultural change and practitioners of a radical curriculum.

XIV.

SLOWER HISTORY

A new generation at Narkompros advanced a vision of schooling far grander than anything proposed earlier by Lunacharsky. School and society together would build the Republic anew; the community and classroom—life and learning—would become one and inseparable. Once again fervent hope proved no match for cruel reality.

Labor Education

Vocational training foundered from neglect and an absence of resources. Economic commissariats, factories, and collective farms refused to provide equipment, teaching personnel, and opportunities for practicums.[1] In late 1931, about 75 percent of secondary schools still had no shops.[2] On August 19, 1931, Sovnarkom of the Russian Republic could do no more than require once again that State agencies obey the law calling for assistance to schools.[3] The real situation was worse than the committee would admit. One factory did agree to accept pupils for on-the-job experience, but at a price; it wanted reimbursement from the school for its efforts.[4] Narkompros demanded just the opposite—that factories reimburse schools for pupils' work and pay students directly if they were over fifteen years of age.[5]

The First Five-Year Plan, which caused some officials at Narkompros to wax enthusiastic about prospects for technical education, proved to be problematic. Industry required particular skills which primary and secondary schools could not possibly provide. The uneven pace of industrialization and collectivization precluded cooperation between economic agencies and Narkompros in determining the types of workers needed. In September 1930,

Sovnarkom devised a detailed but meaningless scheme for such planning at local, regional, and national levels.[6]

Narkompros, the Supreme Economic Council, the Commissariat of Agriculture, and the Collective Farm Center rarely communicated with each other.[7] When they talked, they traded accusations. Narkompros charged that local organs of the Supreme Economic Council did not know their present or future needs.[8] Factory managers insisted that pupils lounged or roamed

Narkompros Gets the Bureaucratic Run-Around

The caption under the cartoon reads "Perpetual motion machine." The desks, clockwise from the top, are Narkompros, Cultural-industrial association, and Vesenkha. The bureaucrats pass papers that read, clockwise from top left, "Place your order," "Give us equipment," and "Provide raw materials." Artist: K. Shaparev.

SOURCE: *Za kommunisticheskoe prosveshchenie,* no. 159 (529) (November 18, 1930), p. 3.

aimlessly about the factory. This was not a major loss, perhaps, since management believed students were only fit for collecting trash.[9] Anything more could be disastrous. In one instance, pupils sounded a factory's fire alarm in order to produce a captive audience for a presentation on alcoholism.[10] An effort by a Factory Seven-Year School to help a Stalingrad tractor factory overcome low productivity deteriorated into harassment of the labor force. Arriving at the plant in the morning, workers encountered a student demonstration demanding fulfillment of the plan. Once inside, they had to put up with more didactics and the observation of their every move by youths determined to protect the machinery and get a day's work for a ruble's pay. Persons charged with absenteeism found that pupils scribbled their names on public blackboards, attached black pennants to their machines at work, and staged demonstrations in front of their homes.[11]

Schools for Collective Farm Youth often had little to do with collective farms. In October 1929, the Bureau of the Komsomol's Central Committee found a "widespread and dangerous attraction" among teachers at these schools toward the "methods and traditions of formal study."[12] Some rural elementary schools and Schools for Collective Farm Youth lacked garden plots, and others rented them out.[13] Teachers did not relate their instruction to agriculture; collective farms returned the favor by paying little attention to the schools.[14]

The law requiring the transfer of the senior division of secondary schools to economic agencies was honored in the breach. The legislation itself was partly to blame. Sovnarkom's order of August 10, 1930, stipulated that the use of equipment and physical facilities be determined by rent agreements between Narkompros and economic organs. It left Narkompros with the responsibility of establishing a minimum of general educational subjects in all technicums.[15] Squabbling over facilities and curricula resulted, as issues of *Za kommunisticheskoe prosveshchenie* repeatedly made clear. Some local departments of education refused to transfer the premises or, after doing so, to maintain them properly.[16] Most senior divisions did not become technicums because they lacked the necessary equipment, shops, and special instructors.[17] They neglected labor as a subject and, in the jargon of the day, "adhered to a scholastic approach isolated from production."[18]

Project Method

Like labor training, the project method in practice resembled only a shadow of its paper self. Judging from the complaints of its supporters, a majority of teachers continued to rely on the class-lesson approach. Conferences on the method acknowledged that traditional instruction still dominated.[19] Teacher training institutions provided no instruction in the project method,[20] and teachers who claimed to use projects often avoided them in fact.[21] Others made a public display of their contrary behavior. One instructor reported on his use of the 100-point grading system and recommended it to others because of its alleged objective nature.[22] Another told of his tightly run, disciplined classroom with its emphasis on proper behavior.[23]

By 1931, the project method's most vociferous advocates acknowledged failure. Rudnev lamented that teachers preferred an adherence to old-fashioned ways. A familiar litany followed: teachers failed to employ activity methods, refused to organize excursions, undermined pupil self-government, and assigned grades.[24] Vsesviatsky, an earlier opponent of curricular compromise, now complained that schools avoided involvement in production and socially useful labor. "In other words, our school is still a copy of the bourgeois school to a well-known degree."[25] Even Shul'gin confessed that teachers resisted the introduction of the new method.[26]

Krupskaya's concerns may be taken as another indication of resistance from below. While she continued to oppose the uncritical adoption of the project method proposed by colleagues at Narkompros, Krupskaya condemned rejection of reform below. She expressed fear that a growing concern for the academic side of life, especially with instruction in arithmetic, grammar, and history, was coming at the expense of a true communist education.[27] In 1929, she criticized the State Academic Council for its failure to promote the theme "Class Struggle and the School."[28] Urban schools avoided socially useful labor; teachers terminated student self-government and applied harsh disciplinary measures.[29] By 1931, Krupskaya had become so concerned that she stooped to crude political language. An effort against teachers who would introduce old methods was part of the class struggle; teachers campaigning for the old school posed a right wing danger.[30]

Teachers

For all of the familiar reasons, teachers rejected the project method. Radical curriculum or traditional, schools needed equipment, buildings, desks, reading matter, paper, and pencils.[31] In Briansk, pupils compensated for a lack of desks and paper by sitting and writing on the floor.[32] In the Lower Volga, schools lacked notebooks.[33] Throughout the Republic, schools could not provide breakfasts, even though the Sovnarkoms of the USSR and Russian Republic demanded on four occasions in 1930 that educational and other agencies supply the utensils and food.[34] Where school kitchens did exist, food often did not arrive.[35] The most optimistic of estimates proved rather disheartening. Of all the pupils enrolled in 1929, only 30 percent received food, 15 percent were given shoes, and little more than half were provided with reading and writing materials.[36] Touted as the showcase of relevancy, Schools for Collective Farm Youth lacked all the usual items, as well as dormitories, teacher-agronomists, agricultural implements, and stipends.[37] When forced to provide the materials to build or add to a school, peasants acted predictably by bringing rotten wood.[38]

Radical methods created confusion. In response to questionnaires distributed at the Polytechnical Congress, delegates called for detailed instructions on implementing new curricula.[39] Teachers believed that the conference's exhibit failed to deal with academic content and with real conditions. Workers thought production was ignored.[40] Local departments of education were also perplexed by changing signals. Unable to decide what reading materials should be used, departments seldom submitted requests to the State Publishing House before August.[41] Shortages of funds and paper induced some departments to accept at least one new device: they ordered journal-texts as a cheap substitute for full-fledged textbooks.[42]

Teachers were hardly better trained to cope with the project method than with the complex. In the mid-1920s, slightly more than 10 percent of all teachers had attended a higher educational institution. Among elementary instructors alone, only 4 percent had done so. The partial census of January 1931 revealed measured but by no means spectacular improvement. Nine percent of the instructors in the primary grades had attended a higher educational institution and 75 percent of them had completed a secondary education. Of secondary schoolteachers, 42 percent had some form of higher education (although not necessarily in pedagogical training); 48 percent had gone no further than the completion of a secondary school.[43]

These improved figures were somewhat misleading. The rapid increase in the number of pupils from 1928 to 1931 led to the adoption of dubious methods for doubling the number of teachers.[44] Many received their training at technicums which prepared primary schoolteachers in four to eight months (instead of the usual three to four years), or at pedagogical institutes which could be completed in eight to ten months (instead of two to four years). Some individuals sallied forth with no preparation at all. The Young Communist League drafted its own members and many others for the teaching profession. Some of these recruits may have previously attended a pedagogical technicum or institute, and even may have taught, but most surely had not. And most of them went right to work. Of 17,000 teachers mobilized in mid-1930, 15,939 did so; of 30,000 drafted in 1931, 25,090 did likewise.[45] One district in the Urals received 68 new teachers, not one of whom had attended a pedagogical technicum.[46] Yet Narkompros expected these instructors to employ radically new techniques and rally themselves, pupils, and parents for campaigns against man, nature, and beast. It was far too much to ask.

Nor did the teaching cadre's experience, or lack of it, predispose it to the new curriculum. The rapid turnover of the inexperienced young, as well as the rugged persistence of the pre-revolutionary old, meant a profession simultaneously unable to employ new techniques and determined to adhere to the familiar. The partial census of January 1931 revealed that 33 percent of primary school teachers and 45 percent of their secondary school counterparts had begun teaching before the 1917 revolution; 31 and 18 percent had launched their careers after 1928.[47]

The same census revealed that neither the social composition nor the political affiliation of teachers inclined them to take up Moscow's programs. From the official point of view, retrenchment had occurred in both areas. In 1925, the government classified 15 percent of the Republic's elementary schoolteachers as originating with the white collar salaried personnel (sluzhashchie) and 16 percent with the free professions; 30 and 15 percent of their secondary school colleagues were so categorized. Six years later, 36 percent of the teachers in the elementary grades and 52 percent in the secondary schools came from the white collar group.[48] The percentage of teachers who belonged to the Party or Young Communist League declined slightly. As the First Five-Year Plan entered its final year, 14 percent of the primary schoolteachers were associated with the Party or its youth arm, a decline from 18 percent in 1927/28.[49]

Whatever their training, experience, political leanings, or intentions, teachers continued to find their job extremely difficult and themselves quite often alone. National and local organs of the government, the Party, and the teachers union were incapable of providing support. Teachers remained subject to late and absent pay, arbitrary dismissals and transfers, and heavy social obligations. More so than before, they suffered arrest, dispossession, and physical abuse.[50]

From 1927 to 1931, the minimum salary guaranteed by the State increased by 50 percent for both elementary and secondary schoolteachers.[51] It was only a paper improvement. Inflation wiped out any advances in those rare instances when teachers received everything promised. Local governments arbitrarily reduced salaries, and refused to provide the special supplements required by law since 1927; in rural areas, local authorities failed to deliver firewood and kerosene mandated as compensation for lower salaries.[52] They also continued to find inventive ways to deprive teachers of their vacations.[53] One report from a district in Nizhnii Novgorod contained many disturbing examples of these abuses: teachers received their salaries five months late and not at all during the summer; the local Party committee diverted a shipment of shoes intended for teachers to cafeteria workers and officials in the soviet; in a practice reminiscent of feudal times, district authorities forced teachers to purchase sixteen kilograms of salt.[54] In a similar case elsewhere, village instructors were required to donate 5 percent of their monthly pay for the purchase of seeds.[55]

Local authorities, especially in rural areas, forced teachers to work as accountants, to copy papers, and to stand by the village telephone.[56] A hint of non-compliance led to transfer and dismissal. Laws prohibiting the practice in 1928 and 1929 indicated nothing short of a full-scale purge in many areas.[57] Teachers themselves pointed out that departments of education and union locals refused to help.[58] Their accusations did not extend to inspectors who were still largely unseen and plagued by inadequate pay, few travel funds, and inexperience caused by high turnover.[59]

Teachers were victimized by the public as well as by local officials. In 1929, at the Congress of Workers of Enlightenment, a teacher from Kaluga

revealed that teachers were expected to participate in the campaign against
kulaks but when they did, sometimes it was the teachers who were beaten
and killed.[60] The press reported many such instances. A certain teacher,
Ivushkin, commanded to go to a "false soviet" to oversee its grain deliveries
to the State, was shot to death.[61] In 1931, *Za kommunisticheskoe prosveshchenie*
published a similar drama in two parts. A husband and wife, the Sinitsynyis,
both teachers, exposed a young man, Belov, as a kulak. Belov and his brother-
in-law went to the school, killed the husband, and then went on to the
couple's apartment where they murdered the wife. The seven-year-old son
managed to save himself by running away from his slower-footed attackers.[62]
All this while many soviets declared teachers to be kulaks, stripping them
of the franchise, their apartments, and their property.[63] Female instructors
experienced special forms of degradation. One drunk official knocked on the
door of the local teacher late at night to demand that she "get up and talk
with the boss."[64] Complaints filed with Soviet judicial organs revealed that
this was not an isolated case.[65]

Central Party and State authorities, Bubnov included, denounced the
behavior of local officials, while ignoring their own culpability. Forced industrialization and collectivization, the rhetoric of class warfare, the campaign
to liquidate the kulaks, and an impulse to maim the intelligentsia came from
the top and set an abusive style to be followed by anyone in authority. A
narrow definition of educational relevance and preoccupation with projects
made teachers both participants and victims of a brutalization of life. At the
Sixteenth Party Congress, while Bubnov spoke sympathetically of teachers
overburdened with civic responsibilities, he demanded that they become
cultural and political agents.[66] When Sovnarkom of the Russian Republic
declared in August 1930 that teachers should not be forced to perform office
work, it also emphasized their eligibility for recruitment into political, social,
and cultural activities.[67] An article in *Vestnik prosveshcheniia* concluded that a
"good pedagogue must be a good socialworker."[68]

Sometimes Moscow directly encouraged atrocities. Once a strong teachers'
advocate, *Uchitel'skaia gazeta* announced in 1930 its unwillingness to defend
a profession consisting of so many "wreckers and enemies."[69] That same
year, Rabkrin acknowledged a purge of the teaching corps, in which its own
apparatus participated.[70] The Young Communist League created more than
its share of misery with its mobilization campaigns. Forced to go to strange
places, many teachers discovered that they were not needed after all. Finding
himself in such circumstances, one inspector wrote home: "Don't write me
in Orenburg since I don't know where they will send me . . . I have fifteen
rubles left."[71] Disillusionment preceded the launching of a teaching career.
Pedagogical technicums and institutes did not pay the stipends promised,
or divided them among so many students that they amounted to no more
than ten to fifteen rubles a month.[72] Shortages and miserable conditions
matched those in schools.[73]

Teachers responded as they had during the 1920s. Like so many of their pupils, they dropped out. Some of them quit teacher training institutions, others refused to report to work upon graduation, and still others walked away from their jobs. In 1929, neither the pedagogical faculty of Smolensk University nor the regional department of education knew what had become of 75 percent of the faculty's recent graduates. Nor did the pedagogical faculty at Saratov University and the regional department of education know anything about any of its 150 graduates.[74] Some pedagogical technicums encouraged an avoidance of teaching by signing contracts to send their graduates to economic agencies.[75] Many teachers quickly found other employment, sometimes departing from their jobs without warning. One instructor left school to fetch some of his things from another village; he kept on going and was not heard from again.[76] Others fled from their personal and professional problems by committing suicide.[77]

Enough instructors vanished to arouse the harshest of official responses. In 1930, *Za kommunisticheskoe prosveshchenie* talked of "desertion at the pedagogical front." It produced its own billboard of shame by periodically listing the names of offenders.[78] The example was infectious. A provincial journal followed suit, and the Narkompros publication *Biulleten' Narkomprosa* spoke of desertion from teacher training institutions.[79] Authorities should have expected no other from a profession which was underpaid, overworked, belittled, and under constant attack. The most conscientious of prospective teachers must have felt little moral obligation to submit to assignment to remote areas. Moscow had justified forced recruitment on the basis of stipends that were not paid. Little wonder that many young citizens chose to pursue other careers less treacherous and more rewarding. In 1930, pedagogical technicums in the Moscow province filled only 50 percent of their vacancies, and the Herzen Pedagogical Institute in Leningrad received 25 percent fewer applications than expected.[80]

The Arithmetic of Success and Failure

For Narkompros, the picture was not entirely bleak. In a period preoccupied with numbers, the educational system boasted of spectacular arithmetical advances. From 1928 through 1930, the number of elementary and secondary schools in the Russian Republic increased from 85,000 to over 102,000, and enrollment from 7.9 to 11.3 million, increases of 20 and 43 percent.[81] Enrollment in the primary grades alone rose by 48 percent—considerably more than the 20 percent increase of children aged eight to eleven—resulting in a near universal enrollment of this group in urban and rural areas. The number of first-graders grew by 62 percent (33 percent in cities and 67 percent in rural areas). Spectacular improvements in the countryside meant that despite the migration of peasants to cities during the period 1927–30, the percentage of all pupils in urban schools in the Soviet Union declined from 28 to 22 percent.[82] Schools now provided something approximating the official academic year. In the academic year 1930/31, over 90 percent of Narkompros's schools operated for at least ten months a year.[83]

Special schools registered impressive gains. Schools for Collective Farm Youth in the Russian Republic increased from 768 with 73,000 students in 1927 to 3,500 with 529,000 pupils in 1930.[84] Factory Seven-Year Schools in the Soviet Union increased from 92 in 1927 to 370 in 1929; and Factory Apprenticeship Schools from 903 with 100,000 students in 1927 to 3,265 with 600,000 in 1930.[85]

Numerical progress occurred in other areas of pedagogical and political importance. The number of pupils taking a grade for a second or third time declined from 20 percent of enrollment during the 1920s to slightly under 10 percent in 1929/30, and to 5 or 6 percent in 1930/31.[86] Grade repetition reached manageable proportions even in elementary grades, declining to 5.9 percent in 1930/31 in urban areas and 9.2 percent in the countryside.[87] Girls now entered and remained in school in unprecedented numbers. From 1927 to 1930, their percentage of enrollment rose from 40 to 46 percent, with most of that advance taking place in rural regions.[88] In 1930, peasant children commanded an equally unprecedented percentage in primary as well as in secondary grades. This development, combined with the increased enrollment of working-class children and the social effects of the First Five-Year Plan (including the destruction of such occupational groups as private traders), ended the domination of non-peasant and non-proletarian children in the secondary school.

Membership in the Young Pioneers ceased its decline of the mid-1920s. It rose from 10 percent of all students in grades one through seven in 1926/27 to 18 percent in 1930/31. Combined with membership in the new organization for the youngest of schoolchildren, the Octobrists, the total number of urban pupils affiliated with the Party's youth arms reached 40 percent of enrollment.[89]

These quantitative successes masked serious problems. In the absence of additional funding, more schools and more pupils created more shortages. Without new construction, existing schools doubled up, straining available material and human resources to the breaking point. In 1930/31, 57 percent of all schools operated in two or three shifts.[90] One frustrated teacher complained that the children of one shift could not put on their coats to go home before the second shift arrived to take theirs off.[91] Increased enrollment

Social Composition
Russian Republic, 1930/1931[92]

	Primary Grades			Secondary Grades		
	Total	Urban	Rural	Total	Urban	Rural
Workers	11.7%	55.2%	3.4%	33.8%	46.0%	11.0%
Collective farmers	16.9	2.9	19.5	16.7	6.0	36.5
Individual peasants	63.3	7.5	74.0	24.6	14.3	43.8
White collar	5.6	24.8	1.9	19.1	25.8	6.7
Others	2.5	9.6	1.2	5.8	7.9	2.0

outstripped an expansion of the teaching corps so that in the primary grades the teacher-pupil ratio increased from 1:39 in 1927/28 to 1:42 in 1930/31.[93] The situation was far worse for teachers who were responsible for two or more grades and for teachers of a first grade that included 35 percent of total school enrollment in 1930/31.[94]

Surveys of fourth- and seventh-graders from 1929 to 1931 and entrance examinations given by technicums found an inadequate grasp of grammar, spelling, history, the sciences, and mathematics.[95] Soviet officials need not have looked beyond their own departments to find an important reason for this poor performance. The State had removed pressure on secondary students by making occupational status and Party affiliations more important than academic ability in gaining access to higher educational institutions.[96] Furthermore, Narkompros had encouraged indiscriminate promotion. Concerned about academic standards in 1929, Glavsotsvos had prohibited the use of socialist competition in reducing grade repetition.[97] One year later, the Commissariat's *Biulleten' Narkomprosa* encouraged its use for exactly that purpose.[98] The Moscow Department of Education devised an "up or out" policy by disallowing repetition of the final year of the major divisions of the school—the fourth, seventh and ninth grades.[99] An angry Blonsky responded that the policy would discriminate against children from the poorest strata of the population. The first to experience academic problems and thereby repeat a grade, they would now be victimized by undeserved promotion or by dismissal from school.[100] Informed by Blonsky's protest, the Moscow Soviet negated the order.[101]

While grade repetition declined, the dropout rate remained high. Many pupils on school rolls were no longer attending at year's end, especially in rural areas.[102] In early 1931, Epshtein pointed to a dismal record in elementary schools. Taking the third grade as an example, he noted that 30 percent of pupils did not proceed to the next grade.[103] Schools for Collective Farm Youth were especially prone to difficulties. In 1930, their staunch advocate, Rudnev, acknowledged unacceptable levels of dropouts and absenteeism.[104] In some cases, 30 to 40 percent of pupils in a particular grade disappeared from one year to the next.[105] So many youngsters withdrew from rural schools that less than half of all children twelve to fourteen years of age were enrolled in December 1930, and most of them in primary schools. Less than 5 percent of all children in this age group attended any secondary grade.[106]

Schools for Collective Farm Youth were established in areas with no collective farms, while there were none in regions fully collectivized, an unremarkable development given the vicissitudes of collectivization. Some regional departments of education, including the Moscow Department, did not know how many of these institutions they supervised.[107] Pupils completing the course disrupted central plans in a way already familiar. They refused to work on collective farms, preferring instead other jobs or the pursuit of an advanced degree.[108] Those few senior divisions that offered some form of vocational training could not do it well, nor could they readily find work for their graduates. In an effort to meet the needs of pupils and industry, schools lacking equipment and teaching personnel nevertheless offered many specializations, even changing them from year to year.[109] One school in Orel' went to the opposite extreme, graduating nothing but poultry breeding technicians, none of whom went to work in the specialty.[110]

The phenomenal expansion of Factory Apprenticeship Schools occurred in part because of an overall reduction in the course of study. In 1924/25, schools with a four-year program comprised 49 percent of the total. Six years later, they all but disappeared as the overwhelming majority featured a course of only two or three years.[111] The change came at the expense of general education, reduced to 25 percent of the entire curriculum.[112] Whatever the course, many pupils were ill-prepared for it. Of total enrollment in 1931, only 19 percent claimed seven years of prior schooling.[113] That same year, 44 percent of the pupils entering apprenticeship schools associated with heavy industry had not gone beyond the elementary school.[114] Like graduates of Schools for Collective Farm Youth, many students who completed their apprenticeship avoided work in the sponsoring factory, instead seeking a job elsewhere, or going on for additional study.[115] Dismayed by these results, the Supreme Economic Council and plant managers preferred short courses and on-the-job training.

In early 1931, Bubnov went before the Fifteenth All-Russian Congress of Soviets to report on the state of education. He referred to a string of successes. Funding was no longer a major problem, schools worked hand in hand with factories and collective farms, the 1930 curriculum was wiping out a scholastic approach to learning, and teachers and pupils willingly participated in the cultural revolution.[116] He knew better. So did Krupskaya. She had seen a draft of Bubnov's resolutions and sent him her criticism, stating that many of his points amounted to "drum-beating." "Delegates from the provinces know how matters actually stand, let them tell about it."[117]

Bubnov ignored her, but Krupskaya need not have worried. The real state of affairs was clear to anyone who cared to notice. Recent policy changes had widened the gap between pretension and reality. The more the radicals of Narkompros and the Young Communist League got their way, the greater the gap. Not unlike the Commissariat under Lunacharsky's direction, Narkompros could point to many plans but to few practical results.

By the spring of 1931, advocates of a radical curriculum acknowledged the need for an adjustment in policy. They and their critics proceeded to fight over the scope and direction of that change.

XV.

POLICY MEETS PRACTICE, 1931

On the eve of the new school year, August 25, 1931, the Central Committee of the Communist Party began to dictate school policy. It condemned Narkompros and its curriculum for their neglect of subjects and content.

> The Central Committee declares that by a large margin the Soviet school does not meet the huge demands placed before it . . . The school's *fundamental defect* at the present time [is] its failure to provide a sufficient level of general-educational knowledge and an unsatisfactory preparation for technicums and higher education of fully literate people who have mastered the fundamentals of science (physics, chemistry, mathematics, native language, geography, etc.). . . . It is necessary to wage a decisive struggle against thoughtless scheming with methods . . . especially against the so-called project method.[1]

Eleven days later, *Pravda* published the decree. Narkompros was given until January 1 to prepare new syllabi. Concerned with a need for systematic instruction, the Central Committee paused only to reject any return to the "old scholastic school."[2]

Many observers then (and later) expressed surprise at the Party's decision. Yet there had been signs of official impatience with the 1930 curriculum and with radical proposals that followed in 1931. This critical concern at the upper levels was reinforced by the opinions and practices of teachers below.

Projects for the Class Struggle

Advocates of the project method sought its unquestioned dominion. In December 1930, they redoubled their efforts in the hope of influencing the next session of the State Academic Council, scheduled for the end of the month. On December 11, Ia. Stepanov, a member of Shul'gin's School Methods Institute, declared in *Za kommunisticheskoe prosveshchenie* that the Council should endorse the project method and brigades as devices to break the old school.[3] A week later, the same message emerged from a three-day Children's Conference on the Project Method organized by the Institute. Despite testimony that all was not well in the classroom, major reports endorsed the method because of its emphasis on relevance and on socially useful labor.[4]

When the State Academic Council convened on December 27, Shokhin equated the worth of a school with its involvement in community life.[5] The majority was not prepared to go that far, but did approve measures much to Shokhin's liking. Labelling itself an "organ of the dictatorship of the proletariat," the Council endorsed projects, brigades, and socialist competition.[6] In an act symbolic of its declarations, the Council held one of its meetings at the Dinamo factory. It agreed to employ thirty shock workers, ten engineers, and ten specialists from the factory, to which Narkompros would then send twenty-seven professors, engineers, and scholars.[7]

Four months later, Shul'gin's organization, renamed the Institute of Marxist-Leninist Pedagogy, organized the Second Republic Conference on the Project Method (April 9–14).[8] Shul'gin raised his favorite contrivance to the level of an ideological principle: "The struggle for the project method is one of the efforts at the front of the class struggle."[9] Support for a radical curriculum continued well into mid-year in other forums. Articles in a new Narkompros journal, *Kommunisticheskoe prosveshchenie* (Communist Enlightenment), praised the project method.[10] Esipov reconfirmed his support of projects, brigades, and journal-texts (as well as a radio-text).[11] In June, *Za kommunisticheskoe prosveshchenie* carried a scathing attack on alleged political errors in existing textbooks. It announced plans for the annual publication of a separate journal-text for each type of school.[12] At the same time, Rudnev stated before the Society of Marxist Pedagogues and at a children's conference that problems with projects arose primarily from faulty teaching practices.[13]

"Looking Reality Squarely in the Eye"

Since 1929, much of the pressure for radicalization of the curriculum originated from outside of Narkompros. It had been the School Methods Institute and the Young Communist League that had sought a merger of education and cultural revolution. Like-minded individuals within Narkompros had largely been on its fringes until the formation of the Methods Sector and Sector for Mass Measures in 1930. Many others at Narkompros remained skeptical of the value of the project method, brigades, socialist competition, and journal-texts. In late 1930 and 1931, they began to act with increasing boldness.

Shul'gin, Rudnev, and Esipov remained unwilling to compromise, but other officials proved more accommodating. L. N. Skatkin, one of Shatsky's teachers at the First Experimental Station, suggested that the method be modified to facilitate the teaching of content.[14] Major articles in the educational press made precisely the same point.[15] On February 19, 1931, at a district Workers Conference on Polytechnical Education in Moscow, Bubnov added his considerable weight to the ongoing reevaluation. While calling for an alliance (smychka) between factory and school, he lectured his audience on the importance of knowledge as a prerequisite for specialized training.[16]

At the same time, Krupskaya took her criticism into the public forum. She began on March 21 at a meeting of educators from Moscow's Krasnopresnensk district. She repeated her earlier opposition to a precipitous implementation of the project method. She warned that projects would be best designed not for multiple grades or for a school as a whole but for specific age groups.[17] The next month, at Shul'gin's Conference on the Project Method, she spoke more aggressively by condemning a preoccupation with the project method and with socially useful activities. In her opinion, the most important task of the school amounted to a "systematic presentation of defined spheres of knowledge."[18]

While the Methods Sector at Narkompros prepared new syllabi featuring projects, the method's critics launched an impressive campaign of their own. On March 26, the Narkompros Collegium refused to endorse the project method to the exclusion of all other approaches.[19] A month later, the Pedagogical Section followed suit. Shul'gin had come in praise of the method's place in the making of the glorious socialist future.[20] A majority disagreed. Epshtein claimed that Shul'gin's theories substituted fancy for the role that school, teacher, and child could play in the educational process. He insisted that Narkompros supervise the method's use to assure concern for content and for the abilities of specific age groups.[21] Recalling efforts in 1926 and 1927 to modify the complex method, Epshtein and most speakers at this session promoted a curriculum that set a minimum level of knowledge and skills to be learned in each grade.[22]

The two most prominent officials at Narkompros, Krupskaya and Bubnov, addressed the Section. Krupskaya acknowledged that the project method was the leading, although not the only, format for instruction. But schools hardly needed projects that "amounted to cabbage"; the project method would have to earn the respect of the people involved.[23] Bubnov was less charitable when he spoke on April 23, stating that "It is necessary to look reality squarely in the eye."[24] The school system was in disarray, its teachers frustrated and disillusioned. Bubnov then turned his attention to Shul'gin, beginning with modest praise. In the struggle against "old bourgeois pedagogy," Shul'gin and the School Methods Institute had played a positive role. He then confessed his own past fondness for the "political spirit" with which the Institute had waged its campaigns.[25] But there followed a sharp denunciation of the theory of the withering away of the school and a condemnation of excesses associated with the use of the project method.[26]

While the Pedagogical Section deliberated in April, teachers and other educators interested in particular subjects rejected new curricula. Instructors of literature in Tver and in Yaroslavl', and experts in the subject at the Communist Academy demanded more attention to vocabulary, history, and the Russian classics of the nineteenth century.[27] The editorial board of the journal *Obshchestvovedenie v shkole* (Social Studies in the School) required that more historical and biographical information be presented in chronological order.[28] Two months later, teachers in Moscow's Dzerzhinsky district declared that the Method Sector's draft curricula for the rural elementary school and Factory Seven-Year School lacked substance.[29]

In July, Bubnov told the Central Committee of the need to improve instruction in schools and in teacher training institutions.[30] On August 9, he appeared before the All-Russian Conference of Heads of Regional Departments of Education to demand that more attention be paid to content in mathematics, chemistry, and physics. He gave two reasons: these subjects were of importance to technicums and higher educational institutions; and teachers were not prepared to rely on projects and activity methods.[31] Now the champion of the Republic's instructors, Bubnov called for the liquidation of Shul'gin's Institute for Marxist-Leninist Pedagogy for its failure to respond to their needs.[32]

One day later, on August 10, Bubnov addressed the All-Russian Conference on Production Instruction in the Factory Seven-Year School. A ritualistic condemnation of the "scholastic school" preceded an equally harsh judgment of the project method. Bubnov clearly identified the method with the heretical theory of the withering away of the school.[33] Other speakers agreed. Rudnev disagreed, choosing to defend the primacy of production instruction, socialist competition, and the project method.[34]

At the end of August and the beginning of September, *Za kommunisticheskoe prosveshchenie* may have attempted to prepare the educational community for the Central Committee's decree. An article of August 26 by T. D. Korneichik, a professor at the Samara Pedagogical Institute, an editorial of August 28, and an unsigned front-page piece of September 1 complained that many pupils lacked basic knowledge in mathematics, native language, chemistry, physics, natural science, and social studies.[35] After denying any desire to return to the scholastic school, the articles called for higher academic standards and more energetic leadership in the classroom. Previewing the spirit as well as some of the language of the Central Committee's own decision, the editorial of August 28 declared that "the school's central task at the present time is the expansion of the volume of knowledge and skills." The article of September 1 required the "subordination of the social work of the school and pupils to an achievement of the school's [academic] program."

On September 5, at the end of the first week of school, the Central Committee made it all very official and public in *Pravda*. A distinct era in the history of Soviet educational policy and practice, and in the relationship between the two, had come to a close.

CONCLUSION

On February 6, 1934, L. M. Kaganovich spoke of schooling at the Seventeenth Party Congress. Prompted by commentary from Stalin, he praised the General Secretary's ability to heal the sick and infirm, including, in 1931, the nation's schools.

> Comrade Stalin found out that instruction went very badly in a certain school: there was no discipline, the teachers were not respected, children learned little. And so from this one fact a whole range of issues were examined and decisions on the school were taken which educational personnel themselves justifiably called truly historical.[1]

Bubnov registered a mild objection: "Didn't we [at Narkompros] nevertheless do something?" Kaganovich would have none of it. "Yes, Comrade Bubnov, you acted only after the Central Committee sharply defined the issues and carefully supervised the implementation of its resolutions."[2]

Kaganovich accurately described conditions in many schools. But decision-making was not as simple as he would have it; the relationship between the Party and Narkompros and between policy and practice was not so tidy, not even in Stalin's Russia.

The Social Dimension

Certainly ideological, political, and, in Stalin's case, perhaps personal, factors contributed to the Central Committee's dictation of school policy in 1931. The Party wanted an educational system in the image of an authoritarian "political Realkultur."[3] It may also have favored a traditional curriculum because it now seemed pointless to think of schools as institutions for social transformation. Structurally, Russia had already been revolutionized by the events of the past three years, but not in a way that Narkompros had expected. The Party had rejected Lunacharsky's humane vision of school and society.

The Party's decision was not reached in isolation from events at Narkompros and at school. The Central Committee knew of the debate over the curriculum and of the problems facing teachers, parents, and pupils. Its members were aware, if only because first Lunacharsky and then Bubnov told them (it is also possible *they* told Bubnov), that over the years policy diverged from classroom practice and expectations from pupils' performance. The Party's involvement in 1931 introduced a new principal element in a larger story consisting, since 1917, of a complex relationship among educational officials, teachers, pupils, and parents. Kaganovich's "Stalinist"

interpretation conveniently ignored this social dimension heretofore important in determining educational policy and practice. Such was the emergent
Stalinist historiography and politics of the period: to substitute a pliant society
for the vitality of social forces.

Policy and Practice

The Commissariat of Enlightenment began with the hope that the school
could remake people and society. Lunacharsky and his colleagues understood
the enormity of their task and foresaw many of the obstacles that lay ahead.
They believed, nevertheless, that teachers, parents, pupils, and society would
share their enthusiasm and help make the new world. Subsequent developments demonstrated that the future could not overcome the traditions of
the past and the difficulties of the present. The school could not be manip-
ulated from above, nor could it manipulate the people it was to serve.
Shortages of material and human resources proved more decisive than originally thought. The distance between the Kremlin and the schoolhouse was
more than a matter of geography. Despite all of its publications, curricula,
and special instructions, Narkompros found it impossible to keep teachers
regularly informed, whether they were in Siberia or in Moscow. And when
it did place its materials in the hands of instructors, it could not make them
read it, understand it, and above all, implement it. Just as teachers responded
to Narkompros initiatives with disdain, so did pupils, parents, and local
officials.

When schools and society failed to match expectations, the Commissariat
of Enlightenment redoubled its efforts to impose change from above. Whether
under Lunacharsky from 1917 to the mid-1920s, or under his successor,
Bubnov, Narkompros sought to mold, by compulsion if need be, teachers
and the people they taught. The Central Committee's intervention in August
1931 continued this pattern of reform by dictate.

There was one striking exception to this authoritarian behavior. In the
realm of education, the NEP period ended with a compromise between
Narkompros and the nation's teachers. It occurred when Narkompros stopped
pursuing a vision in place of responding to reality. Narkompros's leaders
accommodated pressure from teachers, parents, and local departments of
education. As a result, remarkably different curricula emerged in 1926 and
1927. Hope was in the ascendant in Narkompros above and in the classroom
below. Visionaries at Narkompros and practitioners in the schools had found
common ground. An effective combination of new methods favored by Narkompros and traditional content desired by teachers and parents seemed
possible.

As Narkompros compromised with teachers, it forged an alliance with the
Young Communist League against the claims of the technical lobby. Now
Lunacharsky, Krupskaya, and others at Narkompros could realistically hope

to move Russia forward through a gradual process of enlightenment. It might have worked if the main institutions and people involved had functioned in an environment of their own making.

But they did not. Alternative visions of socialism and impatient policies that arose from them ripped asunder the fabric of compromise. The cultural revolution, industrialization, and collectivization resurrected authoritarian behavior at Narkompros, along with efforts to use schools as agents of revolutionary change. Advocates of the project method presumed to dictate policy to the old guard at Narkompros and to teachers. Although never receiving official blessing, they thrived in an environment largely of the Party's making, one hostile to anything less than the transformation of popular culture.

The new radicals at Narkompros were no less successful than their predecessors. Teachers and parents resisted change. A chasm between policy and practice became, once again, a major issue. Krupskaya, Epshtein, and Shatsky, joined by Bubnov in mid-1931, referred to classroom practice in an effort to rein in Rudnev, Shul'gin, and other champions of a "collectivization of life." The Central Committee was not unaware of the debate or the fundamental characteristic of Soviet schooling—the gap between pretense and reality. Although it acted in a most authoritarian manner in August 1931, it moved in concert with elements in Narkompros above and teachers below.

Heroes? Villains?

This has been the story of how Russians stubbornly clung to familiar ways when assaulted from above. Few teachers joined a crusade against academic subjects, class enemies, or moonshiners. This is not to lionize teachers and vilify their antagonists; the history of Soviet schools from 1917 to 1931 contained few heroes or villains. We can sympathize with teachers asked to do the impossible, whether it was Gaidovskaia who apparently gave up, Konovalova who was prepared to keep on trying, or the Sinitsynyis who were murdered. We can also share the anguish of Narkompros during the 1920s when so many schoolteachers rejected its program and its vision. Parents had their own understandable reasons for limiting a child's education to several years. The technical lobby, Young Communist League, and School Methods Institute all acted in predictable ways consistent with their beliefs about Soviet society, present and future.

There were noteworthy differences. Individuals and agencies charged with the rapid development of a backward economy insisted on occupational and specialized education in the schools. Narkompros countered by emphasizing the broader social and economic benefits of a general curriculum. Recent work on developing countries indicates that once it had revised its curriculum in 1926 and 1927, Narkompros may indeed have had the better of the argument.[4] Some teachers rejected the progressive methods out of a strong sense of professional duty; others denied Narkompros its wishes out of an absence of any such commitment.

Although he was unable to create a smoothly functioning apparatus, Lunacharsky possessed many laudable administrative qualities. He combined an infectious vision of enlightenment with an ability to compromise and maneuver. Lunacharsky deserves much of the credit for the Commissariat's success in fending off the claims of the technical lobby, finding common ground with Komsomol, and reaching a compromise with teachers and local departments of education. Krupskaya hoped to strike a balance between radical methods and traditional content. In so doing, she leaned first in one direction, then in another, displeased with anything not in keeping with her views of the moment. Despite his association with experimental schools, Shatsky sympathized with the plight of teachers and was instrumental in the compromise of the late NEP period. Esipov was too arrogant, Shokhin too driven by a sense of a revolution betrayed by Narkompros, and Shul'gin too much the intolerant crusader. Later, when Bubnov and the Party's Central Committee "looked reality squarely in the eye," they demonstrated no interest in establishing procedures for the participation of Narkompros, teachers, and society in decision-making.

Of greatest significance to this study, teachers consistently demonstrated the folly of policies that were far in advance of the capacities, for good or ill, of those citizens required to accept them. A revolutionary state must eventually accommodate the desires of some of its citizens and the persistence of traditional values. Such a reconciliation with reality contributed to a reshaping of Narkompros policy at the close of the NEP period and to the Central Committee's dictate of school policy in 1931.

Past and Present

My work corroborates the scholarship of Roberta Manning, J. Arch Getty, and Lynne Viola, who have pointed to limits on the regime's power over society.[5] Whether purging the Party, pursuing dekulakization, or transforming schools, Soviet authorities could not overcome the autonomous behavior of people and institutions below. Like Kendall Bailes in his study of the technical intelligentsia and Eugene Huskey in his examination of the legal profession, I find that professional standards remained more resistant to change than the Party's leadership would have liked.[6] Teachers never were the pliant instruments that Narkompros had counted on; not all Narkompros officials were willing to cast aside their principles when faced with politicized bullying after 1928.

Parents and the local community were particularly stubborn. My work reaffirms Moshe Lewin's emphasis on the resiliency of peasant culture and its capacity to overpower initiatives from above.[7] For Lewin, collectivization strengthened the peasantry's traditional distrust of political authority and its regard for the family as a production unit (now focusing its attention on the garden plot). Educational policies reinforced and eventually accommodated popular preference for a conventional curriculum.

I share the opinion of David Joravsky, Susan Gross Solomon, Louise Shelley, Peter H. Solomon, Jr., and Richard Taylor that the NEP period achieved viable pluralistic arrangements in a number of fields.[8] Manipulation from above disrupted these years of achievement and a promise of more to come. In education, the cultural revolution destroyed the compromise between Narkompros and teachers by precluding tolerance for differing points of view. Advocates of the project method refused to consider alternatives; a new generation of radicals at Narkompros widened the gap between Moscow's pretense and classroom reality.

I agree that the cultural revolution must be seen in a social and political context that acknowledges a measure of popular support for radical change. Roger Pethybridge, Moshe Lewin, and Sheila Fitzpatrick point to the role of economic, social, and political backwardness, as understood by members of the Party and others, in bringing about the cultural revolution and First Five-Year Plan.[9] Chapter 11 acknowledges the shortcomings of the educational system in 1928 from the perspective of an ideology professing the interests of the proletariat and modernization. And yet the compromises of 1926 and 1927 would have contributed to improved academic performance, greater opportunites for children of workers and peasants, and the inculcation of modern secular values.

Pethybridge argues that the NEP failed because it lacked a solid bridge "between regime and masses, town and country."[10] This was definitely not the case in school education. For Narkompros officials and teachers during the period 1926-28, the future had never been brighter. There was every reason to expect that this "era of good feeling" would lead to institutionalized procedures for the participation of all concerned in the future development of the school system. The cultural revolution intervened to destroy this hope and the curricula upon which it was based.

That hope has been reborn in the current discourse over school reform in the Soviet Union. Advocates of change acknowledge the relevance to their efforts of earlier experiments with activity methods, the complex method, educational soviets, and the blending of academic and labor training. They also recognize that the reforms of the 1920s, handed down by Moscow, collided with the wishes and ability of teachers to do what was expected of them.

The Center for Pedagogical Innovation, formerly the Provisional Research Collective, responsible for many of the recent initiatives to change the authoritarian school system, includes teachers, sociologists, philosophers, and historians. Its head and since June 1990 the Minister of Education of the Russian Republic, E. D. Dneprov, employs the language of the social historian conversant with educational developments in late tsarist and early Soviet

Russia. Schools should serve the needs of society more than those of the State; classroom practice must be considered in devising policy; conflict between those above and below can only be ended by providing teachers, parents, and society a guaranteed role in the adoption of policy.[11] These proposals portend a new era in Soviet schooling. Teachers will have means other than complaint and resistance to influence decisions; policy and practice will draw more closely together.

STATISTICAL APPENDICES

All data are for the Russian Republic (RSFSR). Dashes indicate that no information is available.

Appendix 1. Budget

Source of Funds for All Forms of Enlightenment

Year	RSFSR	Local Government
1923/24	35.1%	64.9%
1924/25	33.9	66.1
1925/26	32.7	67.3
1926/27	29.9	70.1
1927/28	28.3	71.7
1928/29	23.7	76.3
1929/30	25.2	74.8
1931	18.4	81.6

Sources: For 1923/24 through 1926/27, A. Vasil'ev, "Biudzhet narodnogo obrazovaniia v SSSR," *Narodnoe prosveshchenie,* no. 4 (1928), p. 128; for 1927/28 through 1931, *Narodnoe prosveshchenie v RSFSR v osnovnykh pokazateliakh; statisticheskii sbornik (1927/28–1930/31 gg., so vkliucheniem nekotorykh dannykh za 1931/1932 g.)* (Moscow-Leningrad, 1932), p. 134.

Percentage of Funds Designated for Enlightenment Allocated to Primary and Secondary Education by Local Governments

Year	Elementary Grades	Secondary Grades
1924/25*	37.5	13.5
1927/28	38.8	—
1928/29	34.8	—
1929/30	31.3	—
1931	29.1	—

Sources: Pedagogicheskaia entsiklopediia, vol. 1 (Moscow, 1927), cols. 1090–91; *Narodnoe prosveshchenie v RSFSR v osnovnykh pokazateliakh,* p. 145.

*RSFSR excluding its autonomous republics and Orenburg province.

Appendix 2. Schools, Pupils, Teachers

Schools

Year	Total	Grades 1-4	7-letki	ShKM	9[10]-letki	Sec. School
1914/15	77,539	76,256				
1920/21	95,138	91,100	—	—	—	—
1921/22	78,570	75,563	—	—	—	—
1922/23	67,714	65,360	—	—	—	—
1923/24	68,585	66,363	—	—	—	—
1924/25	67,838	64,492	1,507	207	657	975
1925/26	74,396	70,585	1,885	457	617	852
1926/27	79,790	75,410	2,273	589	683	835
1927/28	85,568	80,752	2,437	768	761	850
1928/29	90,293	85,228	2,385	1,030	820	830
1929/30	96,170	90,764	2,191	1,513	903	799
1930/31	109,690	103,167	2,495	3,448	303	277

Source: Massovoe prosveshchenie v SSSR (k itogam pervoi piatiletki) (Moscow, 1933), pp. 6–9.
*7-letki is the Seven-Year School; ShKM, the School for Peasant Youth; 9[10]-letki, the nine- or ten-year school; and the Sec. School, the school with only the junior and senior division.

Pupils

Year	Total	Grades 1-4*	7-letki	ShKM	9[10]-letki	Sec. School
1914/15	5,532,500	5,134,334				
1920/21	7,928,602	7,391,441	—	—	—	—
1921/22	6,500,074	6,015,542	—	—	—	—
1922/23	5,375,059	4,828,611	—	—	—	—
1923/24	5,729,585	5,019,912	—	—	—	—
1924/25	6,423,324	5,283,046	477,029	19,276	382,881	261,092
1925/26	7,045,391	5,689,353	687,805	33,602	376,633	257,998
1926/27	7,362,192	5,813,795	796,400	44,764	437,399	269,834
1927/28	7,757,841	6,045,553	855,514	72,950	492,947	290,877
1928/29	8,241,589	6,413,295	843,123	109,104	561,128	314,939
1929/30	9,134,800	7,150,832	806,709	173,147	676,782	327,330
1930/31	11,930,090	9,638,407	1,418,396	528,515	237,849	106,923

Source: Massovoe prosveshchenie v SSSR (k itogam pervoi piatiletki) (Moscow, 1933), pp. 6–9.
*Includes all pupils enrolled in grades one through four in all types of schools.
†Includes only pupils enrolled in grades five through nine/ten.

Teachers

Year	Total	Grades 1-4	Grades 5-9/10			
			7-letki	*ShKM*	*9[10]-letki*	*Sec. School*
1914/15	—	—				
1920/21	253,462	219,289	—	—	5,466	28,707
1921/22	211,452	176,735	5,633	—	6,849	22,235
1922/23	161,712	125,603	7,675	—	12,623	15,811
1923/24	174,596	129,011	11,439	—	18,284	15,862
1924/25	177,858	128,759	19,208	—	17,366	12,525
1925/26	191,848	136,634	25,001	1,919	16,567	11,727
1926/27	205,287	142,767	28,846	2,505	18,743	12,426
1927/28	227,762	153,893	33,564	4,172	22,013	14,120
1928/29	244,435	163,238	34,499	5,840	25,436	15,422
1929/30	262,141	178,207	32,002	8,272	28,533	15,127
1930/31	315,397	224,486	52,796	21,733	11,791	4,591

Source: Narodnoe prosveshchenie v RSFSR v tsifrakh za 15 let sovetskoi vlasti (Moscow-Leningrad, 1932), p. 31.

Excludes teachers at a small number of special schools included in the original: elementary schools for older youths and forest (lesnye) schools intended primarily for children with respiratory problems.

Female Teachers
(December 1, 1926)

	Grades 1-4	Grades 5-9/10			
		7-letki	*ShKM*	*9[10]-letki*	*Sec. School*
Urban	77.4%	61.5%	22.5%	55.1%	40.4%
Rural	66.1	55.2	24.6	56.9	38.9

Source: Prosveshchenie v RSFSR v 1926/27 uchebnom godu (po materialam: 1) tekushchego obsledovaniia na 1 dekabria 1926 goda; 2) vyborochnogo obsledovaniia biudzheta shkol sotsvosa za 1926/27 uchebnyi god (Moscow, 1928), pp. 122-23.

Appendix 3. Enrollment by Grade (in percent)

In Urban and Rural Areas Combined

		In Elementary School						In Secondary School				
						Total						
Year	*Prep*	*1*	*2*	*3*	*4*	*1-4*	*5-6*	*5*	*6*	*7*	*8*	*9-10*
1924/25	0.46	37.0	27.0	17.0	8.2	89.2	0.5	3.2	2.3	1.7	1.1	0.9
1925/26	0.5	34.0	27.4	18.2	9.6	89.2	0.4	3.9	2.5	1.7	1.9	0.8
1926/27	0.3	33.0	26.0	19.0	11.0	89.0	0.4	4.6	3.1	2.0	1.0	0.7
1927/28	0.2	33.0	25.0	17.5	11.0	86.5	0.3	5.0	3.5	2.3	1.0	0.7
1928/29	0.2	31.0	26.0	18.0	12.0	87.0	0.2	5.0	3.7	2.6	1.0	0.8
1929/30	0.2	31.5	23.8	19.0	12.0	86.3	0.3	5.0	3.6	2.7	1.1	0.8
1930/31*	0.8	35.0	23.0	18.0	13.0	89.0	0.3	5.4	2.9	2.0	0.24	0.25

In Rural Areas Alone

1924/25	0.5	43.7	30.0	16.5	6.3	96.5	0.3	1.2	0.7	0.5	0.2	0.2
1925/26	0.5	34.0	27.4	18.0	9.6	89.0	0.4	4.0	3.0	2.0	1.0	0.8
1926/27	0.3	33.0	26.0	19.0	11.0	89.0	0.4	5.0	3.0	2.0	1.0	0.7
1927/28	0.2	33.0	25.0	18.0	11.0	87.0	0.3	5.0	3.4	2.3	1.0	0.7
1928/29	0.2	36.0	29.0	19.0	10.0	94.0	0.2	2.0	1.2	0.8	0.1	0.9
1930/31*	0.3	38.6	24.6	18.5	13.0	94.7	0.3	3.0	1.1	0.7	0.05	0.04

Source: Massovoe prosveshchenie v SSSR (k itogam pervoi piatiletki) (Moscow, 1933), pp. 40–41.

*Figures are lower than expected for grades 8–10 because of the nominal conversion of the senior division of schools into technicums.

Appendix 4. Problems and Wastage in the Elementary Grades, Late 1920s

Age of Pupils by Grade (in percent)
(December 1,1926)

	Grade 1	Grade 2	Grade 3	Grade 4
Less than eight years of age	3.2	0.1	0.0	0.0
Eight	27.3	3.0	0.1	0.0
Nine	25.1	15.0	2.5	0.1
Ten	21.6	25.5	14.5	3.1
Eleven	12.5	24.4	25.9	16.0
Twelve	7.2	20.3	30.6	31.8
Thirteen	2.3	8.6	18.1	28.0
Fourteen	0.6	2.5	6.6	15.3
Fifteen and older	0.2	0.6	1.7	5.7

Source: *Prosveshchenie v RSFSR v 1926/27 uchebnom godu,* p. 24.

Average Number of Days Absent, 1926/27

Rural Areas	25.1	26.2	24.7	19.7
Urban Areas	19.2	18.0	15.6	13.0

Average Number of Days Attended, 1926/27

Rural Areas	132	132	136	146
Urban Areas	167	171	174	178

Source: *Narodnoe prosveshchenie v SSSR 1926–1927 uchebnyi god* (Moscow, 1929), pp. 24–25.

Percentage of Enrollment Repeating a Grade, 1927/28

Rural Areas	16.7	16.8	16.8	15.7
Urban Areas	15.2	16.8	17.7	18.7

Source: *Vseobshchee obiazatel'noe obuchenie: statisticheskii ocherk po dannym shkol'noi perepisi tekushchei statistiki prosveshcheniia* (Moscow, 1930), p. 86.

Percentage of Enrollment Dropping Out, 1926/27

Rural Areas	22.0	20.8	22.1	19.5
Urban Areas	12.9	10.7	10.7	10.3

Percentage of Pupils Failed at the End of Academic Year, 1926/27
(excluding those who had dropped out during the year)

Rural Areas	16.0	17.8	19.7	19.3
Urban Areas	14.4	17.7	20.1	21.7

Source: *Narodnoe prosveshchenie v RSFSR: statisticheskii sbornik* (Moscow-Leningrad, 1928), pp. 92–99.

Appendix 5. Literacy Rate among the Young, December, 1926 (in percent)

Age Group	RSFSR	European Part of RSFSR	Lower Volga Region
8–11 years of age			
Rural	41.9		37.0
Urban	77.2		70.1
Total	46.8	47.1	41.8
12–15 years of age			
Rural	59.2		53.7
Urban	90.0		84.8
Total	63.8	64.5	58.3

Sources: For RSFSR and Lower Volga Region: *Kul'turnoe sostoianie Nizhe-Volzhskogo kraia (kratkoe opisanie)* (Saratov, 1928), p. 18. For European Russia, N. K. Krupskaya, *Pedagogicheskie sochineniia,* vol. 9 (Moscow, 1960), p. 290.

NOTES

Abbreviations

Journals and Newspapers

Biulleten' MONO: Biulleten' Moskovskogo Otdela Narodnogo Obrazovaniia
Biulleten' NKP: Biulleten' Narodnogo Komissariata Prosveshcheniia
BONO: Biulleten' Otdela Narodnogo Obrazovaniia (Moscow Soviet)
BORS: Biulleten' ofitsial'nykh rasporiazhenii i soobshchenii
Ezhenedel'nik MONO: Ezhenedel'nik Moskovskogo Otdela Narodnogo Obrazovaniia
Ezhenedel'nik NKP: Ezhenedel'nik Narkomprosa RSFSR
KP: Kommunisticheskoe prosveshchenie
Na putiakh: Na putiakh k novoi shkole
NP: Narodnoe prosveshchenie
NU: Narodnyi uchitel'
OTS: Obshchestvovedenie v trudovoi shkole
RP: Rabotnik prosveshcheniia
UG: Uchitel'skaia gazeta
VP: Vestnik prosveshcheniia
VPTO: Vestnik prof-tekhnicheskogo obrazovaniia
ZKP: Za kommunisticheskoe prosveshchenie
ZVO: Za Vseobshchee obuchenie

Other

NO: Narodnoe obrazovanie v SSSR. Sbornik dokumentov, 1917–1973 gg. (Moscow, 1974)
Sobr. uzak. RSFSR: Sobranie uzakonenii i rasporiazhenii raboche-krest'ianskogo pravitel'stva
TsGA RSFSR: Tsentral'nyi gosudarstvennyi arkhiv RSFSR

Introduction

1. F. F. Korolev, *Sovetskaia shkola v period sotsialisticheskoi industrializatsii* (Moscow, 1959); Z. I. Ravkin, *Sovetskaia shkola v period vosstanovleniia narodnogo khoziaistva 1921–1925 g.g.* (Moscow, 1959); and P. I. Pidkasistyi, *N. K. Krupskaya o soderzhanii v sovetskoi shkole* (Moscow, 1962).

2. Marianne Krueger-Potratz, *Absterben der Schule oder Verschulung der Gesellschaft? Die sowjetische Paedagogik in der Kulturrevolution 1928–1931* (Munich, 1987); and "Continuities and Discontinuities in Soviet Educational Theory on the Verge of Stalinism," in *Soviet Education under Scrutiny*, ed. John Dunstan (Glasgow, 1987), pp. 1–10.

3. Timothy Edward O'Connor, *The Politics of Soviet Culture: Anatolii Lunacharskii* (Ann Arbor, 1983); Robert C. Williams, *Artists in Revolution: Portraits of the Russian Avant-garde, 1905–1925* (Bloomington, 1977), pp. 23–58; and *The Other Bolsheviks: Lenin and His Critics, 1904–1914* (Bloomington, 1986). Also Sylvia Russell, "The Philosophy of Education of Anatolii Vasil'evich Lunacharsky, Commissar of Education, 1917–1929," unpublished dissertation (Indiana University, 1970).

4. See the proposals made by the Provisional Research Collective, working directly under the Minister of Education, in *Uchitel'skaia gazeta:* (August 16, 1988), p. 2; and (August 23, 1988), pp. 2–3. See especially several items by the head of the Collective, E. D. Dneprov: "Uchit'sia uchit," *Sovetskaia kul'tura* (November 4, 1987), p. 3; and "Vedomstvennoe samovlastie," *Pravda* (February 13, 1988), p. 3.

Also: Avril Suddaby, "Perestroika in Soviet Education," *Soviet Education Study Bulletin,* vol. 7, no. 1 (Spring 1989), pp. 14–21; and Marianne Krueger-Potratz and Friedrich Kuebart, "Schulreform 'von unten' in der Sowjetunion," *Pad. extra* (December 1987), Heft 12/1987, pp. 4–14.

I. A New School for a New Society

1. For progressive education in the United States, see Lawrence A. Cremin, *The Transformation of the School: Progressivism in American Education, 1876–1957* (New York, 1961). For a Soviet analysis of Western progressive educators: *Pedagogicheskaia entsiklopediia,* vol. 1 (Moscow, 1927), columns 415–40.

2. Nicholas Hans, *The Russian Tradition in Education* (London, 1963); William H. E. Johnson, *Russia's Educational Heritage* (Pittsburgh, 1950), pp. 226ff.; Ronald Hideo Hayashida, "The Pedagogy of Protest: Russian Progressive Education on the Eve of the Revolution," *Slavic and European Education Review* (2) (1978), pp. 11–30; Oskar Anweiler, *Geschichte der Schule und Paedagogik in Russland vom Ende des Zarenreiches bis zum Beginn der Stalin-Aera* (2nd ed.; Berlin, 1978), pp. 50–53, 91–92, 156ff.; and Anna Gock, *Polytechnische Bildung und Erziehung in der Sowjetunion bis 1937* (Wiesbaden, 1985), pp. 14ff.

3. This transformationist goal sharply distinguished Narkompros leaders from the European school reform movement. See the discussion of reform ideas in Europe since the year 1800 in Mary Jo Maynes, *Schooling in Western Europe: A Social History* (Albany, 1985).

4. *The Karl Marx Library,* ed. Saul K. Podover (7 vols.), *On Revolution,* vol. 1 (New York, 1971), p. 505 and *On the First International,* vol. 3 (New York, 1976), pp. 113–14.

5. Marx and Engels, *Collected Works,* vol. 6 (London, 1975), pp. 353–54 (from Engels, "Principles of Communism," 1847); *On Revolution,* p. 506; Karl Marx, *Capital* (London, 1938), p. 494.

6. Marx and Engels, *Collected Works,* vol. 6, p. 353 (from Engels, "Principles of Communism," 1847).

7. *On the First International,* p. 113.

8. Gock, p. 20.

9. On Lunacharsky: Robert C. Williams, *Artists in Revolution: Portraits of the Russian Avant-garde, 1905–1925* (Bloomington, 1977), pp. 23–58; Timothy Edward O'Connor, *The Politics of Soviet Culture: Anatolii Lunacharskii* (Ann Arbor, 1983); the introduction by Isaac Deutscher to Anatoly Vasilievich Lunacharsky, *Revolutionary Silhouettes* (trans. Michael Glenny) (New York, 1967), pp. 9–25; and the autobiographical sketch in Georges Haupt and Jean-Jacques Marie, *Makers of the Russian Revolution: Biographies of Bolshevik Leaders* (New York, 1974), pp. 305–12.

10. A. V. Lunacharsky, *A. V. Lunacharsky o narodnom obrazovanii* (Moscow, 1958), pp. 143–46.

11. Ibid., p. 148.

12. Anatoli Lunacharsky, *On Education: Selected Articles and Speeches* (Moscow, 1981), pp. 168–69.

13. Ibid., p. 169.

14. Ibid., p. 160.

15. Ibid., pp. 221–22, 226–27.

16. N. Krupskaya, "Zadachi shkoly 1-oi stupeni," *Na putiakh k novoi shkole* [henceforth *Na putiakh*], no. 1 (July 1922), p. 35.

17. *Uchitel'skaia gazeta* [henceforth *UG*], no. 36 (263) (March 27, 1929), p. 2.

18. N. Krupskaya, "Klassovaia bor'ba v prosvetitel'nykh uchrezhdeniiakh," *Na putiakh,* no. 6 (June 1929), pp. 7–9.

19. Lenin, "Karl Marks," *Polnoe sobranie sochinenii,* 5th ed. [henceforth *PSS*], vol. 36, pp. 77–81.

20. *Lunacharsky o narodnom obrazovanii,* pp. 39, 46.

21. Lenin, *PSS,* vol. 37, p. 77.

22. *Lunacharsky o narodnom obrazovanii,* pp. 145–46.

23. Lenin, *PSS,* vol. 41, pp. 298–318.

24. Frederic Lilge, "Lenin and the Politics of Education," *Slavic Review,* vol. 27, no. 2 (June 1968), pp. 254–55.

25. See the case made for a gentler Lenin, more concerned than before with developing the educated, cultured personality free of rudeness in Adam B. Ulam, "Lenin's Last Phase," *Survey,* vol. 21, no. 1/2 (94/95) (Winter–Spring 1975), pp. 148–59.

26. Anne D. Rassweiler, *The Generation of Power: The History of Dneprostroi* (New York, 1988), pp. 12–29.

27. Lenin, *PSS,* vol. 45, p. 52.

28. Richard Stites, "Stalin: Utopian or Antiutopian? An Indirect Look at the Cult of Personality," in *The Cult of Power: Dictators in the Twentieth Century,* ed. Joseph Held (Boulder, 1983), pp. 77–93; and Richard Stites, *Revolutionary Dreams: Utopian Vision and Experimental Life in the Russian Revolution* (New York, 1989). Also David Joravsky's discussion of how Bolsheviks could use faith in modern culture as both a prophecy pulling them toward visionary thinking and as an organizing ideology: David Joravsky, "Cultural Revolution and the Fortress Mentality," in *Bolshevik Culture: Experiment and Order in the Russian Revolution,* ed. Abbott Gleason, Peter Kenez, and Richard Stites (Bloomington, 1985), p. 97.

29. James C. McClelland, "Utopianism versus Revolutionary Heroism in Bolshevik Policy: The Proletarian Culture Debate," *Slavic Review,* vol. 39, no. 3 (September 1980), pp. 403–25; and James C. McClelland, "The Utopian and the Heroic: Divergent Paths to the Communist Educational Ideal," in *Bolshevik Culture,* pp. 114–30.

II. In Search of a Policy

1. *Narodnoe obrazovanie v SSSR. Sbornik dokumentov, 1917–1973 gg.* [henceforth *NO*] (Moscow, 1974), pp. 13–14.

2. *NO,* pp. 327, 362. Children with psychological disorders were to be assigned to institutions under the Commissariat of Public Health.

3. Ibid., p. 402.

4. By 1924, the course had expanded from the initial six or nine months to three years; by 1928 it had reached four years. See Fredrika M. Tandler, "The Workers' Faculty (Rabfak) System in the USSR," unpublished dissertation (Columbia University, 1955); and the entry on rabfaks in the *Modern Encyclopedia of Russian and Soviet History,* vol. 30 (Gulf Breeze, Fla., 1982), pp. 124–30.

5. The Statement and Declaration may be found in *NO,* pp. 133–45.

6. *NO,* p. 138.

7. *NO,* p. 133.

8. The constitution: *Sbornik dekretov i postanovlenii po narodnomu khoziaistvu,* vol. 1 (of 3) (Moscow, 1918), p. 1016; the Declaration: *NO,* pp. 133–34.

9. *NO,* pp. 134, 136; *Lunacharsky o narodnom obrazovanii,* p. 122.

10. Tsentral'nyi gosudarstvennyi arkhiv RSFSR [henceforth TsGA RSFSR], f. 2306, op. 4, ed. khr. 384, l. 1.

11. *NO,* p. 144.

12. A. V. Lunacharsky, "Ot narodnogo komissara po prosveshcheniiu," [October 29, 1917] in I. F. Svadkovsky, *Rabochaia kniga po istorii pedagogiki* (Moscow-Leningrad, 1927), p. 408; *NO,* p. 10.

13. Lunacharsky in *Pravda* (March 10, 1918), p. 3. For the discussion: A. I. Fomin, "Sozdanie sovetskogo apparata narodnogo prosveshcheniia po mestam," *Voprosy istorii,* no. 9 (1979), p. 31; *NO,* pp. 14–16.

14. *NO*, p. 316.

15. A. I. Fomin, "Stanovlenie tsentral'nogo sovetskogo apparata gosudarstvennogo rukovodstva narodnym prosveshcheniem," *Voprosy istorii*, no. 12 (1976), pp. 26–27.

16. Gock, pp. 103–19; Sheila Fitzpatrick, *The Commissariat of Enlightenment: Soviet Organization of Education and the Arts under Lunacharsky, October 1917–1921* (London, 1970), pp. 29–31; A. G. Ivanov, "Ocherki po istorii sovetskoi srednei obshcheobrazovatel'noi shkoly (1917–1925 gg.)," in *Uchenye zapiski. Yaroslavskii gosudarstvennyi pedagogicheskii institut*, vyp. 48 (Yaroslavl', 1961), pp. 5–185; Anweiler, *Geschichte*, pp. 112–15.

17. *NO*, p. 138.

18. *NO*, p. 139.

19. *NO*, p. 139–40.

20. *NO*, p. 133, 143.

21. *NO*, p. 143.

22. Materials for history and language are in TsGA RSFSR: f. 2306, op. 4, ed. khr. 96, l. 2; and ed. khr. 98, ll. 1–2; those for physics, music, history, psychology, mathematics, and natural sciences are in TsGA RSFSR, f. 2306, op. 1, ed. khr. 3277. These programs were poorly reproduced and words or entire lines are missing.

23. TsGA RSFSR, f. 2306, op. 4, ed. khr. 96, l. 1. This draft called attention to political history and to biography, but another draft ignored political and diplomatic history: TsGA RSFSR, f. 2306, op. 1, ed. khr. 3277, ll. 23–23 ob.

24. TsGA RSFSR: f. 2306, op. 4, ed. khr. 98, ll. 1–2; and op. 1, ed. khr. 3277, ll. 8–8 ob.

25. TsGA RSFSR, f. 2306, op. 1, ed. khr. 3277, ll. 42–48.

26. TsGA RSFSR, f. 2306, op. 1, ed. khr. 3277, l. 8 ob.

27. TsGA RSFSR, f. 2306, op. 6, ed. khr. 11, l. 23 ob. In April 1919, the collegium representing both bodies voted by a three to two margin against the teaching of subjects in the primary school. A report on the Department of School Reform criticized it for devising programs for academic disciplines: TsGA RSFSR, f. 2306, op. 2, ed. khr. 16, l. 9.

28. *Materialy po obrazovatel'noi rabote v trudovoi shkole*, vyp. 2, *Matematika v shkol'noi rabote na pervom kontsentre* (Moscow, 1919), p. 9.

29. Ibid., p. 4.

30. Ibid., p. 4.

31. Ibid., vyp. 4, *Esteticheskoe razvitie v shkole* (Moscow, 1919), pp. 1–3.

32. Ibid., pp. 6–7. See the Narkompros periodical, *Vestnik nagliadnykh posobii*, published in 1919 and 1920 and replaced by *Pedagogicheskoe delo* in 1921.

33. *Materialy po obrazovatel'noi rabote v trudovoi shkole*, vyp. 1, *Mirovedenie v rabote shkol pervoi stupeni* (Moscow, 1919).

34. *Primernye uchebnye plany dlia I-i i II-i stupeni v edinoi trudovoi shkole* (Moscow, 1920) (only eight pages long).

35. *Primernye programmy po izobrazitel'nym iskusstvam dlia shkol I i II stupeni* (Moscow, 1920).

36. *Primernye programmy po istorii dlia shkol II-stupeni* (Moscow, 1920).

37. *Rodnoi iazyk v shkole I stupeni* (Moscow, 1921).

38. *Primernye uchebnye plany dlia I-i i II-i stupeni v edinoi trudovoi shkole* (Moscow, 1920).

39. *Biulleten' Narodnogo prosveshcheniia M.S.P.D.*, no. 2 (November, 1918), p. 13.

40. *Edinaia trudovaia shkola i primernye plany zaniatii v nei (I-ia stupen' obucheniia)* (Viatka, 1918), especially pp. 13–15, 51–55; *Programmy nachal'noi shkoly (s shestiletnim kursom)* (Malmyzh, 1919).

41. *Programmy nachal'noi shkoly* (Malmyzh, 1919), pp. 82–84.

42. *Narodnaia edinaia trudovaia shkola*, vyp. 2 (Penza, 1919).

43. *Primernye programmy sovetskoi edinoi trudovoi shkoly 1-oi stupeni* (Novonikolaevsk, 1920), pp. 3–25, 58ff.

44. *Vestnik narodnogo prosveshcheniia soiuza Kommun Severnoi oblasti,* no. 4–5 (September–October 1918), pp. 14–23.

45. *Primernaia programma edinoi trudovoi shkoly I stupeni* (Moscow, 1920). It suggested a specific number of hours for six subjects in grades four and five.

III. In Search of a School and a Public

1. *NO,* pp. 137, 144.

2. On late tsarist Russia: Ben Eklof, *Russian Peasant Schools: Officialdom, Village Culture, and Popular Pedagogy, 1861–1914* (Berkeley, 1986); Patrick L. Alston, *Education and the State in Tsarist Russia* (Stanford, 1969); Nicholas Hans, *History of Russian Educational Policy 1701–1917* (New York, 1931); James C. McClelland, *Autocrats and Academics: Education, Culture and Society in Tsarist Russia* (Chicago, 1979); Allen Sinel, *The Classroom and the Chancellery: State Educational Reform under Count Dmitry Tolstoi* (Cambridge, 1973); and William H. E. Johnson, *Russia's Educational Heritage* (Pittsburgh, 1950). For 1914 to 1917: Dimitry M. Odinetz and Paul J. Novgorotsev, *Russian Schools and Universities in the World War* (New Haven, 1929).

3. N. V. Kotriakhov, "Pedagogicheskii ruchnoi trud v russkoi shkole," *Sovetskaia pedagogika,* no. 4 (April 1985), pp. 123–26.

4. D. S. Bershadskaia, *Pedagogicheskie vzgliady i deiatel'nost' S. T. Shatskogo* (Moscow, 1960); Ronald Hideo Hayashida, "The Pedagogy of Protest," pp. 18–23; Carol Gayle Moodie, "S. T. Shatskii and His Essay, 'My Development as an Educator'," *Slavic and European Education Review:* no. 1 (1977), pp. 23–31; and no. 2 (1977), pp. 43–53, a translation of Shatsky's autobiographical essay first published in 1928; and *Modern Encyclopedia of Russian and Soviet History,* vol. 34 (1983), pp. 162–66.

5. Lunacharsky offered Shatsky a seat on the State Education Commission: Bershadskaia, *Pedagogicheskie vzgliady,* p. 63.

6. Moodie, "S. T. Shatskii and His Essay," no. 2, p. 51.

7. TsGA RSFSR, f. 2306, op. 3, ed. khr. 3, l. 10 ob.

8. McClelland, *Autocrats and Academics,* p. 50.

9. Odinetz and Novgorotsev, *Russian Schools and Universities in the World War,* pp. 3–129.

10. Fitzpatrick, *The Commissariat of Enlightenment,* pp. 34–35; *Sovetskaia pedagogika,* no. 1 (January 1973), pp. 139–41; and *Narodnoe obrazovanie,* no. 6 (June 1966), p. 82.

11. "Shkola II-oi stupeni," *Narodnoe prosveshchenie* (Narkompros monthly) [henceforth *NP*], no. 16–17 (November–December 1920), p. 34.

12. *Narodnoe obrazovanie* (Tver), no. 4–5 (March 1–15, 1919), p. 229.

13. M. G. Khitarian, "Nachalo stroitel'stva sovetskoi shkoly v Novonikolaevske (1917–1920 gg)," in *Iz istorii zapadnoi sibiri,* vol. 1 (Novosibirsk, 1961), p. 75.

14. A. Tolstov, "Na rabote po organizatsii trudovoi shkoly," *Narodnoe prosveshchenie,* no. 10 (October 1927), pp. 131–32.

15. TsGA RSFSR, f. 1575, op. 5, ed. khr 13, ll. 121, 128 ob.

16. *Itogi osnovnogo obsledovaniia sostoianiia narodnogo obrazovaniia v Novgorodskoi gubernii na 1-e noiabria 1920 goda* (Novgorod, 1922), pp. 32, 34; *Narodnoe obrazovanie v Severo-Dvinskoi gubernii* (Velikii-Ustiug, 1922), pp. 111, 113, 115.

17. *Narodnyi Komissariat po prosveshcheniiu. 1917–oktiabr'–1920 (kratkii otchet)* (Moscow, 1920), p. 35.

18. *Narodnoe obrazovanie* (Tver), no. 6 (April 1919), p. 283.

19. TsGA RSFSR, f. 2306, op. 1, ed. khr. 3277, l. 143. Also the memoirs by Tolstov, "Na rabote," p. 133; and M. I. Voronkov, "U kolybeli sovetskogo ONO," *NP,* no. 10 (October 1927), p. 163.

20. Ivanov, *Ocherki,* p. 13.

21. Khitarian, "Nachalo stroitel'stva sovetskoi shkoly," p. 69.

22. *Programmy nachal'noi shkoly (s shestiletnim kursom)* (Malmyzh, 1919), pp. 104–109.

23. N. Krupskaya, *Pedagogicheskie sochineniia,* vol. 11 (Moscow, 1963), pp. 192, 736, 751, 753.

24. Ibid., p. 753.

25. Ibid., p. 739.

26. Ibid., pp. 192–93, 733, 740–52.

27. Ibid., p. 738.

28. Ibid., p. 743.

29. *Narodnyi Komissariat po prosveshcheniiu,* pp. 103–104. In the rubles sweepstakes, Narkompros trailed the Supreme Economic Council, the Commissariat of Food, and the Commissariat of Military Affairs.

30. Ibid., p. 104.

31. "Shkola II-oi stupeni," *Narodnoe prosveshchenie,* no. 16–17 (November–December 1920), pp. 32ff. For Novgorod, *Itogi osnovnogo obsledovaniia,* pp. 11, 19, 20, 22–23, 44–45; for Orlov, *Narodnoe obrazovanie Orlovskoi gubernii za 1910–1917, 1920–1923 g.g.* (Orel, 1924), pp. 46–48; and for the Central Statistical Administration, Margaret Kay Stolee, "'A Generation Capable of Establishing Communism': Revolutionary Child Rearing in the Soviet Union, 1917–1928," unpublished dissertation (Duke University, 1982), p. 41. Also: Abraham Epshtein, "The School in Soviet Russia," *School and Society,* vol. 16, no. 406 (October 7, 1922), pp. 398–99.

32. *Narodnyi Komissariat po prosveshcheniiu,* p. 101.

33. Ibid.; *Nadezhda Konstantinovna Krupskaya: biografiia* (Moscow, 1978), p. 200.

34. *Informatsionnyi Builleten' Otdela Narodnogo Obrazovaniia* (Moscow Soviet): no. 3 (March 15, 1921), p. 10; and no. 10–11 (July 1–15, 1921), p. 12. Also: TsGA RSFSR, f. 1575, op. 5, ed. khr. 13, l. 121.

35. *Biulleten' Otdela Narodnogo Obrazovaniia* (Moscow Soviet) [henceforth *BONO*], no. 3 (March 1919), p. 54; *Informatsionnyi Biulleten' Otdela Narodnogo Obrazovaniia* (Moscow Soviet), no. 3 (March 15, 1921), p. 11.

36. *Vospominaniia o Nadezhde Konstantinovne Krupskoi* (Moscow, 1966), p. 77.

37. The memoir by Ol'ga Anikst, "Puti professional'nogo obrazovaniia," *NP,* no. 10 (October 1927), p. 138.

38. Krupskaya, *Pedagogicheskie sochineniia,* vol. 11, p. 741.

39. *Itogi osnovnogo obsledovaniia,* pp. 11, 23.

40. "Shkola II-oi stupeni," p. 36.

41. TsGA RSFSR, f. 2306, op. 1, ed. khr. 3277, l. 150 ob. The third inspector followed a practice that would become common in the 1920s—he limited his activity to administrative tasks.

42. TsGA RSFSR, f. 1575, op. 5, ed. khr. 13, ll. 121, 143.

43. TsGA RSFSR, f. 1575, op. 5, ed. khr. 1 or 13, ll. 37–43; and *Informatsionnyi Biulleten' Otdela Narodnogo Obrazovaniia* (Moscow Soviet), no. 4 (April 1, 1921), p. 10.

44. TsGA RSFSR, f. 1575, op. 5, ed. khr. 1, l. 71.

45. *Narodnoe obrazovanie,* no. 7 (1966), p. 82.

46. Nicholas Hans and Sergius Hessen, *Educational Policy in Soviet Russia* (London, 1930), p. 232.

47. "Shkola II-oi stupeni," pp. 32–33; and *Itogi osnovnogo obsledovaniia,* pp. 6, 21. In Northern Dvinsk in 1920, almost 80 percent of all schools opened some time in October: *Narodnoe obrazovanie v Severo-Dvinskoi gubernii,* p. 40. It is likely that some of these schools existed only on paper in order to draw what funds Moscow might provide. Despite severe shortages, about 20 percent of the schools purportedly existing in Orlov province in 1919 had been founded during the two previous years (*Narodnoe obrazovanie Orlovskoi gubernii,* p. 40). Relying on reports submitted by schools themselves, a 1920 study of Pskov province disclosed that 6.24 percent were not functioning (*Narodnoe obrazovanie v Pskovskoi gubernii* [Pskov, 1921], table 4).

48. "Shkola II-oi stupeni," p. 33; and Krupskaya, *Pedagogicheskie socheniniia,* vol. 11, pp. 736, 740.

49. Krupskaya, *Pedagogicheskie sochineniia,* vol. 11, p. 742.

50. Ibid., pp. 743, 745. She and Narkompros retained their faith in educational soviets: TsGA RSFSR, f. 1575. op. 5, ed. khr. 13, l. 131.

51. Krupskaya, *Pedagogicheskie sochineniia,* vol. 11, p. 738; and TsGA RSFSR, f. 1575, op. 5, ed. khr. 13, l. 121.

52. S. I. Lapshin, "Samoobsluzhivanie v trudovoi shkole," *Narodnoe prosveshchenie,* no. 8 (March 1919), pp. 32–35.

53. "Shkola II-oi stupeni," pp. 35–36.

54. *Programmy nachal'noi shkoly (s shestiletnim kursom)* (Malmyzh, 1919), p. 108.

55. TsGA RSFSR, f. 1575, op. 5, ed. 13, ll. 69, 121, 128, 128 ob., 138–138 ob.; F. F. Korolev, *Ocherki po istorii sovetskoi shkoly i pedagogiki, 1917–1920* (Moscow, 1958), pp. 232–34, 300, 314.

56. TsGA RSFSR, f. 1575, op. 5, ed. 13, l. 69.

57. *Narodnoe obrazovanie* (Tver), no. 2 (February 1–20, 1919), p. 98 and no. 4–5 (March 1–15, 1919), p. 229.

58. *BONO,* no. 3 (March 1919), p. 58.

59. TsGA RSFSR, f. 1575, op. 5, ed. khr. 13, ll. 143–44.

60. *Itogi osnovnogo obsledovaniia,* p. 18.

61. I. Bogdanov, "Nominal'nyi i fakticheskii kurs obucheniia v nachal'noi shkole," *NP,* no. 1 (1925), p. 67.

62. Ibid., p. 66.

63. S. Belousov, "'Vtorogodnichestvo' i ego rol' v zhizni nashei shkoly," *NP,* no. 4–5 (April–May 1926), pp. 144–45.

IV. Narkompros under Siege

1. On June 20, 1919, Sovnarkom ordered all organizations other than Narkompros to abolish organs responsible for education: *Sobranie uzakonenii i rasporiazhenii raboche-krest'ianskogo pravitel'stva RSFSR* [henceforth *Sobr. uzak. RSFSR*], 1919, no. 27, st. 306.

2. *Ezhenedel'nik Narkomprosa RSFSR* [henceforth *Ezhenedel'nik NKP*], no. 1 (November 5, 1918), p. 7.

3. L. N. Dmitrieva, *Partiinoe rukovodstvo professional'no-tekhnicheskim obrazovaniem molodezhi (1917–1936 gg.)* (Leningrad, 1978), p. 17; L. E. Ankudinova, "Podgotovka kadrov molodykh rabochikh," in *Istoriia rabochego klassa Leningrada,* vol. 1 (Leningrad, 1962), pp. 40–46.

4. *Lunacharsky o narodnom obrazovanii,* pp. 88, 541, 543.

5. *Sobr. uzak. RSFSR,* 1920, no. 6, st. 41, 42; Anikst, "Puti professional'nogo obrazovaniia," pp. 138–39; and *Vestnik prof-tekhnicheskogo obrazovaniia* [henceforth *VPTO*], no. 1 (May 1920), p. 9.

6. Glavprofobr followed the lead of the Ukrainian Commissariat of Enlightenment, which limited general education to a seven-year course. The best source for these proposals is *VPTO:* no. 1 (May 1920), pp. 4–19; no. 3–4 (August–September 1920), pp. 6–14, 53, 60; and no. 5–7 (October–December 1920), pp. 42–46, 50. Also James C. McClelland, "The Utopian and the Heroic," pp. 114–30 and P. V. Rudnev, "Iz istorii bor'by za leninskii printsip politekhnicheskogo obrazovaniia (fevral' 1920 g.–fevral' 1921 g.)," in *V. I. Lenin i problemy narodnogo obrazovaniia,* ed. N. K. Goncharov and F. F. Korolev (Moscow, 1961), pp. 244–69.

7. *VPTO:* no. 1 (May 1920), p. 18; and no. 5–7 (October–December 1920), p. 46; E. G. Osovsky, "Trudovoe vospitanie i politekhnicheskoe obuchenie v istorii sovetskoi shkoly," in *Voprosy trudovogo vospitaniia i politekhnicheskogo obucheniia v istorii sovetskoi pedagogiki i shkoly,* vol. 1 (Vologda, 1975), p. 28.

8. For Factory Apprenticeship Schools: Dmitrieva, *Partiinoe rukovodstvo,* pp. 24ff;

and *Professional'no-tekhnicheskoe obrazovanie v Rossii za 1917–1921 gg.: iubileinyi sbornik,* ed. O. G. Anikst (Moscow, 1922), pp. 39, 83–88. In 1921, in the Russian Republic, there were over forty Factory Apprenticeship Schools with 2,000 students: F. L. Blinchevsky and G. I. Zelenko, *Professional'no-tekhnicheskoe obrazovanie rabochikh v SSSR* (Moscow, 1957), p. 38.

9. *Pervyi s"ezd RKSM, 29 oktiabria–4 noiabria 1918 g.* (Moscow, 1934), p. 78.

10. *Vtoroi Vserossiiskii s"ezd RKSM, 5–8 oktiabria 1919 goda. Stenograficheskii otchet* (3rd ed.; Moscow-Leningrad, 1926), pp. 149–52, 162–64, 186.

11. Ibid., pp. 152, 164.

12. Ibid., pp. 149, 152.

13. *Tretii Vserossiiskii s"ezd RKSM, 2–10 oktiabria 1920 goda. Stenograficheskii otchet* (Moscow-Leningrad, 1926), pp. 143–44, 171, 280–86, 312–13.

14. *Vtoroi Vserossiiskii s"ezd RKSM,* pp. 186, 163–64; *Tretii Vserossiiskii s"ezd RKSM,* p. 138.

15. *Vtoroi Vserossiiskii s"ezd RKSM,* p. 186.

16. Ibid., p. 163.

17. *NO,* p. 138.

18. M. Pistrak, "Kak sozdavalis' programmy GUSA," *NP* no. 10 (1927), p. 76.

19. *Lunacharsky o narodnom obrazovanii,* pp. 542–43.

20. *VPTO,* no. 1 (May 1920), p. 14.

21. *Lunacharsky o narodnom obrazovanii,* pp. 143–55.

22. Ibid., pp. 145–46, 155.

23. Ibid., p. 155.

24. *VPTO,* no. 5–7 (October–December 1920), pp. 5–7.

25. *Rabotnik prosveshcheniia* [henceforth *RP*], no. 2–3 (1921), p. 27; and *Pravda* (March 4, 1921), p. 1.

26. Krupskaya's theses are in Krupskaya, *Pedagogicheskie sochineniia,* vol. 4, pp. 35–37; Lunacharsky's in *Prilozhenie k Biulleteniu VIII s"ezda sovetov* (January 10, 1921), pp. 15–16.

27. *Direktivy VKP(b) po voprosam prosveshcheniia* (Moscow-Leningrad, 1930), p. 315.

28. Rudnev, "Iz istorii bor'by," p. 264.

29. Lenin, *PSS,* vol. 42 (Moscow, 1970), p. 87.

30. Ibid., p. 228. Lenin continued to emphasize that vocational instruction be offered principally in the senior classes (p. 230).

31. Ibid., pp. 319, 323.

32. Ibid.

33. See Krupskaya's exchanges with O. Iu. Shmidt, chairman of Glavprofobr, in *Pravda* (February 23, March 4, and March 8, 1921); and Rudnev, "Iz istorii bor'by," pp. 266–68.

34. Lenin, *PSS,* vol. 42, p. 229.

35. Lenin, *PSS,* vol. 42, pp. 319, 326.

36. Lenin, *PSS,* vol. 42, pp. 319–20, 324–25 and vol. 52, pp. 133–34.

37. *Programmy semiletnei edinoi trudovoi shkoly* (Moscow, 1921). The preface was dated September 5.

38. Ibid., pp. 241ff.

39. Ibid., pp. 88ff.

40. *Biulleten' ofitsial'nykh rasporiazhenii i soobshchenii* [henceforth *BORS*], no. 33 (July 22, 1921), pp. 6–7.

41. TsGA RSFSR, f. 2306, op. 1, ed. khr. 3277, l. 71.

42. A. V. Veselov, *Professional'no-tekhnicheskoe obrazovanie v SSSR: Ocherki po istorii srednego i nizshego proftekhobrazovaniia* (Moscow, 1961), p. 147.

43. See complaints registered by nineteen provincial organs of Glavprofobor in *BORS,* no. 5 (December 30, 1922), p. 15.

44. As quoted in Dmitrieva, *Partiinoe rukovodstvo,* p. 34.

V. NEP and the Progressive Curriculum

1. TsGA RSFSR, f. 1575, op. 6, ed. khr. 244, l. 36.

2. Information on funding has been difficult to find and when available, has been contradictory. Statistical bases vary from source to source because of competing definitions of enlightenment and education. The best sources are: *Pedagogicheskaia entsiklopediia,* vol. 1, cols. 1082–98; *Kul'turnoe stroitel'stvo Soiuza sovetskikh sotsialisticheskikh respublik: sbornik diagramm* (2nd ed.; Moscow-Leningrad, 1932), p. 12; *Narodnoe prosveshchenie v RSFSR v osnovnykh pokazateliakh: statisticheskii sbornik (1927/28–1930/31 gg., so vkliucheniem nekotorykh dannykh za 1931/1932 g.)* (Moscow-Leningrad, 1932), pp. 134, 137, 145; *Narodnoe prosveshchenie v RSFSR: statisticheskii sbornik* (Moscow-Leningrad, 1928), pp. 110-11; I. Zakolodkin, "Kul'turnye nozhnitsy," *NP,* no. 10 (October 1928); and A. Vasil'ev, "Biudzhet narodnogo obrazovaniia v SSSR," *NP,* no. 4 (1928), pp. 120–30. See also the study for Orlov province in 1923/24 in *Narodnoe obrazovanie Orlovskoi gubernii,* pp. 111–12. For a discussion of local finance (budget, revenue, expenditures), see E. H. Carr, *Socialism in One Country, 1924–1926,* vol. 2 (New York, 1960), pp. 455-65; and E. H. Carr, *Foundations of a Planned Economy, 1926-1929,* vol. 2 (London, 1971), pp. 223-24, 483, 485.

3. *Pedagogicheskaia entsiklopediia,* vol. I, cols. 1088, 1090, 1092, 1094; *Narodnoe prosveshchenie v RSFSR v osnovnykh pokazateliakh,* p. 145; *Narodnoe prosveshchenie v RSFSR: statisticheskii sbornik,* p. 110; Vasil'ev, "Biudzhet," p. 126. About 30 percent of local funds went to the various activities sponsored by Narkompros.

4. Zakolodkin, "Kul'turnye nozhnitsy," (October 1928), pp. 89–90.

5. *UG,* no. 32 (104) (August 14, 1926), p. 3.

6. *Piatnadtsatyi s"ezd VKP(b), dekabr' 1927 goda: Stenograficheskii otchet,* vol. 2 (Moscow, 1962), p. 1114.

7. *Ezhenedel'nik NKP,* no. 15 (36) (August 1, 1924), p. 7.

8. *Massovoe prosveshchenie v SSSR (k itogam pervoi piatiletki)* (Moscow, 1933), pp. 6–9; *Narodnoe prosveshchenie v RSFSR v tsifrakh za 15 let sovetskoi vlasti* (Moscow-Leningrad, 1932), p. 31. The overall number of pupils decreased by 19 percent. In Orlov province, the number of primary schools declined by 37 percent from January 1922 to January 1923, including a 48 percent decline in urban areas: *Narodnoe obrazovanie Orlovskoi gubernii,* pp. 37–39. Also tables in TsGA RSFSR, f. 1575, op. 5, ed. khr. 49, ll. 48–59.

9. *Vestnik prosveshcheniia* [henceforth *VP*], no. 8 (October 1922), p. 145.

10. Comparing the 1928/29 figures with those of 1920/21, the number of schools had decreased by 5 percent and teachers by 2 percent; the number of pupils had increased by 4 percent: *Massovoe prosveshchenie v SSSR (k itogam pervoi piatiletki),* pp. 6–9; and *Narodnoe prosveshchenie v RSFSR v tsifrakh,* p. 31.

11. *Sobr. uzak. RSFSR,* 1921, no. 64, st. 482.

12. *Vestnik prosveshcheniia* (Tambov), no. 2-3 (April 1922), pp. 2, 7.

13. Fitzpatrick, *The Commissariat of Enlightenment,* pp. 277–78, 286–87; *Ezhenedel'nik NKP,* no. 24 (74) (June 12, 1925), p. 2.

14. TsGA RSFSR, f. 2306, op. 3, ed. khr. 154, l. 2.

15. *BORS,* no. 26 (May 19, 1923), p. 1.

16. *Spravochnaia kniga po narodnomu prosveshcheniiu* (Moscow, 1923), p. 31.

17. M. Epshtein, "Voprosy massovoi obshcheobrazovatel'noi shkoly," *Narodnyi uchitel'* [henceforth *NU*], no. 1 (January 1927), p. 23; and *Ezhenedel'nik NKP,* no. 18 (April 26, 1929), p. 13.

18. *Ezhenedel'nik NKP:* no. 9 (30) (April 24, 1924), p. 2; and no. 24 (74) (June 12, 1925), pp. 2-3; *BORS,* no. 4 (December 23, 1922), p. 7. See also the report on fees in Epshtein, "The School in Soviet Russia," pp. 400–401.

19. *Pedagogicheskaia entsiklopediia,* vol. 2 (Moscow, 1928), col. 283. This data was probably for the year 1925, before the abolition of some fees in 1926 and 1927.

'20. *Ezhenedel'nik NKP,* no. 26b (June 30, 1929), p. 8.

21. *Ezhenedel'nik NKP,* no. 2 (23) (February 1, 1924), p. 14.

22. *Russkii iazyk v sovetskoi shkole,* no. 2 (1929), p. 135.

23. TsGA RSFSR, f. 2306, op. 69, ed. khr. 39, ll. 1–25; *BORS,* no. 27 (May 24, 1923), p. 15; *VP,* no. 5–6 (May–June 1928), p. 125. Reports of such schools and grades were still reaching Narkompros in 1929: *Ezhenedel'nik NKP,* no. 18 (April 26, 1929), p. 13. For similar developments in professional education and a list of private schools for the training of machinists, accountants, and bookkeepers, see *Ezhenedel'nik NKP,* no. 20 (49) (November 5, 1923), p. 11.

24. TsGA RSFSR, f. 2306, op. 3, ed. khr. 154, l. 2.

25. *NO,* p. 22.

26. *Ezhenedel'nik NKP,* no. 24 (June 12, 1925), p. 2

27. *Ezhenedel'nik NKP,* no. 7 (57) (February 20, 1925), p. 8.

28. *NP,* no. 8 (August 1926), p. 4; *Ezhenedel'nik NKP:* no. 7 (February 18, 1927), pp. 2–6; and no. 4 (January 27, 1928), p. 3; *Pedagogicheskaia entsiklopediia,* vol. 2, col. 283.

29. On the heels of this attack on fees, a special educational tax was considered in 1928 by: an educational conference in the Urals *(Ezhenedel'nik NKP,* no. 9 [March 2, 1928], p. 22); an educational conference in Nizhnii Novgorod *(Shkola i zhizn'* [Nizhnii Novgorod], no. 4 [April 1928], p. 91); and the Sixth Congress of Heads of Departments of Education and the Narkompros Collegium *(Ezhenedel'nik NKP,* no. 20–21 [May 18, 1928], p. 15). The Sixth Congress and the Narkompros Collegium also suggested that local communities and parents resort to self-taxation *(Ezhenedel'nik NKP,* no. 20–21 [May 18, 1928], p. 18).

30. For a passionate summary of the problem, see Lunacharsky's report and the resolutions that followed at the November 1926 convocation of the All-Russian Central Executive Committee in *NP,* no. 11 (November 1926), pp. 3–34. Also: A. Radchenko, "Zatrudneniia i dostizheniia massovoi shkoly," *NP,* no. 3 (1926), pp. 71–76; the resolution of the Narkompros Collegium of March 3, 1927, in *NP,* no. 3 (March 1927), pp. 3–7; and the report by the head of the Moscow Deparment of Education, M. Aleksinsky, to a plenary session of the Moscow Soviet, June 25, 1928, *Sostoianie i perspektivy razvitiia narodnogo obrazovaniia v Moskve i moskovskoi gubernii* (Moscow, 1928), especially pp. 3–11, 18–19.

31. See reports in *NU:* no. 3 (March 1924), pp. 66–69; no. 2 (February 1926), p. 47; and no. 4 (April 1926), p. 61. Also the resolution of the All-Russian Central Executive Committee, October 15, 1924, in *NO,* pp. 24–25; Epshtein's report in *NP,* no. 7 (1926), p. 132; Krupskaya's article in *Pravda* (June 24, 1926), p. 1; *NP,* no. 5–6 (1925), p. 76; and *VP,* no. 5 (May 1929), p. 115. Experimental schools fared little better. See the report on a school in Kursk province for the 1922/23 academic year in TsGA RSFSR, f. 1575, op. 4, ed. khr. 159, l. 2; and Stolee, pp. 132–33. In an interview on December 2, 1985, at the Institute of General Pedagogy of the Academy of Pedagogical Sciences in Moscow, M. N. Skatkin, one of Shatsky's co-workers at the First Experimental Station, reported that despite its importance, the Station lacked many essential items. Anweiler found the same to be true: *Geschichte,* p. 322.

32. *NU,* no. 2 (February 1926), p. 47.

33. *Shkola i zhizn',* no. 2 (December 1926), p. 42.

34. N. Sergeeva, "V glushi," *NU,* no. 3 (March 1924), p. 68.

35. F. F. Korolev, *Sovetskaia shkola v period sotsialisticheskoi industrializatsii* (Moscow, 1959), p. 148.

36. *UG,* no. 5 (128) (January 29, 1927), p. 3; *Voprosy shkoly II stupeni; Trudy Pervoi Vserossiiskoi konferentsii shkol II stupeni 5–10 iiulia 1925 g.* (Moscow, 1925), p. 152.

37. *Ezhenedel'nik NKP,* no. 37 (September 17, 1926), p. 1.

38. *Proekty uchebnykh planov tsentral'nykh kursov 1927/1928 g.* (Moscow-Leningrad, 1927), pp. 24–25.

39. A. Lunacharsky, "Narodnoe prosveshchenie v RSFSR," *NP,* no. 7-8 (July-August 1925), pp. 10-11.

40. *NP:* no. 2 (February 1925), p. 177; no. 8 (August 1926), p. 3; and no. 11 (November 1926), p. 7.

41. Zakolodkin, "Kul'turnye nozhnitsy" (October 1928), p. 96; *Massovoe prosveshchenie v SSSR k 15-letiiu oktiabria,* pt. 1 (Moscow-Leningrad, 1932), p. 78; and *Sostoianie i perspektivy,* p. 8.

42. V. Sirotkin, "Kak rabotaiut shkoly Moskovskoi gubernii," in *Kak rabotaiut shkoly Moskovskoi gubernii. Sbornik* (Moscow, 1925), p. 53.

43. See issues of *BORS* and also *Biulleten' Moskovskogo Otdela Narodnogo Obrazovaniia* [henceforth *Biulleten' MONO*], no. 18-19 (September 25, 1924), pp. 3-4, 37-38.

44. TsGA RSFSR, f. 298, op. 1, ed. khr. 45, ll. 1-1 ob. Also: Stolee, pp. 128-130.

45. Lunacharsky, *On Education,* pp. 222, 160.

46. *Uchitel'stvo na novykh putiakh: sbornik statei, dokladov i materialov Vsesoiuznogo s"ezda uchitelei* (Leningrad, 1925), p. 15; and Z. Ravkin, "V bor'be za leninskii stil' raboty Narkomprosa," *Narodnoe obrazovanie,* no. 2 (February 1964), p. 45.

47. V. Shcherbakov, "Ocherednye zadachi shkol'nogo stroitel'stva," *VP,* no. 2 (February 1928), p. 7.

48. In 1923, the Section included: Krupskaya, Shatsky, Blonsky, O. L. Bem, I. I. Glivenko, G. O. Gordon, Ia. G. Kalashnikov, K. N. Kornilov, M. V. Krupenina, A. I. Radchenko, M. G. Rozanov, S. T. Rudneva, A. V. Freiman and I. L. Tsvetkov. See *Spravochnaia kniga po narodnomu prosveshcheniiu,* p. 7.

49. TsGA RSFSR, f. 2306, op. 1, ed. khr. 3277, ll. 71-76 ob.

50. *Na putiakh,* no. 1 (July 1922), pp. 5-43; TsGA RSFSR, f. 298, op. 1, ed. khr. 44, l. 43.

51. *Tezisy k dokladu S"ezdu Gubernskikh ONO o vyrabotannykh programmakh dlia edinoi trudovoi shkoly I i II stupeni,* (Moscow, 1921), pp. 5-6.

52. *Novye programmy edinoi trudovoi shkoly pervoi stupeni (I, II, III i IV gody obucheniia)* (Moscow, 1924), pp. 4-6.

53. *Novye programmy dlia edinoi trudovoi shkoly,* vyp. 1 (Moscow-Petrograd, 1923), especially p. 24; *Novye programmy* (1924) especially pp. 3-4; and *Ezhenedel'nik NKP,* no. 41 (October 9, 1925), pp. 12-15.

54. TsGA RSFSR, f. 2306, op. 3, ed. khr. 154, l. 10.

55. *NO,* pp. 147-48.

56. Ivanov, "Ocherki," p. 179. Pupils could also select a representative.

57. William Heard Kilpatrick, "The Project Method," *Teachers College Record,* vol. 19, no. 4 (September 1918), pp. 319-35.

58. See the Section's instructional letter *Metodicheskie pis'ma. Pis'mo pervoe. O kompleksnom prepodavanii,* (9th ed.; Moscow, 1925), originally published in November 1923; and P. P. Blonsky, *Novye programmy GUS'a i uchitel'* (Moscow, 1924) (32 pp.). Anweiler, *Geschichte,* pp. 266-69, provides a summary of the Soviet justification of the new method.

59. *Novye programmy* (1923), pp. 9-12; and *Novye programmy* (1924), pp. 6-9. Also: "Complex Method of Education," in the *Modern Encyclopedia of Russian and Soviet History,* vol. 7 (Gulf Breeze, Fla., 1978), pp. 237-40.

60. *Metodicheskie pis'ma. Pis'mo pervoe,* p. 10. One enthusiast proudly declared that the Section's 1923 complex programs avoided language, reading, writing, and arithmetic in favor of nature, labor, and society: *NU,* no. 1 (January 1924), p. 41.

61. F. P. Novoselov, *Izuchenie mestnogo kraia v shkole* (Moscow, 1925), pp. 6-7.

62. I. G. Avtukhov and I. D. Martynenko, *Programmy GUS'a i massovaia shkola,* (2nd ed.; Moscow, 1925), pp. 230-31; and B. Zhavoronkov, *Kak rabotat' po obshchestvovedeniiu (na I stupeni)* (Moscow, 1925), pp. 100-101.

63. A. Novikova, "Okh, kompleks!," *NU,* no. 5 (May 1925), pp. 94-98.

64. *Tezisy k dokladu S″ezdu,* pp. 7–8.

65. TsGA RSFSR, f. 2306, op. 1, ed. khr. 3277, ll. 73–73 ob. Eight programs were examined in Tula, Ivanovo-Voznesensk, Simbirsk, Eletsk, Tiumen, Kursk, Moscow, and Viatka. Only the latter three are available among the extensive collection of local curricula at the Library of the Academy of Pedagogical Sciences in Moscow.

66. *Informatsionnyi Biulleten' Otdela Narodnogo Obrazovaniia* (Moscow), no. 12–13 (August 1–15, 1921), pp. 1–34, especially pp. 2–3.

67. *Primernyi plan rabot v shkole I-i stupeni* (Viatka, 1921).

68. TsGA RSFSR, f. 298, op. 1, ed. khr. 45, l. 13.

69. *Novye programmy* (1923), p. 24.

70. Ibid., pp. 98–99.

71. For the circular issued by Glavsotsvos, July 31, 1923, see *Prava uchashchikhsia i uchashchikh. Sbornik deistvuiushchego zakonodatel'stva* (Moscow, 1925), pp. 181–82; and *Metodicheskie pis'ma. Pis'mo pervoe,* p. 9.

72. B. Zhavoronkov, "K voprosu o prorabotke kompleksa so vzroslymi i na II stupeni," *Na putiakh,* no. 10–12 (October–December 1924), pp. 34–35, 44–45.

73. *Metodicheskie pis'ma. Pis'mo pervoe,* p. 15.

74. *Programmy dlia pervogo kontsentra shkol vtoroi stupeni (5, 6 i 7 gody obucheniia)* (Moscow-Leningrad, 1925), p. 13.

75. Ibid., p. 8.

76. Ibid., p. 136.

77. *Metodicheskie pis'ma. Pis'mo tret'e. Ob uchete raboty v shkole I stupeni* (Moscow, 1925). Also: *Prava uchashchikhsia,* pp. 181–82; and *Ezhenedel'nik NKP,* no. 9 (March 4, 1927), p. 17.

78. *Praktika raboty po programme GUS'a; Rabochaia kniga uchitelei I stupeni,* pt. 2 (Moscow, 1926), pp. 28, 37–43.

79. Ibid., p. 40.

80. *Shkola i zhizn',* no. 4 (April 1924), pp. 51–52; "Chto govoriat na mestakh ob uchebnike," *Sovetskoi shkole—novyi uchebnik,* no. 2–3 (1926), pp. 24–26; and S. Dziubinsky, "O rabochei knige," *Sovetskoi shkole—novyi uchebnik,* no. 5 (1926), pp. 70–78. Also: A. P. Belikova, "Siberian Textbooks in the 1920s and Their Role in Developing the Sociopolitical and Labor Activism of Pupils," *Soviet Education,* vol. 24, no. 1 (November 1981), pp. 32–33.

81. V. N. Shul'gin, "Nashi ocherednye zadachi (k Vserossiiskoi konferentsii po knige)," *Na putiakh,* no. 2 (February 1926), pp. 7–12; E. Leonova, "Pervaia Vserossiiskaia konferentsiia po uchebnoi i detskoi knige," *Na putiakh,* no. 7–8 (July–August 1926), pp. 140–43, 146; and *Sovetskoi shkole—novyi uchebnik,* no. 7–8 (1927), pp. 226, 231–32.

82. "Laboratory Plan," *Modern Encyclopedia of Russian and Soviet History,* vol. 18 (Gulf Breeze, Fla., 1980), pp. 232–35. Parkhurst's book, *Education on the Dalton Plan* (New York, 1922), and that of her supporter, Evelyn Dewey, *The Dalton Laboratory Plan* (New York, 1922), were translated into Russian. Krupskaya reviewed them in *Na putiakh,* no. 3 (November 1922), pp. 163–68.

83. *Biulleten' MONO,* no. 12 (June 20, 1924), p. 12.

84. *VP,* no. 2–3 (February–March 1925), p. 235.

85. Harvey Raymond Jahn, "The Development of Soviet Educational Policy During 1917–1936: A Case Study of Mathematics Education at the Elementary and Secondary Levels," unpublished dissertation (University of Michigan, 1968), pp. 16–17.

86. *Novye programmy* (1924), pp. 104–105.

87. *Programmy dlia pervogo kontsentra shkol vtoroi stupeni (5, 6 i 7 gody obucheniia)* (Moscow-Leningrad, 1925), pp. 96–99, 112–13, 124–25, 134–36.

88. Larry E. Holmes, "Two Ideologies: Controversy over Social Studies and

History in the Soviet Schools, 1921–1928," *Slavic and European Education Review,* vol. 9, no. 1–2 (1985), pp. 1–28.

89. Instructions and syllabi in TsGA RSFSR, f. 2306, op. 1, ed. khr. 3277, ll. 76–76 ob.; *Novye programmy* (1923), pp. 103–108; *Novye programmy* (1924), pp. 102–104; *Programmy dlia pervogo kontsentra shkol vtoroi stupeni (5, 6, i 7 gody obucheniia)* (1925), pp. 20ff., 37–59; and *NP:* no. 6–7 (June–July 1924), pp. 46–49; and no. 5–6 (May–June 1925), pp. 61–62. Also the syllabus for teacher repreparation courses in *Ezhenedel'nik NKP,* no. 19 (May 13, 1927), pp. 22–23.

90. M. N. Pokrovsky, "Marksizm v programmakh shkoly I i II stupeni," *Na putiakh,* no. 4–5 (April–May 1924), pp. 161, 163, 165–67, 170; M. Pokrovsky, "O kompleksnom metode," *Na putiakh,* no. 1 (January 1924), pp. 8–11; and *NP,* no. 4–5 (April–May 1923), pp. 66–74.

91. S. Dziubinsky, "Na novye rel'sy," *Na putiakh,* no. 7–8 (July–September 1923), pp. 216–17.

92. S. Singalevich, "Rabota po gazete, kak metod prorabotki materiala po obshchestvovedeniiu," *Na putiakh,* no. 6 (June 1924), pp. 92–97; S. P. Singalevich, *Leninizm v shkole* (Moscow, 1924); S. Singalevich, *Obshchestvovedenie v trudovoi shkole: metodicheskoe rukovodstvo* (Moscow, 1925), pp. 23ff.; B. Zhavoronkov, *Kak rabotat' po obshchestvovedeniiu (na I stupeni)* (Moscow, 1925); and S. Singalevich, "Obshchestvovedenie v shkole I stupeni," in *Pedagogicheskaia entsiklopediia,* vol. I, cols. 167–72.

93. S. Singalevich, "Problema kompleksnosti v obshchestvovedenii," in *Nauchno-pedagogicheskii sbornik,* vol. 1 (Kazan, 1926), p. 85.

VI. Slow History: Classroom Practice

1. *UG:* no. 1 (October 3, 1924), pp. 4–5; and no. 13 (December 25, 1924), p. 3. See, in general, the paper's section "Na putiakh k novoi shkole." By early 1925, the newspaper boasted of 60,000 subscribers (71 percent of whom were teachers), and 800 teacher-correspondents: *UG* (January 22, 1925), p. 7.

2. Ibid., no. 17 (89) (May 1, 1926), p. 5.

3. TsGA RSFSR, f. 298, op. 1, ed. khr. 45, l. 96.

4. See summaries in the publication of the Nizhnii Novgorod Provincial Department of Education and Teachers Union, *Shkola i zhizn',* no. 2–3 (February–March 1927), pp. 173–74, 183; in the publication of the Yaroslavl' Provincial Department of Education, *Nash trud,* no. 1 (January 1927), p. 63; and for Moscow in Sirotkin, "Kak rabotaiut shkoly," pp. 12–88. Also the resolutions of the Third All-Mariiskii Congress on Enlightenment, September 1926, in TsGA RSFSR, f. 2306, op. 69, ed. khr. 878, ll. 3 ob - 4. For accounts that rely extensively on archival materials, see Z. I. Ravkin, *Sovetskaia shkola v gody perekhoda na mirnuiu rabotu po vosstanovleniiu narodnogo khoziaistva (1921–1925 gg.).* Akademiia pedagogicheskikh nauk. *Izvestiia,* vyp. 22 (Moscow, 1949), pp. 69ff.; and Z. I. Ravkin, *Sovetskaia shkola v period vosstanovleniia narodnogo khoziaistva, 1921–1925 gg.* (Moscow, 1959), pp. 65–66, 87–88, 92, 101–104, 120–24.

5. *Biulleten' MONO,* no. 8 (March 10, 1925), p. 14.

6. *UG,* no. 10 (185) (March 2, 1928), p. 4.

7. *Biulleten' MONO,* no. 1 (January 2, 1924), pp. 23–24.

8. Inspectors' reports in Sirotkin, "Kak rabotaiut shkoly," pp. 37, 55, 57; *Shkola i zhizn',* no. 2–3 (February–March 1927), p. 183; *Iz opyta gorodskoi semiletki: sbornik,* ed. E. Kushnir and A. Kolpakova (Moscow-Leningrad, 1927), pp. 13, 22–23; *VP:* no. 1 (January 1927), p. 113; no. 10 (October 1927), p. 98; and no. 5 (May 1929), p. 118; and *V pomoshch' organizatoru narodnogo prosveshcheniia; sbornik po voprosam inspektirovaniia i rukovodstva prosvetitel'noi raboti* (Moscow, 1928), p. 113. Also comments by the Narkompros official, B. Esipov, in *UG,* no. 23 (95) (June 12, 1926), p. 3.

9. *VP,* no. 5 (May 1929), p. 118.

10. *Biulleten' MONO:* no. 1 (January 2, 1924), p. 24; and no. 24–25 (August 25, 1925), p. 20.

11. On homework: *VP:* no. 1 (January 1923), p. 136; no. 2 (February 1923), p. 195; and no. 3 (March 1926), p. 42; Korolev, *Sovetskaia shkola,* pp. 172–73; *Ezhenedel'nik MONO:* no. 5–6 (February 15, 1927), p. 12; and no. 13–14 (April 26, 1927), pp. 3–4. On tests: *Ezhenedel'nik MONO,* no. 48 (December 30, 1926), p. 20; *Ezhenedel'nik NKP,* no. 9 (March 4, 1927), p. 17; *NU,* no. 4 (April 1927), p. 58; E. Gur'ianov, "O testovom uchete v shkole," *VP,* no. 5 (May 1927), pp. 35–36.

12. *VP,* no. 1 (January 1923), p. 136.

13. *Ezhenedel'nik NKP,* no. 6 (35) (July 21, 1923), p. 30.

14. *VP,* no. 10 (October 1927), p. 108.

15. *UG,* no. 10 (185) (March 2, 1928), p. 4.

16. *VP,* no. 10 (October 1927), p. 108.

17. *Ezhenedel'nik NKP,* no. 6 (35) (July 21, 1923), p. 31.

18. A. S. Tolstov to the Pedagogical Section, February 15, 1923, in TsGA RSFSR, f. 298, op. 1, ed. khr. 45, l. 80 ob; a circular from Glavsotsvos in *BORS,* no. 28 (June 2, 1923), p. 7; and *UG:* no. 41 (113) (October 16, 1926), p. 2; and no. 10 (185) (March 2, 1928), p. 4.

19. M. Pistrak, "Komsomol i shkola," *VP,* no. 2 (February 1923), p. 17.

20. TsGA RSFSR, f. 298, op. 1, ed. khr. 45, l. 16.

21. *Biulleten' MONO:* no. 8 (April 15, 1924), pp. 5–6; and no. 36 (December 20, 1925), p. 14.

22. *NP,* no. 7 (1926), p. 133.

23. *Iz opyta gorodskoi semiletki,* p. 17.

24. See the Central Committee on the conflict between teachers and the Party's youth organizations in *NO,* pp. 265–67, 270; and *Direktivy VKP po voprosam prosveshcheniia,* pp. 132, 136.

25. Summary of these complaints in *UG,* no. 6 (129) (February 5, 1927), p. 2.

26. S. Belousov, "'Vtorogodnichestvo' i ego rol'," p. 145.

27. *VP,* no. 7–8 (July–August 1926), p. 10.

28. Ibid.

29. *Shkola i zhizn',* no. 8 (August 1924), p. 53; *Nash trud,* no. 12 (December 1927), p. 9; S. Belousov, "Vtorogodnichestvo v gorodskikh shkolakh," *VP,* no. 5 (May 1927), p. 3; V. Krylov, "Uchashchiesia v shkolakh II stupeni," *NP,* no. 9 (1925), pp. 64, 68, 72; T. Khrushchev, "O vtorogodnichestve," *Na putiakh,* no. 9 (September 1929), p. 46; and *Vseobshchee obiazatel'noe obuchenie: statisticheskii ocherk po dannym shkol'noi perepisi tekushchei statistiki prosveshcheniia* (Moscow, 1930), p. 86.

30. *Norodnoe prosveshchenie v RSFSR v tsifrakh,* p. 26.

31. *Narodnoe prosveshchenie v RSFSR: statisticheskii sbornik,* p. 172.

32. Ibid., p. 173.

33. For the Congress of Teachers: *NP,* no. 2 (February 1925), pp. 187–88; and Avtukhov, *Programmy GUS'a i massovaia shkola,* pp. 80–81. For the conference: *Voprosy shkoly II stupeni,* p. 147.

34. TsGA RSFSR, f. 1575, op. 3, ed. khr. 227, l. 16; *UG:* no. 2 (October 10, 1924), p. 3; and no. 37 (50) (August 6, 1925), p. 3; *Nash trud,* no. 7–8 (July–August 1925), pp. 15–22; *Shkola i zhizn',* no. 5–6 (May–June 1925), p. 86.

35. B. Esipov, "Voprosy uchitelei po povodu programmy GUS'a," *Na putiakh,* no. 7–8 (July–August 1924), pp. 78–95; M. Epshtein, "Shkola, kak ona est'," *NU,* no. 7 (July 1926), pp. 10–22, especially 13–16; and Shatsky's report in S. T. Shatsky, *Pedagogicheskie sochineniia,* vol. 2, pp. 350–53.

36. *UG,* no. 35 (48) (July 23, 1925), p.3.

37. K. Konovalova, "S uchitel'skoi konferentsii," *NU,* no. 4 (April 1926), p. 59.

38. Avtukhov, *Programmy GUS'a i massovaia shkola,* pp. 50–51, 162ff.; N. Leskin, "Sviaz' navykov s kompleksom," *NU,* no. 2 (February 1926), pp. 29–31; *UG,* no.

7 (79) (February 18, 1926), p. 4; Sirotkin, "Kak rabotaiut shkoly," p. 22; and I. P. Kopachev, "Perestroika soderzhaniia raboty shkol Kabardino-Balkarii v 1920–1930 gg.," in *V pomoshch uchiteliu; Sbornik metodicheskikh statei,* vol. 17 (Nal'chik, 1963), p. 14.

39. *Shkola i zhizn',* no. 2–3 (February–March 1927), p. 72.
40. TsGA RSFSR, f. 298, op. 1, ed. khr. 41, ll. 18–19 ob.
41. Shatsky, *Pedagogicheskie sochineniia,* vol. 2, p. 306.
42. Ibid., p. 353.
43. Ibid., p. 354. Also pp. 382–91 and vol. 3, p. 77 for similar criticism.
44. P. Chepikov, "Programmy GUS'a i mestnaia rabota nad nimi," *Shkola i zhizn',* no. 4 (April 1926), p. 24.
45. Epshtein, "Shkola, kak ona est'," p. 16.
46. A. Lunacharsky, "Na bor'bu za narodnoe prosveshchenie," *NP,* no. 2 (February 1926), p. 16.
47. Korolev, *Sovetskaia shkola,* pp. 167–70, 178; and Ivanov, "Ocherki," pp. 132–33.
48. I. Svadkovsky, *Dalton-Plan v primenenii k sovetskoi shkole* (2nd ed.; Moscow-Leningrad, 1926), pp. 138–41. The Dalton Plan was ridiculed in N. Ognyov, *The Diary of a Communist Schoolboy,* trans. Alexander Werth (New York, 1928).
49. See the memoir by a 1930 graduate of the Soviet nine-year school, Vladimir D. Samarin, in George L. Kline, ed., *Soviet Education* (New York, 1957), pp. 26–27; inspectors' reports in *VP,* no. 3 (March 1929), p. 144; no. 10 (October 1927), p. 98; and no. 1 (January 1927), p. 113.
50. *VP,* no. 10 (October 1927), pp. 106–107.
51. TsGA RSFSR, f. 298, op. 1, ed. khr. 41, l. 18 ob.
52. Avtukhov, *Programmy GUS'a i massovaia shkola,* pp. 56–57; Ravkin, *Sovetskaia shkola,* p. 66.
53. *Ezhenedel'nik MONO,* no. 7–8 (February 26, 1927), p. 7.
54. A. Egolin, "Obshchestvenno-neobkhodimaia rabota shkol II stupeni," *Na putiakh,* no. 2 (February 1927), p. 67.
55. M. Pistrak, "Nedopustimye uklony v shkol'nom dele," *Na putiakh,* no. 11 (November 1927), pp. 8–22.
56. Ibid., pp. 10, 17.
57. See information from the 1925 All-Russian Conference of Secondary School-teachers, in *NP,* no. 5–6 (1925), pp. 174-80, 187-89; and *Ezhenedel'nik NKP,* no. 20–21 (May 18, 1928), pp. 23–24; the Conference on Labor in the School in *Ezhenedel'nik NKP,* no. 27 (June 29, 1928), p. 6; the State Academic Council in *Russkii iazyk v sovetskoi shkole,* no. 3 (1929), p. 143; a meeting of the provincial soviet of MONO, March 1929, in *VP,* no. 4 (April 1929), pp. 97–98; and a report by a school inspector in *Iz opyta gorodskoi semiletki,* p. 17.
58. *NP,* no. 7 (1926), p. 131.
59. Sirotkin, "Kak rabotaiut shkoly," p. 22.
60. *Ezhenedel'nik NKP,* no. 20–21 (May 18, 1928), p. 24; *VP,* no. 5 (May 1929), p. 115.
61. *Biulleten' MONO,* no. 24–25 (August 1925), p. 20; A. Kirienko, "Soveshchanie po voprosam stroitel'stva fabrichno-zavodskoi semiletki," *Na putiakh,* no. 7–8 (July-August 1928), p. 87.
62. *Ezhenedel'nik NKP,* no. 14 (64) (April 4, 1925), p. 13.
63. *Ezhenedel'nik NKP:* no. 20–21 (May 18, 1928), p. 26; and no. 30 (July 20, 1928), pp. 12–13.
64. *Ezhenedel'nik NKP:* no. 30 (July 20, 1928), p. 12; and no. 14 (64) (April 4, 1925), p. 13; *Shkola i zhizn',* no. 12 (December 1926), p. 42.
65. *UG,* no. 32 (45) (July 2, 1925), p. 5.
66. Ibid., no. 39 (51) (August 13, 1925), p. 3.

67. *Shkola i zhizn'*, no. 4 (April 1927), p. 34.

68. *Nash trud*, no. 1 (January 1927), p. 63; *Biulleten' MONO*, no. 5 (March 1, 1924), p. 26.

69. *VP*, no. 1 (January 1923), p. 163.

70. *Voprosy shkoly II stupeni*, pp. 19, 44, 73, 93, 119, 159.

71. *Biulleten' MONO*, no. 1 (January 2, 1924), p. 23.

72. Ibid., no. 5 (March 1, 1924), p. 26.

73. Ibid., no. 22-23 (August 10, 1925), p. 38.

74. See a series of reports for the earlier period 1920 to 1921, most of them quite positive, but a few revealing serious difficulties: TsGA RSFSR, f. 1575, op. 5, ed. khr. 13. More serious problems are revealed in questionnaires returned by 120 experimental schools: *Programmy GUS'a i obshchestvenno-politicheskoe vospitanie*, ed. E. Rudneva (Moscow, 1925); and N. V. Chekhov, "Programmy GUS'a v tsentral'nykh opytno-pokazatel'nykh shkolakh NKP," in *Programmy GUS'a i mestnaia rabota nad nim*, ed. S. T. Shatsky (Moscow, 1925), pp. 59-62.

75. TsGA RSFSR, f. 298, op. 1, ed. khr. 45, ll. 27ff., especially ll. 29-29 ob. The memorandum is not dated, but Krupskaya probably submitted it in March.

76. Ibid., ll. 36-36 ob. It did so on April 3, 1923.

77. *VP*, no. 2-3 (February-March 1924), p. 143; *UG*, no. 36 (108) (September 11, 1926), p. 4; and *Ezhenedel'nik NKP*, no. 21 (May 28, 1926), p. 11.

78. *VP*, no. 2-3 (February-March 1925), p. 229.

79. *Programmy GUS'a i obshchestvenno-politicheskoe vospitanie*, p. 60.

80. *Russkii iazyk v sovetskoi shkole*, no. 3 (1929), pp. 144-45.

81. *Ezhenedel'nik NKP*, no. 6 (July 21, 1923), pp. 17-20: *Shkola i zhizn'*, no. 5-6 (May-June 1925), p. 76.

82. *UG*, no. 9 (132) (February 26, 1927), p. 5.

83. *VP*, no. 3 (March 1928), p. 129. Vocational and professional schools "continued to work on the basis of subjects": E. G. Osovsky, *Razvitie teorii professional'no-tekhnicheskogo obrazovaniia v SSSR (1917-1940)* (Moscow, 1980), p. 224.

84. Richard Stites, "Adorning the Russian Revolution: The Primary Symbols of Bolshevism, 1917-1918," *Sbornik* of the Study Group on the Russian Revolution, no. 10 (Summer 1984), pp. 39-42; and Stites, *Revolutionary Dreams*, pp. 64-72.

85. *Biulleten' MONO*, no. 16-17 (June 5, 1925), p. 24.

86. *Ezhenedel'nik NKP*, no. 44 (October 26, 1928), p. 5.

87. *UG*, no. 43 (218) (October 19, 1928), p. 6.

VII. Teachers: A Preference for the Customary

1. *NU*, no. 2 (February 1924), pp. 68, 87; *UG*, no. 4 (October 24, 1924), p. 6; *Ezhenedel'nik NKP*, no. 27 (47) (December 11, 1924), p. 11; *Shkola i zhizn'*, no. 2 (February 1926), p. 64. Narkompros complained to this effect in *Ezhenedel'nik NKP*: no. 20-21 (May 18, 1928), p. 22; no. 51 (December 10, 1928), p. 2; and no. 47 (November 22, 1929), p. 2.

2. *Ezhenedel'nik NKP*: no. 51 (December 10, 1928), p. 2; and no. 52 (December 14, 1928), pp. 4-5; *VP*, no. 1 (January 1929), p. 150; *Ezhenedel'nik NKP*, no. 47 (November 22, 1929), p. 2.

3. *VP*, no. 1 (January 1929), p. 150.

4. Sirotkin, "Kak rabotaiut skholy," p. 49.

5. *Nash trud*, no. 1 (January 1927), p. 63.

6. *BORS*, no. 73 (March 15, 1923), p. 3.

7. *Pedagogicheskaia entsiklopediia*, vol. 1, col. 1077; for complaints by the Narkompros Collegium, *Ezhenedel'nik NKP*, no. 7 (57) (February 20, 1925), p. 10; and no. 28 (48) (December 18, 1924), p. 2.

8. A. A. Shatalov, "Narkompros v pervye gody posle Oktiabria (1917-1920)," *Sovetskaia pedagogika*, no. 11 (November 1988), p. 98.

9. *VP,* no. 2 (February 1928), p. 136.

10. *Kommunisticheskoe prosveshchenie* [henceforth *KP*], no. 5 (1935), p. 65.

11. *Pedagogicheskaia entsiklopediia,* vol. 1, col. 1081. Also incomplete information in N. Kostromin, "Kadr rukovodiashchikh rabotnikov po narodnomu obrazovaniiu," *NP,* no. 5 (May 1928), pp. 121–22; *Proekty uchebnykh planov,* p. 22; *Sostoianie i perspektivy,* p. 24.

12. *BORS,* no. 69 (February 15, 1922), pp. 1–2; *Ezhenedel'nik NKP:* no. 3 (24) (February 14, 1924), p. 7; and no. 22–23 (42–43) (October 30, 1924), p. 12.

13. *UG,* no. 50 (225) (December 7, 1928), p. 2.

14. *UG,* no. 47 (170) (November 18, 1927), p. 2.

15. TsGA RSFSR, f. 298, op. 1, ed. khr. 74, l. 36 ob.

16. *Ezhenedel'nik NKP,* no. 8 (37) (August 4, 1923), pp. 3–5; *Proekty uchebnykh planov,* p. 22.

17. *BORS,* no. 13 (February 24, 1923), pp. 1–2; *Ezhenedel'nik NKP,* no. 11 (61) (March 23, 1925), p. 3; *VP,* no. 2 (February 1928), p. 136; *Pedagogicheskaia entsiklopediia,* vol. 1, col. 1078.

18. *Sostoianie i perspektivy,* p. 24; *Proekty uchebnykh planov,* p. 22; and especially *V pomoshch' organizatoru,* p. 54.

19. *UG:* no. 13 (26) (February 19, 1925), p. 5; and no. 15 (28) (March 5, 1925), p. 2. Also *Ezhenedel'nik NKP,* no. 15 (36) (August 1, 1924), pp. 9–10.

20. *UG,* no. 16 (29) (March 12, 1925), p. 2.

21. Sirotkin, "Kak rabotaiut shkoly," p. 81.

22. *UG,* no. 35 (107) (September 4, 1926), p. 2.

23. Ibid.

24. *Ezhenedel'nik NKP,* no. 51 (December 8, 1925), p. 5.

25. *RP,* no. 1 (January 1926), p. 28; *UG,* no. 11 (24) (February 5, 1925), p. 3.

26. TsGA RSFSR, f. 298, op. 1, ed. khr. 41, l. 20.

27. *Ezhenedel'nik NKP,* no. 8 (37) (August 4, 1923), pp. 3–5; *Proekty uchebnykh planov,* p. 22.

28. *UG,* no. 13 (26) (February 19, 1925), p. 5.

29. Epshtein, "Shkola, kak ona est'," p. 20.

30. *BORS,* no. 22 (April 25, 1923), p. 16; *Ezhenedel'nik NKP,* no. 8 (February 27, 1925), pp. 10–12; and no. 12 (April 2, 1926), pp. 44–45.

31. *UG,* no. 36 (108) (September 11, 1926), p. 4.

32. *UG,* no. 13 (188) (March 23, 1928), p. 3.

33. *Narodnoe prosveshchenie v SSSR 1926–1927 uchebnyi god,* p. 17. Schools with three grades and two instructors tended to combine grades two and three, but those with two teachers and four grades combined either one and three or two and four.

34. For teacher-pupil ratios in the mid-1920s, see V. A. Popov, *Shkoly sotsial'nogo vospitaniia: g. Moskvy i Moskovskoi gubernii. Statisticheskii obzor* (Moscow, 1930), pp. 88–89; *Kul'turnoe stroitel'stvo SSSR: statisticheskii sbornik* (Moscow-Leningrad, 1940), p. 66; and *Narodnoe obrazovanie v Ul'ianovskoi gubernii za 1914–1924 gg.* (Ul'ianovsk, 1927), p. 8.

35. *Ezhenedel'nik NKP,* no. 19 (May 8, 1925), pp. 10–11; *Prosveshchenie v RSFSR v 1926/27 uchebnomu godu* (Moscow, 1928), p. xvi; *Narodnoe prosveshchenie v SSSR 1926–1927 uchebnyi god,* pp. 23–26; *Sostoianie i perspektivy,* p. 13; *Ezhenedel'nik NKP,* no. 20–21 (May 18, 1928), p. 21.

36. *Biulleten' MONO,* no. 2 (January 15, 1924), p. 23; B. Esipov, "Voprosy uchitelei," pp. 78–95; *Shkola i zhizn',* no. 5–6 (May–June 1925), p. 86. For the same at the All-Mariiskii Congress on Enlightenment: TsGA RSFSR, f. 2306, op. 69, ed. khr. 878, ll. 3 ob - 4.

37. N. Iordansky, "K predstoiashchemu s"ezdu," *VP,* no. 12 (December 1924), pp. 11–12.

38. Avtukhov, *Programmy GUS'a i massovaia shkola,* p. 90.

39. *Uchitel'stvo na novykh putiakh,* pp. 176–77.

40. See the account by a teacher, N. Demin, in *Narodnoe obrazovanie,* no. 6 (June 1968), p. 114.

41. *Programmy GUS'a i obshchestvenno-politicheskoe vospitanie,* p. 61.

42. L. Lysiakov, "Iz grudy uchitel'skikh stikhov," *NU,* no. 5–6 (May–June 1927), p. 67.

43. Ibid.

44. The problems experienced by teachers were similar to the hardships of an earlier period in Western and Central Europe. Local officials and the community distrusted and abused teachers. They demanded instruction in literacy, numeracy, and obeisance, but were reluctant to provide the means for doing so. See Anthony J. La Vopa, *Prussian Schoolteachers: Profession and Office, 1763–1848* (Chapel Hill, 1980); and Theodore Zeldin, *France, 1848–1945: Intellect and Pride* (New York, 1980), pp. 159ff.

45. I. S. Kantsenelenbaum, *Trudovye prava prosveshchentsev* (Moscow, 1928), pp. 71–86.

46. For salary schedules: *Ezhenedel'nik NKP:* no. 27 (47) (December 11, 1924), p. 2; no. 19 (69) (May 8, 1925), p. 3; no. 46 (November 13, 1925), pp. 2–3; no. 35 (September 3, 1926), p. 2; and no. 30 (July 29, 1927), p. 3.

47. *Kul'turnoe stroitel'stvo Soiuza,* p. 16.

48. *NO,* p. 449.

49. *Zakonodatel'stvo o trude rabotnikov prosveshcheniia* (Moscow, 1931), pp. 105–11.

50. Ibid., p. 106.

51. Detailed information on teaching experience for December 1926 in *Narodnoe prosveshchenie v SSSR 1926–1927 uchebnyi god,* p. 242.

52. *NP,* no. 11 (November 1926), p. 20.

53. *Lunacharsky o narodnom obrazovanii,* p. 306.

54. I. Zakolodkin, "Kul'turnye nozhnitsy," (October 1928), p. 100.

55. *Sostoianie i perspektivy,* p. 17.

56. See n. 46 above. For a comparison of salaries: Roger A. Clark, *Soviet Economic Facts, 1917–1970* (New York, 1972), p. 26.

57. *NP,* no. 11 (November 1926), p. 20.

58. Zakolodkin, "Kul'turnye nozhnitsy," (October 1928), p. 100. The average worker was probably paid a lower wage than that guaranteed to teachers. See information on average workers' pay in Alec Nove, *An Economic History of the U.S.S.R.* (New York, 1969), p. 114; and E. H. Carr, *Socialism in One Country, 1924–1926,* vol. 1 (New York, 1958), p. 374.

59. *UG,* no. 34 (106) (August 28, 1926), p. 5.

60. *Ezhenedel'nik NKP,* no. 51 (December 24, 1926), pp. 1–2; *RP,* no. 1 (January 1926), p. 29; *Ezhenedel'nik NKP:* no. 25 (June 25, 1926), pp. 1–2; no. 3–4 (January 18, 1929), p. 9; and no. 7 (57) (February 20, 1925), pp. 7–8; *Prava uchashchikhsia i uchashchikh,* p. 243; *UG:* no. 51 (61) (November 7, 1925), p. 7; no. 4 (76) (January 28, 1926), p. 3; and no. 21 (93) (May 29, 1926), p. 5.

61. *Prava uchashchikhsia i uchashchikh,* p. 243.

62. *NU,* no. 10 (October 1924), p. 81.

63. Ibid., no. 5–6 (May–June 1927), p. 177.

64. *Lunacharsky o narodnom obrazovanii,* pp. 281–82; A. Lunacharsky, "Narodnoe prosveshchenie v RSFSR," *NP,* no. 7–8 (July–August 1925), pp. 13–14.

65. *NP,* no. 11 (November 1926), pp. 36–37.

66. *UG,* no. 43 (56) (September 17, 1925), p. 3.

67. *UG,* no. 31 (103) (August 7, 1926), p. 5.

68. *UG,* no. 32 (104) (August 14, 1926), p. 3.

69. *UG,* no. 16 (191) (April 13, 1928), p. 5.

70. *BORS:* no. 4 (December 23, 1922), p. 8; and no. 27 (May 24, 1923), p. 15; *UG:* no 4 (October 24, 1924), p. 6; no. 29 (42) (June 11, 1925), p. 5; and no. 56 (69) (December 10, 1925), p. 2.

71. *Statisticheskii sbornik po narodnomu prosveshcheniiu RSFSR 1926 g.,* pp. 76-77, 88-89, 102-103, 114-15, 122-24; and the partial census of December 1926 in *Prosveshchenie v RSFSR v 1926/27 uchebnom godu,* pp. 122-23. Even in urban areas, less than 10 percent of the elementary teachers had other work.

72. Income for 1927/28 in *Vseobshchee obiazatel'noe obuchenie: statisticheskii ocherk po dannym shkol'noi perepisi tekushchei statistiki prosveshcheniia* (Moscow, 1930), p. 68.

73. E. Lunin, "O chem pishet narodnyi uchitel'," *NU,* no. 6 (June 1924), p. 109; and *Ezhenedel'nik NKP,* no. 13 (34) (June 30, 1924), p. 2.

74. *Narodnoe prosveshchenie v SSSR 1926-1927 uchebnyi god,* pp. 37-40.

75. See the Central Committee's circular of September 9, 1921, and letter to all Party committees of September 18, 1921, in *NO,* p. 444. From Narkompros, in *Ezhenedel'nik NKP:* no. 21 (41) (October 15, 1924), p. 8; no. 7 (57) (February 20, 1925), p. 11; no. 25 (June 19, 1925), p. 11; and no. 31 (August 6, 1926), p. 3. Also issues of *UG:* no. 44 (57) (September 24, 1925), p. 7; and no. 49 (62) (0ctober 22, 1925), p. 3. Some inspectors arbitrarily transferred and dismissed teachers as reported in *UG:* no. 11 (24) (February 5, 1925), p. 3; no. 19 (32) (April 2, 1925), p. 3; and no. 20 (33) (April 9, 1923), p. 3.

76. *UG,* no. 42 (55) (September 10, 1925), p. 4; no. 35 (158) (August 26, 1927), p. 3; and no. 20 (195) (May 11, 1928), p. 5.

77. *UG,* no. 34 (209) (August 17, 1928), p. 4; and no. 35 (210) (August 24, 1928), p. 3.

78. *Pravda* (March 20, 1923), p. 4. For the results of the competition for which 400 teachers were nominated, *Narodnoe obrazovanie,* no. 1 (January 1960), pp. 106-107.

79. *UG:* no. 11 (24) (February 5, 1922), p. 6; no. 18 (31) (March 26, 1925), p. 3; no. 24 (37) (May 5, 1925), p. 6; no. 37 (50) (August 6, 1925), p. 4; and no. 55 (68) (December 3, 1925), p. 4. Also *RP,* no. 1 (January 1926), p. 30; *NU:* no. 2 (February 1925), pp. 86-89; and no. 2 (February 1926), p. 48; Sirotkin, "Kak rabotaiut shkoly," pp. 62-66; *BORS,* no. 29 (June 9, 1923), pp. 2-4.

80. *Ezhenedel'nik NKP,* no. 7 (57) (February 20, 1925), p. 5; *NP,* no. 11 (November, 1926), pp. 6, 36-37; and *Rezoliutsii piatogo Vserossiiskogo s"ezda zaveduiushchikh otdelami narodnogo obrazovaniia* (Moscow, 1926), p. 5.

81. Sirotkin, "Kak rabotaiut shkoly," p. 63.

82. *Narodnoe prosveshchenie v SSSR 1926-1927 uchebnyi god,* p. 42.

83. *NP,* no. 7 (1926), p. 13.

84. *Narodnoe prosveshchenie v SSSR 1926-1927 uchebnyi god,* p. 42.

85. Popov, *Shkoly sotsial'nogo vospitaniia,* p. 91; *Statisticheskii sbornik po narodnomu prosveshcheniia RSFSR 1926 g.,* pp. 76-77, 88-89, 102-103, 114-15, 122-24; and *Prosveshchenie v RSFSR v 1926/27 uchebnomu godu,* pp. 122-23.

86. *UG,* no. 15 (87) (April 17, 1926), p. 5.

87. *UG:* no. 43 (218) (October 19, 1928), p. 4; and no. 45 (220) (November 2, 1928), p. 6.

88. *Ezhenedel'nik NKP,* no. 52 (December 14, 1928), p. 38.

89. *Zakonodatel'stvo o trude,* p. 170.

90. P. Romanenko, "Uchitel'stvo i zhizn'," *NU,* no. 6 (June 1925), p. 90. See also similar problems in *UG,* no. 14 (86) (April 10, 1926), p. 2.

91. *UG,* no. 35 (158) (August 26, 1927), p. 3.

92. TsGA RSFSR, f. 298, op. 1, ed. khr. 45, l. 96.

93. See the summary of these reports by N. Ruberts, Academic Secretary of the Methods Bureau of the Novgorod Provincial Department of Education, in *Materialy po razrabotke programm GUS'a v sel'skoi shkole* (Novgorod, 1925), p. 15.

94. Esipov, "Voprosy uchitelei," p. 94.

95. Epshtein, "Shkola, kak ona est'," p. 20.

96. *NP,* no. 7 (1926), p. 132.

97. For example, *UG:* no. 8 (November 20, 1924), p. 3; and no. 46 (59) (October 3, 1925), p. 5.

98. *UG,* no. 4 (October 24, 1924), p. 6.

99. *Programmy GUS'a i obshchestvenno-politicheskoe vospitanie,* p. 73.

100. Avtukhov, *Programmy GUS'a i massovaia shkola,* p. 10.

101. *Materialy po razrabotke programm,* p. 16.

102. *VP,* no. 3 (March 1928), p. 129.

103. S. Dziubinsky, "O rabochei knige," *Sovetskoi shkole—novyi uchebnik,* no. 5 (1926), p. 74.

104. *Ezhenedel'nik NKP,* no. 20–21 (May 18, 1928), pp. 23–24.

105. TsGA RSFSR: f. 298, op. 1, ed. khr. 45, l. 96; and f. 298, op. 1, ed. khr. 41, l. 18 ob. See also the report by N. Ruberts in *Materialy po razrabotke programm,* p. 18; *RP,* no. 1 (January 1926), p. 28; *Biulleten' MONO,* no. 16–17 (June 25, 1925), p. 33; *Shkola i zhizn':* no. 5–6 (May–June 1925), p. 86; and no. 7–8 (July–August 1925), pp. 50–51; teachers' queries to inspectors in *V pomoshch' organizatoru,* p. 111; and Esipov's comments in Esipov, "Voprosy uchitelei," p. 94. See the following issues of *UG:* no. 8 (November 20, 1924), p. 3; no. 37 (50) (August 6, 1925), p. 3; and no. 38 (110) (September 25, 1926), p. 3. In 1925, Tomsk teachers voiced their opposition to the complex method because of its deleterious effect on the fundamentals: *Narodnoe obrazovanie v Tomskoi oblasti za sorok let sovetskoi vlasti* (Tomsk, 1957), p. 23. Even local experimental schools sought ways to focus on skills within the complex method: TsGA RSFSR, f. 1575, op. 10, ed. khr. 243, ll. 74–75.

106. V. Sirotkin, "Kak rabotaiut shkoly," p. 24; *UG,* no. 13 (December 25, 1924), p. 3.

107. *Shkola i zhizn',* no. 5–6 (May–June 1925), pp. 74–75.

108. M. Katlinsky, "Kak provesti normal'nyi uchebnyi god," *NU,* no. 9 (September 1927), pp. 15–16.

109. *VP,* no. 7 (July 1925), pp. 23–32; and *Voprosy shkoly II stupeni,* p. 147.

110. Korolev, *Sovetskaia shkola,* pp. 82–83. Journals appeared for: Russian language; Russian literature; foreign language; social studies; natural sciences; and for physics, chemistry, mathematics, and technology.

111. *VP:* no. 3–5 (March–May 1922), pp. 23–26; and no. 9 (September 1923), pp. 170–72.

112. *VP,* no. 4 (April 1928), pp. 139–40; and *Russkii iazyk v sovetskoi shkole,* no. 2 (1929), p. 134.

113. K. Ganshina, "Eshche ob organizatsii prepodavaniia inostrannykh iazykov," *VP,* no. 4–6 (April–June 1924), pp. 135–40; A. L. Lamakina, "Prepodavanie inostrannykh iazykov v trudovoi shkole," *NU,* no. 5–6 (May–June 1928), pp. 174–75; and the First All-Russian Conference of Teachers of Foreign Languages, Moscow, September 10, 1927, in *Inostrannyi iazyk v sovetskoi shkole,* ed. M. V. Sergievsky (Moscow, 1929).

114. *VP,* no. 3 (March 1926), pp. 48–49.

115. Ben Eklof, "The Adequacy of Basic Schooling in Rural Russia: Teachers and Their Craft, 1880–1914," *History of Education Quarterly,* vol. 26, no. 2 (Summer 1986), p. 206; and Eklof, *Russian Peasant Schools,* pp. 194-206.

116. Eklof, "The Adequacy of Basic Schooling," pp. 203–204.

117. *Statisticheskii ezhegodnik: sostoianie narodnogo obrazovaniia v SSSR (bez avtonomnykh respublik) za 1924/25 uch. god* (Moscow, 1926), p. xcvii; *Na poroge vtorogo desiatiletiia,* p. 78; and *NP,* no. 11 (November 1926), p. 30.

118. *Statisticheskii ezhegodnik: sostoianie narodnogo obrazovaniia v SSSR,* p. XCVII.

119. *Statisticheskii sbornik po narodnomu prosveshcheniiu RSFSR 1926 g.* (Moscow, 1927), pp. 76–77.

120. Popov, *Shkoly sotsial'nogo vospitaniia,* p. 91; and *Sostoianie i perspektivy,* p. 16.

121. *Statisticheskii sbornik po narodnomu prosveshcheniiu RSFSR 1926 g.,* pp. 82–83, 94–95, 108–109, 120–21, 124–25; *Narodnoe prosveshchenie v SSSR 1926–1927 uchebnyi god,* p. 242. See the 1926 survey of eighty-eight teachers in ten seven-year and secondary schools in the province of Nizhnii Novgorod in *Shkola i zhizn',* no. 12 (December 1926), p. 45. According to this survey, 16 percent had eleven to fifteen years of experience, 30 percent had fifteen or more years.

122. *Statisticheskii sbornik po narodnomu prosveshcheniiu RSFSR 1926 g.,* pp. 76–77, 88–89, 102–103, 114–15, 122–24.

123. *UG,* no. 6 (November 7, 1924), p. 7.

124. TsGA RSFSR, f. 1575, op. 5, ed. khr. 49, l. 26; *UG:* no. 20 (33) (April 9, 1925), p. 6; and no. 52 (175) (December 23, 1927), p. 4; *Shkola i zhizn',* no. 5–6 (May–June 1925), p. 76; *Ezhenedel'nik NKP,* no. 6 (35) (July 21, 1923), pp. 17–20.

125. TsGA RSFSR, f. 1575, op. 5, ed. khr. 49, l. 12 ob.

126. *Ezhenedel'nik NKP,* no. 2 (31) (June 23, 1923), p. 13.

127. *UG,* no. 5 (October 31, 1924), p. 5; and the earlier complaint that Narkompros and provincial departments of education had little control over the content of repreparation efforts: TsGA RSFSR, f. 1575, op. 5, ed. khr. 49, ll. 12 ob. - 13.

128. *NU,* no. 2 (February 1924), p. 68; *Shkola i zhizn',* no. 1 (January 1927), pp. 68–69.

129. E. Agalakova, "Teni uchitel'skoi zhizni," *NU,* no. 10 (October 1924), p. 81.

130. TsGA RSFSR, f. 1575, op. 5, ed. khr. 49, l. 2; *Ezhenedel'nik NKP:* no. 8 (March 5, 1926), p. 34; and no. 6 (February 11, 1927), pp. 4–5.

131. *Ezhenedel'nik NKP,* no. 35 (August 25, 1928), p. 14. The archives contain a particularly distressing account of a one-month course arranged in July 1922 by Narkompros for teachers of Turkish peoples. Of the ten provinces invited to send teachers, only six did so. Of the twenty-four individuals who actually came, two left after two days because of a lack of means and two more came down with typhus: TsGA RSFSR, f. 1575, op. 5, ed. khr. 49, l. 27.

132. TsGA RSFSR, f. 1575, op. 6, ed. khr. 244, l. 15.

133. In 1925/26 in the Russian Republic, little more than 50 percent of the teachers came from the peasantry and working class combined. In primary schools, over 50 percent of teachers were classified as children of the peasantry; 15 percent were children of salaried white collar employees (sluzhashchie), and 16 percent came from families in the free professions (doctors, lawyers, writers). For the secondary grades, 30 percent were categorized as children of salaried employees and 15 percent represented the free professions: *Statisticheskii sbornik po narodnomu prosveshcheniiu RSFSR 1926 g.,* pp. 82–83, 94–95, 108–109, 120–21. The next generation of teachers promised to be more representative of the working class and salaried personnel. In the mid-1920s, about 50 percent of the students in pedagogical technicums of the RSFSR were classified as peasantry in origin, slightly less than 10 percent as workers, and about 22 percent as intelligentsia. During the late 1920s, in pedagogical institutions, about 20 percent of the student body was categorized as workers, 33 percent as peasant, and about 35 percent as white collar: *Narodnoe prosveshchenie v RSFSR v osnovnykh pokazateliakh,* pp. 88, 90. In 1924/25, about 6 percent of the teachers in the Russian Republic were full or candidate members of the Party or Komsomol. One year later, the figure had risen to 8 percent and grew more rapidly after that: *Narodnoe prosveshchenie v RSFSR v tsifrakh,* p. 31; and *Statisticheskii sbornik po narodnomu prosveshcheniiu RSFSR 1926 g.,* pp. 82–83, 94–95, 108–109, 120–21, 124–25. By 1927/28, over 18 percent of the Republic's elementary teachers and over 12 percent of its secondary instructors were listed as full or candidate members of the Party or Komsomol: *Narodnoe prosveshchenie v RSFSR v tsifrakh,* p. 31; *Proveshchenie v RSFSR v 1926/27 uchebnom godu,* pp. 122–23. Simultaneously, the number of Komsomolites enrolled in the pedagogical technicums of the RSFSR grew from 23 percent of all

students in 1924/25 to over 43 percent in 1928/29: *Narodnoe prosveshchenie v RSFSR v osnovnykh pokazateliakh,* p. 88.

VIII. The ABC's beyond the School

1. Richard Stites, "Stalin: Utopian or Antiutopian?," pp. 85–86.
2. S. Shumov, "O chem pishet narodnyi uchitel'," *NU,* no. 5 (May 1925), pp. 90–91; and *UG,* no. 24 (199) (June 5, 1928), p. 3.
3. *UG,* no. 35 (158) (August 26, 1927), p. 3.
4. N. Kubantsev, "V glukikh uglakh," *NU,* no. 6 (June 1925), p. 84.
5. *UG,* no. 7 (79) (February 18, 1926), p. 4.
6. *UG,* no. 19 (194) (May 4, 1928), p. 5.
7. Romanenko, "Uchitel'stvo i zhizn'," pp. 88–89.
8. See complaints at the conference of its correspondents in *UG,* no. 12 (84) (March 25, 1926), p. 4; and also *NP,* no. 2 (1923), p. 63.
9. *Pravda:* (December 2, 1922), p. 3; (January 14, 1923), p. 5; and January 17, p. 5. *Zhurnalist,* no. 3 (1922), p. 38. William Burgess alerted me to this incident.
10. *UG,* no. 19 (32) (April 2, 1925), p. 5.
11. *UG,* no. 10 (185) (March 2, 1928), p. 3.
12. Katerina Clark, "The City versus the Countryside in Soviet Peasant Literature of the Twenties: A Duel of Utopias," in *Bolshevik Culture,* pp. 183–84.
13. *UG:* no. 34 (209) (August 17, 1928), p. 4; no. 35 (210) (August 24, 1928), p. 3; no. 24 (37) (May 5, 1925), p. 6; and no. 49 (62) (October 22, 1925), p. 3.
14. *NU,* no. 2 (February 1925), p. 12.
15. On January 1, 1925, Party members held 12 percent of the union's posts at the cantonal level, 36 percent at the district (uezd) level, and 56 percent at the provincial level. They comprised 87 percent of the membership of the union's Central Committee and 100 percent of its presidium: Ibid., p. 13. From 1926 to 1928, the number of communists holding district administrative posts grew from 40.9 percent to 44.6 percent of the total: V. R. Veselov, "Sozdanie i ukreplenie profsoiuza rabotnikov prosveshcheniia," *Sovetskaia pedagogika,* no. 7 (July 1985), p. 108.
16. Jeffrey Brooks, *When Russia Learned to Read: Literacy and Popular Literature, 1861–1917* (Princeton, 1985), pp. 3–34.
17. E. Lunin, "O chem pishet narodnyi uchitel'," p. 109; *Shkola i zhizn',* no. 2 (February 1926), p. 61; *UG,* no. 38 (110) (September 25, 1926), p. 3. For similar developments earlier in France, see Zeldin, *France,* p. 188.
18. *VP,* no. 3 (March 1929), pp. 22–24.
19. *VP,* no. 5 (May 1929), p. 119.
20. *Narodnoe prosveshchenie v RSFSR v osnovnykh pokazateliakh,* p. 28.
21. *Biulleten' MONO,* no. 7 (March 1, 1925), p. 12.
22. *VP,* No. 3 (March 1929), p. 21.
23. *Narodnoe prosveshchenie v RSFSR: statisticheskii sbornik,* p. 177; *Massovoe prosveshchenie v SSSR k 15-letiiu oktiabria,* p. 68.
24. *NU,* no. 1 (January 1924), p. 81.
25. *Shkola i zhizn',* no. 2 (February 1926), p. 61; and no. 5 (May, 1926), p. 56.
26. *UG,* no. 55 (68) (December 3, 1925), p. 4.
27. B. Gur'ianov, "Po stantsam Dona," *NU,* no. 7 (July 1926), p. 73. Peasants before the revolution distrusted any new methods of instruction, preferring an emphasis on literacy and numeracy: Ben Eklof, "Peasant Sloth Reconsidered: Strategies of Education and Learning in Rural Russia before the Revolution," *Journal of Social History,* vol. 14, no. 3 (Spring 1981), pp. 371–77.
28. *UG,* no. 12 (December 18, 1924), p. 3.
29. *VP:* no. 4–6 (April–June 1924), p. 197; and no. 4 (April 1925), p. 157; *Nash trud,* no. 7–8 (July–August 1925), p. 46.

30. Sirotkin, "Kak rabotaiut shkoly," p. 22.

31. Shumov, "O chem pishet narodnyi uchitel'," p. 88; *RP,* no. 1 (January 1926), p. 28; *VP,* no. 3 (March 1929), pp. 22–24, 25; Konovalova, "S uchitel'skoi konferentsii," p. 58. See comments in *UG* on letters it received from workers, peasants, and parents, complaining of the lack of discipline: *UG,* no. 6 (129) (February 5, 1927), p. 2.

32. *VP,* no. 3 (March 1929), p. 26.

33. N. Rosnitsky, *Litso derevni* (Moscow-Leningrad, 1926), p. 93. Peasants in mid-nineteenth-century France reacted similarly. A recent study has observed that these peasants "were not opposed to learning as such; they were opposed to sending their children to schools brought in by authorities from outside the community whose values and purposes, and in some cases even language, were different and suspect." See Laura S. Strumingher, *What Were Little Girls and Boys Made Of? Primary Education in Rural France, 1830–1880* (Albany, 1983), p. 35. And for the Russian peasantry of the late nineteenth century, Eklof, *Russian Peasant Schools.*

34. Rosnitsky, *Litso derevni,* p. 94.

35. Ibid., p. 95.

36. Ibid., p. 94.

37. Ibid., p. 98.

38. TsGA RSFSR, f. 298, op. 1, ed. khr. 41, l. 22; Avtukhov, p. 39; *VP,* no. 1 (January 1926), p. 20.

39. A. Lunacharsky, "Printsipi postroeniia trudovoi shkoly i programmy GUS'a," *NU,* no. 2 (February 1926), p. 28.

40. Shatsky, *Pedagogicheskie sochineniia,* vol. 2, p. 359; and vol. 3, p. 150.

41. Ibid., vol. 3, p. 150.

42. Ibid.

43. TsGA RSFSR, f. 298, op. 1, ed. khr. 45, l. 16 ob.

44. A. Kancheev, "O podgotovke k vysshei shkole," *Izvestiia* (November 3, 1926), p. 7.

45. A. I. Abinder, "Itogi vstupitel'nykh ispytanii v vysshie uchebnye zavedeniia RSFSR v 1927 g.," *Nauchnyi rabotnik,* no. 10 (October 1927), pp. 42–43, 45–48.

46. Ibid., pp. 49–51; I. I. Loboda, "Zametki ob ekzamenakh po obshchestvovedeniiu," *Nauchnyi rabotnik,* no. 10 (October 1927), pp. 55–57.

47. *Voprosy shkoly II stupeni,* p. 41.

48. *VP,* no. 1 (January 1927), p. 102; I. Veksler, "Po shkolam Leningrada," *NP,* no. 1 (January 1927), pp. 33–35, 37.

49. Veksler, "Po shkolam," p. 36.

50. S. Orshantsev, "Materialy k izucheniiu sovremennogo shkol'nika," *Na putiakh,* no. 7–8 (July–August 1927), pp. 78–79; *Trudy Pervoi Vsesoiuznoi konferentsii istorikov-marksistov* (Moscow, 1930), vol. 2, p. 474.

51. *VP,* no. 10 (October 1927), p. 106.

52. See, for example, reports by Narkompros inspectors in Gur'ianov, "Po stantsam Dona," p. 74; *VP,* no. 10 (October 1927), pp. 106–107; and Veksler, "Po shkolam Leningrada," pp. 35–36.

53. Kancheev, "O podgotovke," p. 7.

54. Biographical information is quite scarce. Mamet, born in 1899, headed the Methodology Section and lectured at the Communist University of Laborers of the East. Fridliand (1896–1941) helped Pokrovsky found the Society of Marxist Historians and taught at Sverdlov Communist University. Ioannisiani, if not at this time, would soon teach at the Moscow State Pedagogical Institute. Slutsky gained prominence in 1931, when one of his articles prompted Stalin's celebrated letter to the journal *Proletarskaia revoliutsiia.*

55. *Istorik-Marksist,* vol. 2 (1926), p. 288; A. Ioannisiani, "Istoriia v shkole II stupeni," *Istorik-Marksist,* vol. 3 (1927), p. 153; L. P. Mamet, "Prepodavanie istorii v industrial'no-tekhnicheskikh vuzakh," *Istorik-Marksist,* vol. 2 (1926), p. 236.

56. S. S. Krivtsov, "Mesto istorii v programmakh obshchestvenno-ekonomicheskikh vuzov," *Istorik-Marksist,* vol. 2 (1926), p. 233; Mamet, "Prepodavanie istorii," pp. 236–37; A. Ryndich, "Laboratornyi plan i prepodavanie istorii," *Istorik-Marksist,* vol. 3 (1927), pp. 179–80; *Trudy Pervoi Vsesoiuznoi konferentsii istorikov-marksistov,* vol. 2, pp. 478, 500, 586.

57. Ryndich, "Laboratoryni plan," pp. 179–80; Mamet, "Prepodavanie istorii," pp. 236–37; Ioannisiani, "Istoriia v shkole," p. 154; A. V. Shestakov, "Laboratornyi plan i rabochie tetradi po istorii," *Istorik-Marksist,* vol. 4 (1927), pp. 201–202; "Otchet o dokladakh, prochitannykh v O-ve za pervoe polugode 1928 g.," *Istorik-Marksist,* vol. 9 (1928), pp. 125–26; A. Ioannisiani, "Rabochie knigi po obshchestvovedeniiu," *Istorik-Marksist,* vol. 7 (1928), pp. 212, 214; *Istorik-Marksist,* vol. 6 (1927), pp. 295–96.

58. *Istorik-Marksist,* vol. 2 (1926), p. 287; A. Ioannisiani, "Istoriia v shkole," p. 165; A. Ioannisiani, "Rabochie knigi," pp. 207–208.

59. *Pravda* (January 4, 1921), p. 1. The article was titled "Pedagogical Futurism and the Tasks of the Soviet School."

60. *Kommunisticheskaia partiia Sovetskogo Soiuza v rezoliutsiiakh i resheniiakh, s"ezdov, konferentsii i plenumov TsK* [henceforth *KPSS v rezoliutsiiakh*], vol. 2 (8th ed.; Moscow, 1970), p. 246.

61. *Pravda* (November 21, 1923), p. 1.

62. I. V. Stalin, *Sochineniia,* vol. 7 (Moscow, 1952), pp. 87–88.

63. *NO,* pp. 265–67, 270; and *Direktivy VKP po prosveshcheniiu,* p. 136.

64. Konovalova, "S uchitel'skoi konferentsii," pp. 58–59.

65. Lysiakov, "Iz grudy," p. 67.

66. E. Gaidovskaia, "Pervye shagi," *NU,* no. 7 (July 1926), pp. 76–78.

67. *Trudovoe zakonodatel'stvo o rabotnikakh prosveshcheniia* (Moscow, 1930), p. 22.

68. *UG,* no. 12 (84) (March 25, 1926), p. 4.

69. *NP,* no. 7 (1926), p. 133.

70. *NO,* p. 414.

71. *UG,* no. 43 (115) (October 30, 1926), p. 5.

72. *KP,* no. 3 (1934), p. 17.

73. *UG:* no. 38 (110) (September 25, 1926), p. 4; and no. 3 (126) (January 15, 1927), p. 3.

74. "Vsesoiuznyi s"ezd rabotnikov prosveshcheniia SSSR," *Na putiakh,* no. 3 (March 1929), p. 46.

75. *UG,* no. 56 (69) (December 10, 1925), p. 2.

76. *UG,* no. 20 (195) (May 11, 1928), p. 5.

77. *Voprosy shkol II stupeni,* p. 35.

78. *UG,* no. 51 (64) (November 7, 1927), p. 6.

79. *Podgotovka kadrov v SSSR 1917–1931 gg.* (Moscow-Leningrad, 1933), p. 37.

80. *Biulleten' Narodnogo Komissariata Prosveshcheniia* [henceforth *Biulleten' NKP*], no. 18 (March 25, 1932), p. 13.

81. *NU,* no. 1 (January 1925), p. 41.

82. As quoted by B. Esipov, "Perekhod massovoi shkoly k rabote po novym programmam," in *Programmy GUS'a i obshchestvenno-politicheskoe vospitanie* (Moscow, 1925), p. 186.

IX. Policy Running After Practice

1. TsGA RSFSR, f. 298, op. 1, ed. khr. 41, ll. 1–3; *Ezhenedel'nik NKP:* no. 25 (45) (November 27, 1924), p. 12; and no. 12 (62) (March 27, 1925), p. 12. The Moscow Department of Education registered the same complaint in *Biulleten' MONO,* no. 18–19 (September 25, 1924), pp. 26ff.

2. TsGA RSFSR, f. 298: op. 1, ed. khr. 45, ll. 16, 96; op. 1, ed. khr. 41, l. 20; and op. 1, ed. khr. 41, l. 22.

3. Stolee, pp. 59–62.

4. TsGA RSFSR, f. 298, op. 1, ed. khr. 41, ll. 1–3.

5. Ibid., l. 4.

6. See TsGA RSFSR, f. 298, op. 1, ed. khr. 21, ll. 40, 50 ob, 83–83 ob. 100–100 ob., 111 for problems between the Political and Pedagogical Sections of the State Academic Council and within the Pedagogical Section.

7. Ia. Bauer, "Pervye itogi chistki Narkomprosa," *NP,* no. 2 (1930), pp. 1–3.

8. TsGA RSFSR, f. 298, op. 1, ed. khr. 45, l. 8 ob.

9. *BORS,* no. 28 (June 2, 1923), p. 7.

10. TsGA RSFSR, f. 298, op. 1, ed. khr. 45, l. 16 ob.

11. *BORS,* no. 15 (March 10, 1923), p. 6.

12. *UG,* no. 3 (October 17, 1924), p. 7.

13. *Ezhenedel'nik NKP,* no. 27 (47) (December 11, 1924), p. 10.

14. I. G. Avtukhov and I. D. Martynenko, *Programmy GUS'a i massovaia shkola* (2nd ed.; Moscow, 1925).

15. I. G. Avtukhov (compiler), *Kak prorabatyvat' uchitel'stvu programmy GUS'a: dlia shkol pervoi stupeni* (Moscow, 1926).

16. Avtukhov, *Programmy GUS'a i massovaia shkola,* pp. 14–17, 35, 64, 99–108.

17. Ibid., p. 11. Also Avtukhov, *Kak prorabatyvat' uchitel'stvu,* pp. 9–10.

18. Avtukhov, *Programmy GUS'a i massovaia shkola,* pp. 65–79.

19. Ibid., pp. 81 ff.

20. Ibid., p. 39.

21. *UG,* no. 58 (71) (December 24, 1925), p. 5.

22. *Programmy GUS'a i obshchestvenno-politicheskoe vospitanie,* pp. 79–81, 94.

23. Ibid., p. 250.

24. *Pravda* (June 24, 1926), p. 1.

25. *NP,* no. 11 (November 1926), p. 41.

26. B. P. Esipov, "Chto nam davalo obshchenie s Nadezhdoi Konstantinovnoi Krupskoi," *Sovetskaia pedagogika,* no. 2 (February 1964), p. 44.

27. *Programmy GUS'a i obshchestvenno-politicheskoe vospitanie,* pp. 180–81; B. Esipov, "O novykh programmakh dlia shkol I stupeni," *NU,* no. 7 (July 1924), pp. 60–65; *UG:* no. 42 (55) (September 10, 1925), p. 2; and no. 41 (54) (September 3, 1925), p. 4.

28. *UG:* no. 2 (October 10, 1924), p. 3; and no. 44 (57) (September 24, 1925), p. 4.

29. *UG,* no. 2 (October 10, 1924), p. 3.

30. Esipov, "Voprosy uchitelei," p. 87.

31. Ibid., p. 85.

32. B. Esipov, "O mestnykh kompleksnykh programmakh" and "O nekotorykh sovremennykh napravleniiakh v ponimanii kompleksnosti" in *Programmy GUS'a i mestnaia rabota nad nim,* pp. 9–58. Also: TsGA RSFSR, f. 1575, op. 10, ed. khr. 243, ll. 5–6.

33. Esipov, "O nekotorykh sovremennykh napravleniiakh," p. 44.

34. Esipov, "Voprosy uchitelei," p. 86.

35. At the Library of the Academy of Pedagogical Sciences in Moscow, I examined many curricula issued by provincial departments of education during the 1920s. They are catalogued by year. Those adhering to the plans of the Commissariat of Enlightenment were published in Viatka, Tsaritsyn, and Orenburg in 1921; in Orel and Tula in 1923; in Tula in 1924; and in Ust'sy sol'sk, Vladivostok, Novgorod, and Syzran in 1925.

36. See curricula at the Library of Academy of Pedagogical Sciences published in Kursk in 1921 and 1922; in Perm', Moscow, Vladimir, Velikii Ustiug, Roslavl', and Novgorod in 1922; in Petrograd, Ivanovo-Voznesensk, Vladivostok, and Ekaterinburg in 1923; in Ekaterinburg in 1924; in Leningrad in 1925; and in Saratov and Penza in 1926.

37. *Programmy-minimum dlia edinoi trudovoi shkoly 1-i i 2-i stupeni* (Petrograd, 1923), p. v.

38. *Programmy dlia shkol semiletok i pervykh trekh grupp shkol II-oi stupeni* (Ekaterinburg, 1924); *Programmy dlia III i IV grupp shkol I stupeni* (Ekaterinburg, 1924).

39. *Programmnyi material dlia shkol I-i stupeni po III-mu i IV-mu godam obucheniia* (Ivanovo-Voznesensk, 1927), especially pp. 6, 8, 91, 94ff. Although printed in 1927, this curriculum was designed before receipt of the pivotal curriculum that year from Narkompros.

40. *Programmy I-i stupeni edinoi trudovoi shkoly* (Saratov, 1922), p. 3; *Uchebnyi plan i programmy edinoi trudovoi shkoly I stupeni (4-kh letki)* (Samara, 1922), p. iii; *Programmy dlia shkol pervoi i vtoroi stupeni* (Ivanovo-Voznesensk, 1923), pp. 3-4; *Programma minimum dlia shkoly I stupeni s chetyrekhletnim kursom obuchenii* (Ekaterinburg, 1923), pp. 3-7; *Novye programmy 1 i 2 godov obucheniia shkol I-i stupeni* (Nikol'sk, 1924), p. 5; *Programmy edinoi trudovoi shkoly II stupeni (5, 6, 7, 8 i 9 gody obucheniia)* (Khabarovsk-Vladivostok, 1926), p. 3.

41. *Programmy dlia shkol 1-i stupeni, Vladimirskoi gubernii* (Vladimir, 1922), p. 7.

42. *Programmnye materialy dlia edinoi trudovoi shkoly I stupeni (chetyrekhletki)* (Samara, 1923), p. 3.

43. *Novye programmy 1, 2, 3 i 4 godov obucheniia shkol I-i stupeni* (V. Ustiug, 1925), p. 7.

44. *Kompleksnye programmy shkol I stupeni na 1925-26 uchebnyi god* (Ust'sy sol'sk, 1925), p. iii.

45. *VP*, no. 8 (October 1, 1922), pp. 180-81.

46. E. Gur'ianov, "Standartizatsiia shkol'noi uspeshnosti," *NU*, no. 6 (June 1926), p. 22.

47. Sirotkin, "Kak rabotaiut shkoly," pp. 86-87.

48. TsGA RSFSR, f. 298, op. 1, ed. khr. 41, l. 4 ob.

49. *Informatsionnyi Biulleten' Otdela Narodnogo Obrazovaniia* (Moscow), no. 12-13 (August 1-15, 1921), pp. 1-34.

50. *VP*, no. 4 (April 1923), pp. 1-2, 203-204.

51. Ibid., pp. 7-9.

52. Ibid., no. 10 (October 1923), pp. 226-27.

53. Ibid., no. 11 (November 1924), p. 99.

54. *Programmy V, VI i VII grupp shkoly 7-letki gor. Moskvy i Moskovskoi gubernii* (Moscow, 1925); *VP*, no. 6 (June 1925), p. 133.

55. *VP*, no. 1 (January 1926), pp. 24-32.

56. *Praktika raboty po programme GUS'a; rabochaia kniga uchitelei I stupeni*, vol. 1 (Moscow, 1926), p. 6, and vol. 2 (Moscow, 1926), p. 6.

57. Ibid., vol. 1, p. 50; vol. 2, pp. 46-47.

58. Ibid., vol. 1, p. 51; vol. 2, pp. 46, 48.

59. *VP*, no. 10 (October 1926), pp. 20ff.

60. *Programmy dlia vtorogo kontsentra shkoly semiletki (V, VI i VII gody obucheniia)* (Moscow, 1926), p. 12.

61. *Ezhenedel'nik Moskovskogo Otdela Narodnogo Obrazovaniia* [henceforth *Ezhenedel'nik MONO,*], no. 48 (December 30, 1926), p. 20.

62. *Ezhenedel'nik MONO:* no. 5-6 (February 15, 1927) pp. 12-14; and no. 13-14 (April 26, 1927), pp. 3-4.

63. I found only two curricula specifically associating systematic instruction with preparation of students for higher education: *Programmy dlia shkol 1-i stupeni, Vladimirskoi gubernii* (Vladimir, 1922), p. 4; *Programma semiletnei trudovoi shkoly* (Roslavl', 1922), p. 1.

64. *NO*, p. 150.

65. *Direktivy .VKP(b) po voprosam prosveshcheniia*, pp. 283-84.

66. *Programmy GUS'a i obshchestvenno-politicheskoe vospitanie*, p. 117. Also: *Uchitel'stvo na novykh putiakh*, pp. 181-82.

67. P. I. Pidkasistyi, *N. K. Krupskaia o soderzhanii v sovetskoi shkole* (Moscow, 1962), pp. 56–57, based on archival records.

68. TsGA RSFSR, f. 298, op. 1, ed. khr. 41, ll. 4 - 4 ob.

69. *Voprosy shkoly II stupeni,* pp. 132–34, 158.

70. TsGA RSFSR, f. 298, op. 1, ed. khr. 41, l. 5.

71. A. Radchenko, "Zatrudneniia v rabote po novym programmam i puti k ikh razresheniiu," in *Programmy GUS'a i mestnaia rabota nad nim,* p. 91.

72. *UG,* no. 42 (155) (September 10, 1925), p. 2.

73. TsGA RSFSR, f. 298, op. 1: ed. khr. 34, ll. 22–23, 34; ed. khr. 35, ll. 16 ob., 20; ed. khr. 59, ll. 14, 28, 31, 48–76.

74. Ibid., ed. khr. 41, ll. 18–19.

75. Ibid., ll. 19 ob - 20.

76. Ibid., l. 18.

77. Ibid., ll. 24–25. It also hoped that the commission would encourage manufacture and distribution of these items.

78. Ibid., ll. 60–60 ob, 65–84.

79. Ibid., ll. 62–64, 87.

80. Ibid., l. 62.

81. Ibid., l. 95.

82. Ibid., l. 62.

83. TsGA RSFSR, f. 2306, op. 69, ed. khr. 660, 1.2.

84. From my interview with Mikhail Nikolaevich Skatkin at the Institute of General Pedagogy of the Academy of Pedagogical Sciences, Moscow, December 2, 1985. Oskar Anweiler points out that Shatsky was more concerned with practicality than ideology or pedagogical theory. Oskar Anweiler, "Leben und Wirksamkeit des Russischen Paedogogen Stanislaw Teofilowitsch Shazkij," *International Review of Education,* vol. 10, no. 2 (1964), pp. 141–61; and Anweiler, *Geschichte,* pp. 321–29.

85. Shatsky, *Pedagogicheskie sochineniia,* vol. 2, pp. 330–91; vol. 3, pp. 25–30, 74–104; and especially the article "Blizhe k uchiteliu," vol. 4, pp. 164–75.

86. Ibid., vol. 2, pp. 366, 373.

87. Ibid., p. 257. Shatsky was further discouraged by efforts to cut the number of schools and personnel at his Experimental Station: Shatsky, *Pedagogicheskie sochineniia,* vol. 4, p. 256.

88. Ibid., vol. 4, p. 198.

89. Ibid., vol. 2, p. 275.

90. See n. 85 above.

91. *Voprosy shkoly II stupeni,* p. 164. Of the sixty-eight teachers who could vote, 47 percent were members of the Communist Party and 39 percent taught social studies and literature.

92. Ibid., pp. 176–77, 180–81, 183.

93. Ibid., pp. 188–90.

94. Ibid., pp. 191–201.

95. Ibid., p. 204.

96. "Iz raboty Nauchno-Pedagogicheskoi Sektsii," *Na putiakh,* no. 5–6 (May–June 1926), pp. 61–63. Krupskaya repeated this appeal in her article, "K voprosu o prepodavanii literatury v II stupeni," *Na putiakh,* no. 12 (December 1926), pp. 3–5.

97. "Iz raboty Nauchno–Pedagogicheskoi Sektsii," pp. 64–66, 85.

98. Ibid., pp. 66–69.

99. Ibid., p. 75.

100. Pokrovsky's presentation to a Conference of Social Science Teachers in Moscow, September 1926, in M. N. Pokrovsky, "Istoriia i sovremennost'," *Na putiakh,* no. 10 (October 1926), pp. 94–111; M. Pokrovsky, "Ob obshchestvovedenii," *Kommunisticheskaia revoliutsiia,* no. 19 (October 1926), pp. 51–61; and M. Pokrovsky, "K

preopodavaniiu obshchestvovedeniia v nashikh shkolakh," *Na putiakh,* no. 11 (November 1926), pp. 40–45. Also Pokrovsky's comments at sessions of the Methodology Section of the Society of Marxist Historians: *Istorik-Marksist,* vol. 3 (1927), pp. 167–71; and vol. 4 (1927), pp. 195–98.

101. Pokrovsky, "Istoriia i sovremennost'," pp. 97–98; Pokrovsky, "Ob obshchestvovedenii," pp. 56–60; Pokrovsky, "K prepodavaniiu obshchestvovedeniia," p. 44; *Istorik-Marksist,* vol. 3 (1927), pp. 167–71; and vol. 4 (1927), pp. 196–98.

102. *Istorik-Marksist,* vol. 3 (1927), pp. 170–71.

103. Pokrovsky, "Istoriia i sovremennost'," p. 101; Pokrovsky, "Ob obshchestvovedenii," p. 61; Pokrovsky, "K prepodavaniiu obshchestvovedeniia," p. 45; *Istorik-Marksist,* vol. 4 (1927), p. 196. Others shared Pokrovsky's concern: M. Pistrak, "O kharaktere programm po obshchestvovedeniiu dlia 5, 6 i 7 godov obucheniia," *Obshchestvovedenie v trudovoi shkole* (henceforth *OTS*), no. 1 (1927), p. 14.

104. *Istorik-Marksist,* vol. 3 (1927), pp. 167, 170; Pokrovsky, "Istoriia i sovremennost'," p. 109.

105. Pidkasistyi, *N. K. Krupskaia,* p. 57; Ravkin, *Sovetskaia shkola,* p. 99.

106. TsGA RSFSR, f. 298, op. 1, ed. khr. 41, ll. 36–38, 124–27 ob. See the summary of the May 19 session in *UG,* no. 20 (92) (May 22, 1926), p. 2.

107. TsGA RSFSR, f. 298, op. 1, ed. khr. 41, ll. 124–124 ob, 36.

108. Ibid, l. 38.

109. Ibid., ll. 126 ob - 127.

110. Ibid., l. 38.

111. Archival records refer to Esipov's attendance and not to any remarks he may have made.

112. TsGA RSFSR, f. 298, op. 1, ed. khr., 37, l. 209. *UG,* no. 26 (149) (June 24, 1927), p. 3, and no. 29 (152) (July 15, 1927), p. 3. See also *V pomoshch' organizatoru,* pp. 113–14, 123.

113. TsGA RSFSR, f. 298, op. 1, ed. khr. 41, ll. 37, 125 ob - 126.

114. Ibid., ll. 37, 125–26.

115. Epshtein, "Shkola, kak ona est'," pp. 21–22.

116. *NP,* no. 7 (July 1926), p. 134.

117. Ibid.

118. *Programmy GUS'a dlia pervogo i vtorogo godov sel'skoi shkoly I stupeni (s izmeneniiami, sdelannymi na osnovanii ucheta opyta)* (Moscow, 1926). See Esipov's summary of the major changes in *UG,* no. 34 (106) (August 28, 1926), p. 3.

119. *Proekty programm shkoly II stupeni (I kontsentr—5, 6, i 7 gody obucheniia)* (Moscow, 1926), pp. 32, 55ff.

120. Ibid., pp. 33ff.

121. "Zamechaniia k programme po obshchestvovedeniiu (dlia 1-go kontsentra II stupeni, 5, 6 i 7-i gg. obucheniia)," *Na putiakh,* no. 9 (September 1926), pp. 77–78.

122. *UG,* no. 46 (118) (November 20, 1926), p. 3.

123. These instructions were reprinted a year later in *Programmy i metodicheskie zapiski edinoi trudovoi shkoly,* Vyp. 2: *Gorodskie i sel'skie shkoly I stupeni. Metodicheskie zapiski k programmam* (Moscow-Leningrad, 1927), pp. 262–63.

124. *Ezhenedel'nik NKP,* no. 14 (April 8, 1927), p. 7. The Collegium hoped in part to accommodate entrance requirements of higher educational institutions and technicums.

125. *NP,* no. 3 (March 1927), p. 3.

126. For primary schools: *Programmy i metodicheskie zapiski edinoi trudovoi shkoly,* vyp. 1: *Gorodskie i sel'skie shkoly I stupeni. Programmy* (Moscow-Leningrad, 1927) and *Programmy i metodicheskie zapiski edinoi trudovoi shkoly,* vyp. 2: *Gorodskie i sel'skie shkoly I stupeni. Metodicheskie zapiski k programmam* (Moscow-Leningrad, 1927). For grades five through seven: *Programmy i metodicheskie zapiski edinoi trudovoi shkoly,* vyp. 3: *1-i kontsentr*

gorodskoi shkoly II stupeni (Moscow-Leningrad, 1927). For grades eight and nine: *Programmy i metodicheskie zapiski edinoi trudovoi shkoly,* vyp. 6: *2–i kontsentr shkoly II stupeni. Programmy spetsial'nykh predmetov* (Moscow-Leningrad, 1927).

127. *Programmy i metodicheskie zapiski,* vyp. 3, p. 18.

128. Ibid., p. 24.

129. *OTS:* no. 1 (1927), pp. 18–39, 49–73; and no. 2–3 (1927), pp. 109–16.

130. *Programmy i metodicheskie zapiski,* vyp. 1, p. 14.

131. *Programmy i metodicheskie zapiski,* vyp. 2, p. 155.

132. *Programmy i metodicheskie zapiski,* vyp. 1, p. 16.

133. *Programmy i metodicheskie zapiski,* vyp. 3, p. 15.

134. Ibid., p. 36.

135. Ibid., p. 31.

136. Ibid., p. 30.

137. *Programmy i metodicheskie zapiski,* vyp. 1, p. 4.

138. Ibid., pp. 5, 7; *Programmy i metodicheskie zapiski,* vyp. 3, pp. 26–29.

139. *UG,* no. 2 (177) (January 6, 1928), p. 5.

140. *Shkola i zhizn',* no. 1 (January 1928), p. 99.

141. *Programmy III i IV godov obucheniia dlia sel'skoi shkoly I stupeni* (Kursk, 1927); *Sibirskii variant programm GUS'a (dlia gorodskikh shkol I stupeni sibirskogo kraia)* (Novosibirsk, 1927), especially pp. 48–51; and *Sibirskii variant programm GUS'a (dlia sel'skikh shkol I stupeni Sibirskogo kraia)* (Novosibirsk, 1927). One program, however, lagged behind developments with an unusual adherence to a thematic approach: *Programmy dlia shkol I–i stupeni Sverdlovskogo okruga* (Sverdlovsk, 1927).

142. *Programmy-minimum dlia V, VI, VII godov obucheniia shkoly-semiletki sotsvosa* (Moscow, 1927).

143. Ibid., p. 6.

144. Ibid., p. 51.

145. *Shkola i zhizn',* no. 5–6 (May–June 1928), p. 6.

146. M. Epshtein, "Voprosy massovoi obshcheobrazovatel'noi shkoly," *NU,* no. 1 (January 1927), p. 26; *UG,* no. 47 (170) (November 18, 1927), p. 3; and no. 4 (179) (January 20, 1928), p. 3.

147. M. Krupenina, "O vospitatel'nykh zadachakh shkoly II stupeni," *Na putiakh,* no. 9 (September 1928), p. 20.

X. Komsomol and the Technical Lobby

1. I. V. Chuvashev, "Voprosy trudovogo i politekhnicheskogo vospitaniia," *NU,* no. 2 (February 1930), p. 74.

2. *Chetvertyi s"ezd RKSM,* p. 238.

3. Ibid., p. 241.

4. *Piatyi Vserossiiskii s"ezd RKSM, 11–19 oktiabria 1922 goda. Stenograficheskii otchet* (Moscow-Leningrad, 1927), p. 261.

5. Ibid., p. 206.

6. Ibid., p. 215.

7. Ibid., p. 317.

8. *Shestoi s"ezd Rossiiskogo leninskogo kommunisticheskogo soiuza molodezhi, 12–18 iiulia 1924 goda. Stenograficheskii otchet* (Moscow-Leningrad, 1924), p. 131.

9. *Chetvertyi s"ezd RKSM,* p. 250; *Piatyi s"ezd RKSM,* pp. 317–18; *Rezoliutsii i postanovleniia VI Vsesoiuznogo s"ezda RLKSM* (Moscow, 1924), pp. 137–39; the Third Conference of Commissariats of Enlightenment, December 1923, in "Tret'e soveshchanie narkomprosov soiuznykh i avtonomnykh respublik SSSR," *NP,* no. 1 (10) (1924), pp. 70, 78; and comments by Komsomol delegates Rudnev and Tarasov at the Conference of Secondary Schools, July 1925, in *Voprosy shkoly II stupeni,* pp. 44, 93.

10. *Piatyi s"ezd RKSM,* p. 317; *Shestoi s"ezd RLKSM,* pp. 128–29; *Sed'moi Vsesoiuznii s"ezd leninskogo kommunisticheskogo soiuza molodezhi, 11–22 marta 1926 goda. Stenografi-cheskii otchet* (Moscow-Leningrad, 1926), p. 505; Andrei Shokhin, "Osnovy polozh-eniia o shkolakh fabzavucha," *NP,* no. 2 (1923), p. 51.

11. *Ezhenedel'nik NKP,* no. 1 (30) (June 16, 1923), p. 15.

12. TsGA RSFSR, f. 298, op. 1, ed. khr. 45, l. 61; and *Shestoi s"ezd RLKSM,* pp. 229–30, 271. See also Shokhin's *Komsomol'skaia derevnia,* (2nd ed.; Moscow-Petrograd, 1923), pp. 63–64.

13. *Rezoliutsii i postanovleniia VI Vsesoiuznogo s"ezda,* pp. 14–15.

14. Krupskaya, *Pedagogicheskie sochineniia,* vol. 10, p. 491; *NP,* no. 6–7 (15–16) (1924), pp. 49–53. On the number: I. V. Chuvashev, "Voprosy trudovogo i poli-tekhnicheskogo vospitaniia," *NU,* no. 12 (December 1929), p. 128.

15. Rudnev's comments in *Voprosy shkoly II stupeni,* pp. 137–42.

16. *NO,* pp. 23, 25–29, 34–36, 41.

17. *Na poroge vtorogo desiatiletiia,* pp. 49–50; *Pedagogicheskaia entsiklopediia,* vol. 2 (Moscow, 1928), col. 282; *Massovoe prosveshchenie v SSSR (k itogam pervoi piatiletki),* pp. 40–41.

18. Blinchevsky, *Professional'no-tekhnicheskoe obrazovanie,* p. 38; Dmitrieva, *Partiinoe rukovodstvo,* p. 34; *Prosveshchenie v RSFSR v 1926/27 uchebnom godu,* p. 66.

19. *Podgotovka kadrov v SSSR,* p. 19; Veselov, *Professional'no-tekhnicheskoe obrazovanie,* pp. 190, 208, 261; B. Makovsky, "Klientura fabzavucha," *NP,* no. 4 (1928), p. 119; Zakolodkin, "Kul'turnye nozhnitsy" (December 1928), p. 70.

20. V. M. Khachaturian, "Formirovanie shkoly krest'ianskoi molodezhi (ShKM) kak shkoly novogo tipa," *Doklady Akademii Pedagogicheskikh nauk RSFSR,* no. 1 (1963), p. 66.

21. Study of 286 ShKMs in December 1925 in *NP,* no. 1 (1927), pp. 61–62.

22. R. Kharitonov, "Fabrichno-semiletka i zadachi klassovogo vospitaniia detei rabochikh," *NP,* no. 1 (January 1929), pp. 70–71.

23. *Lunacharsky o narodnom obrazovanii,* p. 176.

24. Lunacharsky's comments from 1923 to 1925 in "Tret'e soveshchanie narkom-prosov," p. 70; and *Lunacharsky o narodnom obrazovanii,* pp. 214, 287; *Chetvertyi s"ezd RKSM,* pp. 218, 227–29; *Piatyi s"ezd RKSM,* pp. 222–23. Also Krupskaya's embrace of the FZU at the Fifth Komsomol Congress, pp. 211–12.

25. "Tret'e soveshchanie narkomprosov," pp. 66–78; Svadkovsky, *Rabochaia kniga,* pp. 474–76; *Voprosy shkoly II stupeni.*

26. "Tret'e soveshchanie narkomprosov," p. 65.

27. *Ezhenedel'nik NKP,* no. 2 (50) (November 13, 1923), p. 7.

28. *Ezhenedel'nik NKP:* no. 27 (July 4, 1926), pp. 6–9; no. 31 (August 1, 1926), pp. 5–6; and no. 28 (July 5, 1928), pp. 4–8.

29. *Ezhenedel'nik NKP,* no. 27 (July 4, 1926), p. 7; no. 28 (July 5, 1928), p. 7.

30. *Ezhenedel'nik NKP,* no. 36 (September 9, 1927), pp. 8–9.

31. *Ezhenedel'nik NKP,* no. 1 (22) (January 15, 1924), pp. 36–37.

32. *NP,* no. 6–7 (15–16) (1924), pp. 49–52; *Ezhenedel'nik NKP,* no. 21 (71) (May 22, 1925), pp. 10–18.

33. *Shestoi s"ezd RLKSM,* p. 22.

34. Korolev, *Sovetskaia shkola,* pp. 74–76; and Korolev, *Ocherki, 1921–31,* pp. 88–90.

35. Makovsky, "Klientura fabzavucha," p. 119.

36. Dmitrieva, *Partiinoe rukovodstvo,* p. 69.

37. Makovsky, "Klientura fabzavucha," p. 115.

38. *Ezhenedel'nik NKP:* no. 9 (August 16, 1923), p. 7; and no. 22 (72) (May 31, 1925), pp. 8–9; the 1924 statute in *NO,* pp. 378–79; and Veselov, *Professional'no-tekhnicheskoe obrazovanie,* p. 232.

39. *Materialy po proftekhnicheskomu obrazovaniiu v shveinoi promyshlennosti* (Moscow,

1926); *Metodicheskie materialy po proftekhnicheskomu obrazovaniiu metallopromyshlennosti* (Moscow-Leningrad, 1927); and *Materialy po proftekhnicheskomu obrazovaniiu v kozhpromyshlennosti* (Moscow, 1927). Veselov, *Professional'no-tekhnicheskoe obrazovanie,* pp. 242–45, for a discussion of teaching methods.

40. TsGA RSFSR, f. 298, op. 1, ed. khr. 45, l. 8.

41. Svadkovsky, *Rabochaia kniga,* p. 474; *Ezhenedel'nik NKP,* no. 16 (37) (August 8, 1924), pp. 1–3. For circumstances surrounding this session, Fitzpatrick, *Education and Social Mobility,* p. 56.

42. Svadkovsky, *Rabochaia kniga,* p. 476.

43. Ibid., p. 475; *Ezhenedel'nik NKP,* no. 16 (37) (August 8, 1924), p. 3.

44. Svadkovsky, *Rabochaia kniga,* p. 476.

45. Ibid.

46. *Ezhenedel'nik NKP,* no. 22–23 (42–43) (October 30, 1924), pp. 15–16.

47. TsGA RSFSR, f. 298, op. 1, ed. khr. 41, ll. 49 ob - 50; *Uchitel'stvo na novykh putiakh,* p. 186; "Rabota nauchno-pedagogicheskoi sektsii GUS'a," *NP,* no. 7–8 (July-August 1925), p. 220; A. Lunacharsky, "Narodnoe prosveshchenie v RSFSR," *NP,* no. 7–8 (July-August 1925), p. 20; M. Pistrak, "K voprosu o professionalizatsii II kontsentra II stupeni," *NP,* no. 10–11 (1925), pp. 134–147; *Ezhenedel'nik NKP,* no. 38 (September 18, 1925), pp. 13–16. *Vserossiiskii s"ezd zaveduiushchikh otdelami narodnogo obrazovaniia,* p. 7; *Biulleten' MONO,* no. 20–21 (July 20, 1925), p. 26.

48. *Biulleten' MONO,* no. 20–21 (July 20, 1925), p. 26.

49. *Voprosy shkoly II stupeni,* pp. 45–46, 52, 55, 57, 75. On this point, Komsomol's representatives agreed: p. 45.

50. Ibid., pp. 52, 57.

51. Ibid., p. 75.

52. *Ezhenedel'nik NKP,* no. 38 (September 18, 1925), pp. 13–16.

53. *Programmy i metodicheskie zapiski edinoi trudovoi shkoly,* vyp. 6: *2-i kontsentr shkoly II stupeni. Programmy spetsial'nykh predmetov* (Moscow-Leningrad, 1927), pp. 14–16; *Programmy i metodicheskie zapiski edinoi trudovoi shkoly,* vyp. 5: *2-i kontsentr shkoly II stupeni. Programmy obshcheobrazovatel'nykh predmetov* (2nd ed.; Moscow-Leningrad, 1927), pp. 3–8.

54. *Programmy i metodicheskie zapiski edinoi trudovoi shkoly,* vyp. 5, pp. 10–11.

55. *Programmy i metodicheskie zapiski,* vyp. 5, p. 3. Of the time devoted to general educational subjects, mathematics took 15, natural sciences 11, and chemistry 7 percent of the total. Social science and language-literature took up 17 and 15 percent respectively, physics only 11 percent.

56. *Lunacharsky o narodnom obrazovanii,* p. 391.

57. Remarks by A. I. Svidersky, deputy commissar of agriculture of the RSFSR and rector of the Timiriazev Agricultural Academy, at the Sixth Komsomol Congress, in *Shestoi s"ezd RLKSM,* pp. 265–67; Lunarcharsky's comments in *NP,* no. 7–8 (July-August 1925), p. 16; the article by R. I. Berzin, an official in the Commissariat of Agriculture, "Shkola krest'ianskoi molodezhi v sisteme sel'skokhoziaistvennogo obrazovaniia," *NP,* no. 5 (May 1927), pp. 39–40.

58. *Ezhenedel'nik NKP,* no. 16 (66) (April 16, 1925), pp. 1–3; and *Podgotovka kvalifitsirovannoi rabochei sily,* ed. Ol'ga Anikst (Moscow, 1926), pp. 13–15, 19.

59. *Sed'moi s"ezd VLKSM,* pp. 383–84.

60. *Rabochaia molodezh' i ee shkola* (Petersburg, 1922), p. 26.

61. *Ezhenedel'nik NKP,* no. 14 (April 8, 1927), p. 17, and no. 15 (April 15, 1927), p. 22.

62. Stites, *Revolutionary Dreams,* pp. 149–55; Kurt Johansson, *Aleksej Gastev: Proletarian Bard of the Machine Age* (Stockholm, 1983); Patricia Carden, "Utopia and Anti-Utopia: Aleksei Gastev and Evgeny Zamyatin," *Russian Review,* vol. 46, no. 1 (January 1987), pp. 1–18; Charles Rougle, "'Express': The Future According to Gastev," *Russian History,* vol. 11, nos. 2–3 (Summer–Fall 1984), pp. 258–68.

63. Kendall E. Bailes, "Alexei Gastev and the Soviet Controversy over Taylorism, 1918–1924," *Soviet Studies,* vol. 29, no. 3 (July 1977), pp. 373–94; V. V. Mel'nikov, "Leninskii komsomol—pomoshchik partii v podgotovke kadrov massovykh professii dlia promyshlennosti i sel'skogo khoziaistva (1927–1936 gg.)," in *Pozyvnye istorii: uchenye zapiski po istorii VLKSM,* vol. 4 (Moscow, 1975), p. 53; Osovsky, *Razvitie,* pp. 134, 143–49.

64. TsGA RSFSR: f. 298, op. 1: ed. khr. 45, ll. 9 - 9 ob; and ed. khr. 41, ll. 7–17.

65. TsGA RSFSR, f. 298, op. 1, ed. khr. 41, ll. 9 - 10 ob.

66. Ibid., ll. 13 ob, 15 and TsGA RSFSR, f. 298, op. 1, ed. khr. 53, ll. 12 ob., 14.

67. TsGA RSFSR, f. 298, op 1, ed. khr. 41, l. 15 ob. The same response occurred at a session of the presidium of the Pedagogical Section, November 8, 1923: TsGA RSFSR, f. 298, op. 1, ed. khr. 45, l. 90.

68. *Voprosy shkoly II stupeni,* p. 36. Komsomol delegates agreed.

69. *Vserossiiskii s"ezd zaveduiushchikh otdelami narodnogo obrazovaniia,* pp. 42, 48.

70. Veselov, *Professional'no-tekhnicheskoe obrazovanie,* pp. 213–14.

71. *Chetvertyi s"ezd RKSM,* pp. 161, 241.

72. *Piatyi s"ezd RKSM,* pp. 204–05; *Shestoi s"ezd RLKSM,* p. 270; *Rezoliutsii i postanovleniia VII Vsesoiuznogo s"ezda VLKSM* (Moscow-Leningrad, 1926), p. 140.

73. *Sed'moi s"ezd VLKSM,* pp. 369–71.

74. Ibid., p. 375.

75. Ibid., p. 382.

76. Ibid., pp. 133–34; 346–53; 382–85; *Rezoliutsii i postanovleniia VII Vsesoiuznogo s"ezda,* pp. 33–36.

77. *Ezhenedel'nik NKP,* no. 39 (89) (September 25, 1925), p. 12; Veselov, *Professional'no-tekhnicheskoe obrazovanie,* pp. 222–24; and information based on Rabkrin investigations from 1921 to 1925 in Dmitrieva, *Partiinoe rukovodstvo,* p. 71.

78. *Ezhenedel'nik NKP,* no. 39 (September 25, 1925), p. 13.

79. *Ezhenedel'nik NKP:* no. 11 (March 16, 1928), p. 5; and no. 42 (October 16, 1925), pp. 24–25.

80. *Ezhenedel'nik NKP,* no. 35 (85) (August 28, 1925), p. 28.

XI. A Threat of Failure

1. *NO,* p. 134.

2. Ibid., p. 105.

3. Ibid., p. 108.

4. *Vsesoiuznaia perepis' naseleniia 17 dekabria 1926 g. Kratkie svodki,* vyp. 5: *Vozrast i gramotnost'. Evropeiskaia chast' RSFSR. Belorusskaia SSR* (Moscow, 1928), pp. iv–vi.

5. *Rezoliutsii piatogo Vserossiiskogo s"ezda zaveduiushchikh otdelami,* p. 29.

6. Belousov, "'Vtrorogodnichestvo' i ego rol'," p. 148; and Bogdanov, "Nominal'nyi i fakticheskii kurs," p. 67. Bogdanov provides this information in a variety of ways including data for particular provinces (pp. 71, 73). Also similar figures for Novgorod province in early 1924 in *Shkol'noe obrazovanie na 1-i stupeni obucheniia v Novgorodskoi gubernii po sostoianiiu na 1-e ianvaria 1924 goda* (Novgorod, 1924), pp. 29–30.

7. Bogdanov, "Nominal'nyi i fakticheskii kurs," p. 66.

8. Ibid., p. 66.

9. *NP,* no. 4 (April 1925), p. 116.

10. Ibid., p. 117. For the four-year period ending in 1924/25, 26.9 percent finished the elementary school, while 29.9 percent had done so during the years 1920 to 1923.

11. *Narodnoe prosveshchenie v RSFSR: statisticheskii sbornik,* p. 111.

12. *Narodnoe prosveshchenie v RSFSR v osnovnykh pokazateliakh,* p. 128. Figures for the USSR for the years 1923/24 to 1926/27 were no better: *Narodnoe prosveshchenie v SSSR 1926–1927 uchebnyi god,* p. 19; and *Massovoe prosveshchenie v SSSR k 15-letiiu oktiabria,* pp. 63, 65.

13. *Narodnoe prosveshchenie v RSFSR: statisticheskii sbornik,* p. 177. In 1927/28, the average period of study was 2.6 years in rural and 3.8 years in urban regions: *Massovoe prosveshchenie v SSSR k 15-letiiu oktiabria,* p. 68.

14. *Massovoe prosveshchenie v SSSR k 15-letiiu oktiabria,* p. 67.

15. Korolev, *Sovetskaia shkola,* p. 54.

16. *Ezhenedel'nik NKP,* no. 36 (September 9, 1927), p. 7.

17. Korolev, *Sovetskaia shkola,* p. 54; *Prosveshchenie v RSFSR v 1926/27 uchebnom godu,* p. xvi; *Narodnoe prosveshchenie v SSSR 1926–1927 uchebnyi god,* pp. 23–24.

18. *Ezhenedel'nik NKP,* no. 19 (69) (May 8, 1925), pp. 10–11.

19. *Narodnoe obrazovanie Orlovskoi gubernii,* p. 48.

20. *NP,* no. 11 (November 1926), p. 28.

21. *Sostoianie i perspektivy,* p. 13; and *Ezhenedel'nik NKP,* no. 20–21 (May 18, 1928), p. 21. Reduced instruction occurred most often in the subject areas of labor, physical education, fine arts, and foreign languages.

22. *Narodnoe prosveshchenie v SSSR 1926–1927 uchebnyi god,* pp. 24–25.

23. Ibid., pp. 27–28.

24. Belousov, "'Vtorogodnichestvo' i ego rol'," p. 146; Belousov, "Vtorogodnichestvo v gorodskikh shkolakh," p. 3; *Na poroge vtorogo desiatiletiia,* p. 35; *Narodnoe prosveshchenie v RSFSR v tsifrakh,* p. 26; Popov, *Shkoly sotsial'nogo vospitaniia,* p. 39; *Vseobshchee obiazatel'noe obuchenie,* p. 86. For Nizhnii Novgorod province, *Shkola i zhizn',* no. 12 (December 1926), p. 43; for Yaroslavl', *Nash trud,* no. 12 (December 1927), pp. 8–11; and for Moscow, *VP,* no. 7–8 (July–August 1926), p. 10.

25. *Na poroge vtorogo desiatiletiia,* p. 36.

26. *Narodnoe prosveshchenie v RSFSR: statisticheskii sbornik,* pp. 92–99, and the summary on p. 173.

27. *Shkola i zhizn',* no. 8 (August 1924), p. 53.

28. *Narodnoe prosveshchenie v RSFSR: statisticheskii sbornik,* pp. 92–99, with summary on p. 172.

29. Ibid., p. 173. These figures are high and had a devastating impact on Narkompros. It should be said that a highly industrialized nation such as the United States experiences analogous problems.

30. *Narodnoe prosveshchenie v RSFSR: statisticheskii sbornik,* p. 170; and *Narodnoe prosveshchenie v SSSR. I. Predvaritel'nye itogi shkol'noi perepisi. 15 dekabria 1927 goda. II. Dannye tekushchei statistiki 1927–28 uchebnogo goda* (Moscow, 1929), p. 10. Also I. M. Bogdanov, "Vazhneishie itogi perepisei naseleniia shkol'noi v prilozhenii k zaprosam prosveshcheniia," *NP,* no. 5 (May 1928), p. 117.

31. *Prosveshchenie v RSFSR v 1926/27 uchebnom godu,* p. 24.

32. *Ezhenedel'nik NKP,* no. 2 (50) (November 13, 1923), p. 7.

33. I. Zakolodkin, "Kul'turnye nozhnitsy," *NP,* no. 11 (November 1928), p. 110; *Narodnoe prosveshchenie v RSFSR: statisticheskii sbornik,* p. 170; *Pedagogicheskaia entsiklopediia,* vol. 3, col. 803–804; *Narodnoe prosveshchenie v SSSR. I. Predvaritel'nye itogi shkol'noi perepisi,* p. 12; and *Kul'turnoe stroitel'stvo Soiuza,* p. 27.

34. *Massovoe prosveshchenie v SSSR k 15-letiiu oktiabria,* p. 29.

35. For an excellent treatment of an earlier period, Ben Eklof, "The Myth of the Zemstvo School: The Sources of the Expansion of Rural Education in Imperial Russia, 1864–1914," *History of Education Quarterly,* vol. 24, no. 4 (Winter 1984), pp. 578–81.

36. *Piatnadtsatyi s"ezd VKP(b): dekabr' 1927 goda. Stenograficheskii otchet,* vol. 2 (Moscow, 1961), p. 1115.

37. Krupskaya, *Pedagogicheskie sochineniia,* vol. 9 (Moscow, 1960), pp. 289–90.

38. Ibid., vol. 5 (Moscow, 1959), p. 259.

39. *Kul'turnoe sostoianie Nizhe-Volzhskogo kraia (kratkoe opisanie)* (Saratov, 1928), p. 18; *Pedagogicheskaia entsiklopediia*, vol. 3 (Moscow, 1930), col. 787–88.

40. Bogdanov, "Vazhneishie itogi," p. 112.

41. Alston, *Education and the State*, p. 129.

42. *Sbornik dekretov i postanovlenii po narodnomu khoziaistvu*, vol. 1 (Moscow, 1918), p. 1016.

43. Alston, *Education and the State*, p. 289; Hans, *History of Russian Educational Policy*, p. 236.

44. *Narodnoe obrazovanie Orlovskoi gubernii*, pp. 58–61; *Narodnoe obrazovanie v Ul'ianovskoi gubernii*, p. 35; *Shkola i zhizn'*, no. 12 (December 1926), p. 43.

45. From I. M. Bogdanov, "Kharakteristika sotsial'nogo sostava uchashchikhsia na raznykh stupeniakh obucheniia v sisteme sotsvosa i profobra," *NP*, no. 5 (May 1929), pp. 71, 73. Bogdanov's figures are based on about 10 percent of the schools in the Russian Republic. It is difficult to determine just what was meant by a particular social category, especially when dealing with such vague classifications as "sluzhashchie" and "others." The group "others" included members of the free professions, pensioners, and some non-laboring elements. When they worked in institutions dominated by white-collar personnel, furnace men, laundresses, and janitors were classified as white-collar. A postman was white collar, but a conductor was categorized as a worker. Some children of workers dropped out of school, waited a while, and then continued their education in a lower vocational school. For comments regarding problems of classification, see Bogdanov, "Kharakteristika," pp. 70–71, 77; and A. Belozerov, "O sotsial'nom sostave uchashchikhsia shkol sotsvosa," *NP*, no. 6 (June 1929), pp. 59–61.

46. Popov, *Shkoly sotsial'nogo vospitaniia*, p. 77. Adjustments have been made for several arithmetical errors in the original. The category "other" includes those classified in the original as children of: landless agricultural workers and domestics; members of the free professions; traders; owners of industrial establishments; and "others." A minute number in grades 1, 3, 4, and 5 was listed as "unknown."

47. Bogdanov, "Kharakteristika," p. 75.

48. *Deiatel'nost' partiinykh organizatsii urala i zapadnoi sibiri po razvitiiu narodnogo obrazovaniia* (Sverdlovsk, 1979), p. 5.

49. TsGA RSFSR, f. 1575, op. 6, ed. khr. 244, l. 65. Glavsotsvos ordered an investigation.

50. Ibid., pp. 73–74; S. Gaisinovich, "K peresmotru sistemy narodnogo obrazovaniia," *Na putiakh*, no. 12 (December 1928), p. 55.

51. Zakolodkin, "Kul'turnye nozhnitsy" (December 1928), p. 73; F. F. Korolev, "Sovetskaia shkola v period sotsialisticheskoi industrializatsii i v pervye gody sploshnoi kollektivizatsii (1926–1930/31 uchebnye gody)," *Sovetskaia pedagogika*, no. 10 (October 1949), p. 93.

52. Kharitonov, "Fabrichno-zavodskaia semiletka," p. 72.

53. Gaisinovich, "K peresmotru sistemy," p. 53.

54. Ibid.; and *Ezhenedel'nik NKP*, no. 26 (June 30, 1927), p. 16.

55. *Na poroge vtorogo desiatiletiia*, p. 219; and *Ezhenedel'nik NKP*, no. 31 (August 1, 1926), p. 4.

56. *Ezhenedel'nik NKP*, no. 31 (August 1, 1926), p. 4.

57. *Statisticheskii ezhegodnik; sostoianie narodnogo obrazovaniia v SSSR*, p. xxviii. See somewhat lower figures for Ul'ianovsk province in 1924/25 in *Narodnoe obrazovanie v Ul'ianovskoi gubernii*, p. 10. Declining enrollment of girls meant that in Penza province some schools were all-male institutions: Rosnitsky, *Litso derevni*, p. 92.

58. Bogdanov, "Nominal'nyi i fakticheskii kurs," pp. 66–67.

59. *Statisticheskii ezhegodnik: sostoianie narodnogo obrazovaniia v SSSR*, p. xxviii.

60. *Lunacharsky o narodnom obrazovanii*, p. 344.

61. *Massovoe prosveshchenie v SSSR (k itogam pervoi piatiletki)*, p. 50.

62. *NP*, no. 11 (November 1926), pp. 31–32.

63. Ibid., pp. 54–58.

64. Ibid., p. 22.

65. For Sovnarkom's decrees, see *Ezhenedel'nik NKP*, no. 30 (July 29, 1927), pp. 10–11, and no. 34 (August 26, 1927), p. 2.

66. *Prava uchashchikhsia i uchashchikh*, p. 177; and *Ezhenedel'nik NKP*, no. 31 (July 27, 1928), p. 11.

67. Popov, *Shkoly sotsial'nogo vospitaniia*, pp. 58–59; *Ezhenedel'nik NKP*, no. 31 (80) (July 24, 1925), p. 9; T. Khrushchev, "O vtorogodnichestve," *Na putiakh*, no. 9 (September 1929), p. 47; and Kharitonov, "Fabrichno-zavodskaia semiletka," p. 73.

68. *Ezhenedel'nik MONO*, no. 5–6 (February 15, 1927), p. 5.

69. *Pis'mo shkol'niku i shkol'nitse 1-i stupeni* (Moscow, 1925).

70. *NP*, no. 1 (January 1927), pp. 62, 66–67.

71. TsGA RSFSR, f. 2306, op. 69, ed. khr. 1141, l. 13.

72. *Vseobshchee obiazatel'noe obuchenie*, pp. 48–51; *Deiatel'nost' partiinykh organizatsii urala*, p. 8.

73. *Biulleten' MONO*, no. 36 (December 20, 1925), p. 3.

74. *VP*, no. 5 (May 1929), p. 118.

75. *Ezhenedel'nik NKP*, no. 13–14 (April 26, 1927), p. 4; *VP*, no. 3 (March 1929), pp. 18–20; Kharitonov, "Fabrichno-zavodskaia semiletka," p. 73; Krylov, "Uchashchiesia v shkolakh II stupeni," p. 71.

76. Study of Tver's secondary schools in Krylov, "Uchashchiesia v shkolakh II stupeni," pp. 64, 72.

77. Popov, *Shkoly sotsial'nogo vospitaniia*, p. 58; *Narodnoe prosveshchenie v SSSR 1926–1927 uchebnyi god*, p. 28. Figures for urban and secondary schools were somewhat lower: 17 to 33 percent of the withdrawals in the city of Moscow, 33 percent in secondary grades in rural localities, and 20 percent of all grades in urban areas throughout the Russian Republic.

78. Krylov, "Uchashchiesia v shkolakh II stupeni," pp. 69–71.

79. *Prava uchashchikhsia i uchashchikh*, p. 176; *Ezhenedel'nik NKP*, no. 31 (July 27, 1928), p. 11.

80. *Ezhenedel'nik NKP*, no. 14 (35) (July 15, 1924), p. 7; *Prava uchashchikhsia i uchashchikh*, p. 182; *Ezhenedel'nik NKP*, no. 23 (June 11, 1925), p. 5; *Ezhenedel'nik NKP:* no. 35 (September 2, 1927), p. 2; and no. 2 (January 14, 1927), p. 6.

81. *Ezhenedel'nik NKP*, no. 27 (July 9, 1926), p. 8.

82. Popov, *Shkoly sotsial'nogo vospitaniia*, p. 60.

83. Ibid., p. 60. Applicants in this most opprobrious of categories amounted to 4.7 percent of all children seeking admission.

84. *Biulleten' MONO*, no. 26 (September 28, 1928), p. 4.

85. *Ezhenedel'nik NKP*, no. 36 (September 9, 1927), p. 7; *Biulleten' MONO*, no. 25 (August 27, 1928), p. 22.

86. *Narodnoe prosveshchenie v SSSR 1926–1927 uchebnyi god*, p. 28.

87. *Ezhenedel'nik NKP*, no. 35 (September 3, 1926), p. 11.

88. *Nash trud*, no. 12 (December 1927), p. 11; Korolev, *Sovetskaia shkola*, p. 238; S. P. Egorov, *Antireligioznoe vospitanie v nachal'noi shkole* (Moscow-Leningrad, 1929), p. 10.

89. *UG*, no. 20 (195) (May 11, 1928), p. 3; Egorov, *Antireligioznoe vospitanie*, pp. 10–11, 19; *VP*, no. 3 (March 1929), p. 144; M. Markovich, "Protiv primirenchestva v antireligioznoi bor'be," *NP*, no. 2 (February 1929), pp. 114–16.

90. Nina Tumarkin, *Lenin Lives! The Lenin Cult in Soviet Russia* (Cambridge, Mass., 1983), pp. 229–30, 241. Also K. Bendrikov, "Religioznoe natsional'noe i politicheskoe predstavleniia detei shkol'nikov," *NP*, no. 1 (January 1929), pp. 126ff.

91. Anweiler, *Geschichte*, pp. 241–42; and M. Al'bitsky, "Ideologiia sovetskogo shkol'nika," *VP*, no. 10 (October 1927), pp. 48–53.

92. *UG,* no. 26 (201) (June 22, 1928), p. 3.

93. *Narodnoe prosveshchenie v RSFSR v tsifrakh,* p. 25; and *Statisticheskii ezhegodnik: sostoianie narodnogo obrazovaniia v SSSR,* p. 34.

94. *Prosveshchenie v RSFSR v 1926/27 uchebnom godu,* pp. xviii, 25.

95. *Shkola i zhizn',* no. 12 (December 1926), p. 44.

96. On Factory Seven-Year Schools: *Ezhenedel'nik NKP,* no. 27 (July 9, 1926), p. 7; Kharitonov, "Fabrichno-zavodskaia semiletka," pp. 73–76; and Kirienko, "Soveshchanie," p. 84. On Schools for Peasant Youth: *Ezhendel'nik NKP,* no. 12 (62) (March 27, 1925), pp. 8–9; and R. I. Berzin, "Shkola krest'ianskoi molodezhi v sisteme sel'skokhoziaistvennogo obrazovaniia," *NP,* no. 5 (May, 1927), p. 41. On Factory Apprenticeship Schools: Dmitrieva, *Partiinoe rukovodstvo,* pp. 49–52; and Veselov, *Professional'no-proftekhnicheskoe obrazovanie,* p. 210.

97. Berzin, "Shkola krest'ianskoi molodezhi," p. 41; *NP,* no. 1 (January 1927), p. 65; Veselov, *Professional'no-proftekhnicheskoe obrazovanie,* pp. 264–65; and Dmitrieva, *Partiinoe rukovodstvo,* p. 55.

98. *NP,* no. 6–7 (15–16) (1924), p. 35; and Makovsky, "Klientura fabzavucha," p. 119.

99. *Ezhenedel'nik NKP:* no. 31 (July 27, 1928), p. 11; and no. 36 (August 31, 1928), p. 10.

100. *Ezhenedel'nik NKP,* no. 18 (May 8, 1926), p. 26.

101. Kirienko, "Soveshchanie," p. 84; *Ezhenedel'nik NKP,* no. 26 (June 30, 1927), p. 16; *Narodnoe prosveshchenie v RSFSR: statisticheskii sbornik,* p. 175; *Podgotovka kadrov v SSSR,* p. 32.

102. Veselov, *Professional'no-tekhnicheskoe obrazovanie,* p. 210; Blinchevsky, *Professional'no-tekhnicheskoe obrazovanie,* pp. 231–32; Anikst, *Podgotovka,* p. 20.

103. *Ezhenedel'nik NKP,* no. 14 (April 6, 1928), p. 11.

104. *Voprosy shkoly II stupeni,* p. 30.

105. *NP,* no. 5–6 (May-June 1925), p. 67; *Ezhenedel'nik NKP,* no. 22 (72) (May 31, 1925), p. 29.

106. O'Connor, *The Politics of Soviet Culture,* p. 104.

107. *NP,* no. 7 (July 1926), pp. 131–33; and Epshtein, "Shkola, kak ona est'," pp. 10–12.

108. TsGA RSFSR, f. 2306, op. 69, ed. khr. 1141, l. 10.

109. *Ezhenedel'nik NKP,* no. 20–21 (May 18, 1928), p. 17.

XII. Compromise Betrayed

1. *Cultural Revolution in Russia, 1928–1931,* ed. Sheila Fitzpatrick (Bloomington, 1978). See especially Fitzpatrick's introduction to what she calls a "period of contradictions" (p. 2).

2. Ibid. Especially essays by Katerina Clark, "Little Heroes and Big Deeds: Literature Responds to the First Five-Year Plan," pp. 189–206; Sheila Fitzpatrick, "Cultural Revolution as Class War," pp. 8–40; and George M. Enteen, "Marxist Historians during the Cultural Revolution: A Case Study of Professional In-Fighting," pp. 154–68. Also Edward J. Brown, *The Proletarian Episode in Russian Literature, 1928–1932* (New York, 1950) and David Joravsky, *Soviet Marxism and Natural Science, 1917–1932* (London, 1961).

3. See Sheila Fitzpatrick's articles "The Emergence of Glaviskusstvo: Class War on the Cultural Front, Moscow, 1928–29," *Soviet Studies,* vol. 23 (October 1971), pp. 236–53; and "The 'Soft' Line on Culture and Its Enemies: Soviet Cultural Policy, 1922–1927," *Slavic Review,* vol. 23 (June 1974), pp. 267–87. Also Joravsky, *Soviet Marxism and Natural Science,* pp. 211–13, 229, 240–43; Hugh D. Judson, Jr., "The Association of Contemporary Architects in Revolutionary Russia," *Jahrbuecher fuer Geschichte Osteuropas,* vol. 34, no. 4 (1986), pp. 557–78; and Peter Kenez, "The

Cultural Revolution in Cinema," *Slavic Review,* vol. 47, no. 2 (Fall 1988), pp. 414–33. Anweiler ascribes changes in school policy from 1928 to 1931 to a utopian maximalism unleashed by the First Five Year Plan: Anweiler, *Geschichte,* pp. 285, 339; and Oskar Anweiler, "Erziehungs- und Bildungspolitik," in *Kulturpolitik der Sowjetunion,* ed. Oskar Anweiler and Karl-Heinz Ruffman (Stuttgart, 1973), pp. 48–49.

4. I. Stalin, *Sochineniia,* vol. 11 (Moscow, 1952), pp. 74–75.

5. Ibid., p. 76.

6. Ibid., pp. 74, 76–77.

7. *NO,* pp. 415–18; *KPSS v rezoliutsiiakh,* vol. 4, pp. 334–45; *Ezhenedel'nik NKP,* no. 26 (June 28, 1929), p. 10; *Na putiakh,* no. 8–9 (August–September 1930), p. 5.

8. *NO,* p. 418; *KPSS v rezoliutsiiakh,* vol. 4, p. 341.

9. *UG,* no. 52 (227) (December 21, 1928), p. 1; and in the Saratov journal, *Nizhe-Volzhskii prosveshchenets,* no. 4 (December 1928), p. 3. Also *UG,* no. 5 (232) (January 11, 1929), p. 2; and *Ezhenedel'nik NKP,* no. 8–9 (February 15, 1929), pp. 51–52.

10. *UG:* no. 78 (305) (July 9, 1929), p. 2; no. 79 (306) (July 11, 1929), p. 2; no. 80 (307) (July 13, 1929), p. 2.

11. *Vtoroe Vsesoiuznoe partiinoe soveshchanie po narodnomu obrazovaniiu. Stenograficheskii otchet* (Moscow, 1931), resolutions on pp. 290–317.

12. *VIII Vsesoiuznyi s"ezd VLKSM, 5–16 maia 1928 goda. Stenograficheskii otchet* (Moscow, 1928), pp. 227ff., 257, 276–77, 571.

13. Ibid., pp. 62–63.

14. Ibid., pp. 120–38.

15. Ibid., p. 154.

16. Ibid., p. 278.

17. Ibid., p. 279.

18. Ibid., p. 280.

19. The best source of information on Shul'gin is Anweiler, *Geschichte,* pp. 414–23. Also the critical but informative account in I. V. Chuvashev, "Politekhnicheskoe vospitanie v reshauiushchem godu," *NU,* no. 12 (December 1931), pp. 157–59; Fitzpatrick, *Education and Social Mobility,* pp. 139–44; Gail Warshofsky Lapidus, "Educational Strategies and Cultural Revolution: The Politics of Soviet Development," in *Cultural Revolution in Russia, 1928–1931,* pp. 94–99; Gock, *Polytechnische Bildung,* pp. 109–110, 213–18; and Krueger-Potratz, "Continuities and Discontinuities," pp. 4–9.

20. Anweiler, *Geschichte,* p. 415.

21. TsGA RSFSR, f. 298, op. 1, ed. khr. 41, l. 36.

22. TsGA RSFSR, f. 298, op. 1, ed. khr. 41, ll. 60, 65–84.

23. V. N. Shul'gin, "Eshche i eshche raz ob obshchestvennoi rabote," *NU,* no. 3 (March 1927), pp. 43–46.

24. See his comments to the Narkompros Collegium, December 3, 1928, in *Spornye voprosy marksistkoi pedagogiki. Stenogramma rasshirennogo zasedaniia Kollegii Narkomprosa 3-XII 1928 g.* (Moscow, 1929); V. Shul'gin, "O shkol'nykh programmakh," *UG,* no. 5 (232) (January 11, 1929), p. 2. Also comments at a March 16, 1930, session of the Society of Marxist Pedagogues in *Sistema narodnogo obrazovaniia v rekonstruktivnyi period: soveshchanie Obshchestva Pedagogov marksistov pri Kommunisticheskoi akademii 7/II–16/III* (Moscow, 1930), pp. 46–51; and articles in *Spornye problemy marksistskoi pedagogi. Sbornik statei* (Moscow, 1930). He gave full vent to his utopian notions in V. N. Shul'gin, *Piatiletka i zadachi narodnogo obrazovaniia* (Moscow, 1930).

25. "XV s"ezd kompartii i zadachi narodnogo prosveshcheniia," in *Lunacharsky o narodnom obrazovanii,* pp. 403, 405; *VIII Vsesoiuznyi s"ezd VLKSM,* pp. 121–24; "Vospitatel'nye zadachi sovetskoi shkoly," in *Lunacharsky o narodnom obrazovanii,* pp. 443–44; A. V. Lunacharsky, "Problema podgotovki rabochikh kadrov," *Na putiakh,* no.

10–11 (October–November 1928), pp. 3–10. Also A. Lunacharsky, "Kul'tura na zapade i u nas," *NU,* no. 10 (October 1928), pp. 15–31.

26. *VIII Vsesoiuznyi s"ezd VLKSM,* p. 124.

27. *VIII Vsesoiuznyi s"ezd VLKSM,* p. 128.

28. For the December 3 address, *Lunacharsky o narodnom obrazovanii,* p. 463; and for the January presentation, *Lunacharsky o vospitanii i obrazovanii* (Moscow, 1976), p. 197.

29. *Lunacharsky o narodnom obrazovanii,* pp. 459, 563; *Lunacharsky o vospitanii i obrazovanii,* p. 195.

30. *Sovetskaia pedogogika,* no. 1 (January 1989), p. 118.

31. *UG,* no. 36 (263) (March 27, 1929), p. 2; and *Pravda* (June 8, 1929), the latter in Krupskaya, *Pedagogicheskie sochineniia,* vol. 2 (Moscow, 1958), pp. 380–83.

32. *NO,* p. 108.

33. Krupskaya, *Pedagogicheskie sochineniia,* vol. 2, pp. 380, 382.

34. The final version appeared as "Sistema narodnogo obrazovaniia RSFSR," *Na putiakh,* no. 6 (June 1929), pp. 10–20.

35. M. Aleksinsky, "Voprosy obshcheobrazovatel'noi shkoly," *VP,* no. 5–6 (May–June 1928), pp. 3–13; S. Gaisinovich, "K peresmotru sistemy," pp. 51, 57; S. Gaisinovich, "Narkompros, VSNKh i TsIT o politekhnizme," *Na putiakh,* no. 3 (March 1929), pp. 48–52.

36. *UG,* 52 (227) (December 21, 1928), p. 6.

37. *Na putiakh,* no. 1 (January 1929), p. 97.

38. Ibid., pp. 97–98.

39. *Ezhenedel'nik NKP,* no. 14 (April 1, 1926), p. 7; *Russkii iazyk v sovetskoi shkole,* no. 3 (1929), p. 141; "Sistema narodnogo obrazovaniia RSFSR," pp. 10–20; and I. V. Chuvashev, "Voprosy trudovogo i politekhnicheskogo vospitaniia," *NU,* no. 1 (January 1930), p. 95; Fitzpatrick reported on trips by Lunacharsky, Epshtein, and Iakovleva in *Education and Social Mobility,* pp. 146–47. Lunacharsky gave twelve speeches in January, thirty-nine in February, twenty-six in March, five in April, sixteen in May, and fifteen in the first half of June: *Novye formy i metody prosvetitel'noi raboty,* p. 31. During the campaigning, the theses went through several near-identical drafts: *Na putiakh:* no. 3 (March 1929), pp. 33–40; and no. 6 (June 1929), pp. 10–20; *UG:* no. 46 (273) (April 18, 1929), p. 3; no. 47 (274) (April 20, 1929), p. 2; no. 79 (306) (July 11, 1929), p. 2; and no. 80 (307) (July 13, 1929), p. 2.

40. *Ezhenedel'nik NKP,* no. 20–21 (May 17–24, 1929), pp. 20–23.

41. *Piatiletnii plan kul'turnogo stroitel'stva,* (Moscow-Leningrad, 1929), p. 42.

42. Ibid., p. 43.

43. Ibid., pp. 63–64.

44. Ibid., pp. 58, 60.

45. Ibid., p. 61.

46. Ibid., pp. 95–99, 126.

47. Ibid., p. 126.

48. Ibid., pp. 131–37.

49. *Ezhenedel'nik NKP:* no. 20–21 (May 18, 1928), p. 15; and no. 26b (June 30, 1929), p. 8.

50. *Narodnoe prosveshchenie v RSFSR v osnovnykh pokazateliakh,* p. 134. On February 15, 1930, Narkompros ordered the transfer of a number of institutions including museums and technicums to the local budget: *Ezhenedel'nik NKP,* no. 7 (March 1, 1930), p. 2.

51. *Narodnoe prosveshchenie v RSFSR v osnovnykh pokazateliakh,* p. 145.

52. Ibid. On inflation: Harry Schwartz, *Russia's Soviet Economy* (2nd ed.; New York, 1954), pp. 446, 476; Nove, *An Economic History,* p. 204.

53. *Ezhenedel'nik NKP,* no. 2 (February 1929), p. 115.

54. *Nash trud:* no. 9 (September 1927); and no. 10 (October 1927).

55. *Shkola i zhizn'*, no. 7 (1928).

56. Ibid., no. 8 (1928), pp. 1–5.

57. *UG*, no. 147 (365) (December 19, 1929), p. 4.

58. *VP*, no. 10 (October 1928), p. 5.

59. Ibid., p. 144.

60. *Programmy i metodicheskie zapiski shkol krest'ianskoi molodezhi* (Moscow-Leningrad, 1928).

61. *Povyshennaia shkola i oborona strany. Sbornik materialov dopolnenii i poiasnenii programmam narkomprosa* (Moscow-Leningrad, 1928).

62. *Ezhenedel'nik NKP:* no. 5 (February 1, 1929), pp. 4–5; no. 14 (April 1, 1929), pp. 16–21; no. 18 (April 26, 1929), pp. 16, 84; and no. 20–21 (May 17–24, 1929), pp. 16–27.

63. *Ezhenedel'nik NKP*, no. 27 (July 5, 1929), pp. 4–6. Also *Resheniia okruzhnogo soveshchaniia po prosveshcheniiu* (Minusinsk, 1929), p. 27.

64. *Programmy edinoi trudovoi shkoly I stupeni. Dlia fabrichno-zavodskoi i gorodskoi shkoly* (Moscow, 1929); and *Programmy edinoi trudovoi shkoly I stupeni. Dlia sel'skoi shkoly* (Moscow, 1929). Also "Kompleksnye programmy sel'skoi shkoly I stupeni," *VP*, no. 7 (July 1929), pp. 51–122.

65. *Programmy edinoi trudovoi shkoly I stupeni*, pp. 1–2. Also *VP*, no. 7 (July 1929), pp. 43–50.

66. *VP*, no. 11 (November 1929), pp. 85–157.

67. *Programmy GUS'a v sel'skoi shkole: metodicheskoe posobie dlia sel'skikh uchitelei* (Moscow-Leningrad, 1929). Consisting of 398 pages, the second edition appeared in September in a run of 10,000 copies. Its popularity led to a second printing the following month.

XIII. Purges and Projects, 1929–1930

1. *Izvestiia* (September 13, 1929), p. 2.

2. S. Frederick Starr, *Red and Hot: The Fate of Jazz in the Soviet Union, 1917–1960*, (New York, 1983), p. 92.

3. Alexander Vucinich, *The Empire of Knowledge: The Academy of Sciences of the USSR (1917–1970)* (Berkeley, 1984), p. 126.

4. The speech is in *Na putiakh*, no. 3 (March 1929), pp. 4–10; criticism in *UG*, no. 11 (238) (January 25, 1929), p. 5.

5. As quoted in S. A. Fediukin, *Sovetskaia vlast' i burzhuaznye spetsialisty* (Moscow, 1965), p. 244. The letter is in the Central Party Archives.

6. Fitzpatrick, *Education and Social Mobility*, p. 133.

7. *Lunacharsky o vospitanii i obrazovanii*, p. 197; *Ezhenedel'nik NKP*, no. 14 (April 1, 1929), p. 7.

8. *Ezhenedel'nik NKP*, no. 14 (April 1, 1929), p. 8.

9. The Collegium's membership, as appointed by Sovnarkom RSFSR, October 15, 1929, did appear in *Ezhenedel'nik NKP*, no. 43 (October 24, 1929), p. 3. It consisted of Lunacharsky, the deputy commissars (Pokrovsky, Krupskaya, Epshtein, V. A. Kurts) and heads of the Commissariat's chief administrative branches, including A. Ia. Vyshinsky from Glavprofobr, K. A. Popov from the State Academic Council, and A. Ia. Golyshev from Glavpolitprosvet.

10. *NP:* no. 5 (May 1929), pp. 129–40; and no. 8–9 (August–September 1929), pp. 191–92.

11. *Novye formy i metody prosvetitel'noi raboty*, pp. 14, 16.

12. Ibid., p. 17.

13. Ibid., p. 27. At some point in 1929, at least thirty workers from Moscow factories took up positions in Narkompros: Ia. Bauer, "Pervye itogi chistki Narkomprosa," *NP*, no. 2 (1930), p. 2.

14. It is not certain just when Lunacharsky was removed, although it is likely that he departed well before the announcement in *Izvestiia*. Fitzpatrick believes that he may have left office in April or at the beginning of May: Fitzpatrick, *Education and Social Mobility*, p. 290. Lunacharsky, however, seemed to represent the Commissariat in mid-June at the plenary session of the central committee of the teachers union.

15. A. S. Bubnov, *Stat'i i rechi o narodnom obrazovanii* (Moscow, 1959), pp. 22–25, 40–105; *XVI s"ezd Vsesoiuznoi Kommunisticheskoi partii (b)* (Moscow-Leningrad, 1931), pp. 181–85.

16. *Pravda* (November 5, 1929), p. 2; also *NO,* pp. 452–53.

17. Bauer, "Pervye itogi," p. 2.

18. *NU,* no. 9 (September 1929); *Ezhenedel'nik NKP,* no. 36 (September 16, 1929).

19. *UG,* no. 150 (368) (December 26, 1929), p. 3.

20. Bauer, "Pervye itogi," p. 2.

21. Compare *UG,* 150 (368) (December 26, 1929), p. 3 with: *Izvestiia* (May 14, 1930, p. 3; and Ia. Bauer, "Itogi chistki Narkomprosa RSFSR," *NP,* no. 6 (1930), pp. 12–14.

22. Bauer, "Itogi," pp. 12–13.

23. Bauer, "Pervye itogi", p. 2.

24. *UG:* no. 3 (373) (January 9, 1930), p. 3; no. 5 (375) (January 14, 1930), p. 3; and no. 9 (379) (January 22, 1930), p. 3.

25. Bauer, "Pervye itogi," p. 2; Bauer, "Itogi," pp. 12–14.

26. *NP,* no. 3–4 (March–April 1929), p. 235.

27. On the Pedagogical Section: Ibid., p. 236; *Ezhenedel'nik NKP,* no. 16–17 (April 19, 1929), pp. 37–38. Its Political Section had 112 members; its Nationalities-Method Commission had 38. On the Council: Bauer, "Pervye itogi," pp. 1–2. See also a similar assessment by Tikhomirov, "Kakim dolzhen byt' Narkompros," *NP,* no. 2 (1930), p. 8.

28. *Vecherniaia Moskva:* (February 24, 1930), p. 1.; (March 14, 1930), p. 3; and (March 19, 1930), p. 1. This source came to my attention in Fitzpatrick, *Education and Social Mobility*, p. 137.

29. Narkompros was criticized for failing to arrange special courses for the thirty workers who did arrive: Bauer, "Pervye itogi," p. 2. Also: *NP,* no. 5 (May 1929), p. 140.

30. *Novye formy i metody prosvetitel'noi raboty,* p. 34.

31. Krupskaya, *Pedagogicheskie sochineniia,* vol. 11, p. 358. She charitably observed that their efforts, though lacking in clarity and purposefulness, produced good results.

32. *Vospominaniia o Nadezhde Konstantinovne Krupskoi,* ed. A. M. Arsen'ev, V. S. Dridzo and A. G. Kravchenko (Moscow, 1966), p. 206.

33. *Na putiakh,* no. 7 (July 1930), p. 91.

34. P. Rudnev in *Vospominaniia o Nadezhde Konstantinovne Krupskoi,* p. 229. Rudnev's role is mentioned in *Programmy i metodicheskie zapiski shkol kolkhoznoi molodezhi: programmnye materialy* (Moscow-Leningrad, 1930); and *Proekt programm sel'skoi nachal'noi shkoly* (Moscow, 1931). Shatsky had come under heavy-handed criticism. In a letter to Krupskaya, February 21, 1929, he referred to charges in the newspaper *Vecherniaia Moskva* that he was an "ideologue of the right wing of Moscow pedagogues" (Shatsky, *Pedagogicheskie sochineniia,* vol. 4, pp. 285, 312). A year later, he expressed to her his fear of a "new legend about the right deviation of Shatsky" (Ibid., p. 259).

35. *NP:* no. 2 (1930), pp. 11–13; and no. 5 (1930), pp. 10–14.

36. *NP,* no. 2 (1930), pp. 11–13.

37. *NP,* no. 5 (1930), p. 11.

38. *Vtoroe Vsesoiuznoe partiinoe soveshchanie,* p. 23, with resolutions on pp. 290–302.

39. *NP,* no. 5 (1930), p. 8. The School for Communal Services was to prepare cadres for municipal water works, electrical power stations, and cafeterias.

40. Ibid.

41. *Na putiakh,* no. 8–9 (August–September 1930), pp. 5–6; and *NO,* p. 112.

42. *Pervyi Vserossiiskii s"ezd po politekhnicheskomu obrazovaniiu.* See summaries in *Biulleten' NKP,* no. 26 (September 20, 1930), pp. 31–37; and *Russkii iazyk v sovetskoi shkole,* no. 5 (1930), pp. 176–80.

43. *UG,* no. 73 (443) (June 16, 1930), p. 2; and *Vospominaniia o Nadezhde Konstantinovne Krupskoi,* p. 229.

44. *Pervyi Vserossiiskii s"ezd po politekhnicheskomu obrazovaniiu,* pp. 491, 500.

45. *Vtoroe Vsesoiuznoe partiinoe soveshchanie,* p. 23.

46. M. Aleksinsky, "O reorganizatsii organov narodnogo obrazovaniia," *Na putiakh,* no. 6 (June 1930), pp. 23–26.

47. *Sistema narodnogo obrazovaniia,* pp. 11, 31–32; *Vtoroe Vsesoiuznoe partiinoe soveshchanie,* pp. 84–86, 195ff.; *Pervyi Vserossiiskii s"ezd po politekhnicheskomu obrazovaniiu,* pp. 19–34, 139–44; also in Krupskaya, *Pedagogicheskie sochineniia,* vol. 4, pp. 267–303.

48. *Pervyi Vserossiiskii s"ezd po politekhnicheskomu obrazovaniiu,* p. 103.

49. Ibid., pp. 112–13, 545.

50. A. Liubimov praised Krupskaya as Narkompros's "single warrior for the polytechnical school": Ibid., p. 545.

51. Comments by A. Savaniuk: Ibid., p. 123.

52. Ellsworth Collings, *An Experiment with a Project Curriculum* (New York, 1923).

53. See programs designed in 1923/24 in TsGA RSFSR, f. 298. op. 1, ed. khr. 45, l. 85 and l. 99; *Novye programmy* (1924); *UG,* no. 2 (74) (January 14, 1926), p. 4; *Programmy i metodicheskie zapiski krest'ianskoi molodezhi* (Moscow-Leningrad, 1928), p. 266; and *Programmy i metodicheskie zapiski edinoi trudovoi shkoly,* vyp. 3 (1927), p. 18. Also: I. Troianovskii and S. Tiurbert, "Chto takoe 'Proekt metod'," *VP,* no. 11 (November 1924), pp. 76–86.

54. *Russkii iazyk v sovetskoi shkole,* no. 1 (1930), pp. 156, 158.

55. Ibid., p. 159.

56. *Biulleten NKP:* no. 10 (March 31, 1930), p. 49; and no. 21 (July 20, 1930), p. 36.

57. *Programmy i metodicheskie zapiski shkol kol'khoznoi molodezhi: programmnye materialy,* vyp. 1 (Moscow-Leningrad, 1930); and *Programmy fabrichno-zavodskoi semiletki* (Moscow-Leningrad, 1930), p. 39.

58. *Na putiakh,* no. 7 (July 1930), pp. 83–87.

59. *Na putiakh,* no. 7 (July 1930), p. 87.

60. *Biulleten' NKP,* no. 21 (July 20, 1930), p. 36. The locus of critical concern was probably the State Academic Council.

61. Krupskaya, *Pedagogicheskie sochineniia,* vol. 2, pp. 419–21.

62. *Na putiakh,* no. 7 (July 1930), pp. 82–83.

63. Krupskaya, *Pedagogicheskie sochineniia,* vol. 10, pp. 311–16, 326–32, 754; Pidkasistyi, *N. K. Krupskaia,* pp. 60–62, 100, 109.

64. *Programmy nachal'noi shkoly': sel'skii variant* (Moscow, 1930), pp. 7–8; *Programmy nachal'noi shkoly: gorodskoi variant* (Moscow, 1930), pp. 7–8; *Programmy fabrichno-zavodskoi semiletki* (Moscow-Leningrad, 1930), pp. 16–24. The curriculum for the School for Collective Farm Youth praised projects "as the single method of school work": *Programmy i metodicheskie zapiski shkol kolkhoznoi molodezhi: programmnye materialy,* vyp. 1 (Moscow, 1930), p. 27.

65. *Programmy kolkhoznoi molodezhi,* pp. 35, 178; *Programmy fabrichno-zavodskoi semiletki,* pp. 33–34; and *Russkii iazyk v sovetskoi shkole,* no. 3 (1930), pp. 182–83.

66. *Programmy kolkhoznoi molodezhi,* p. 46.

67. *Programmy fabrichno-zavodskoi semiletki,* pp. 16–24; and *Russkii iazyk v sovetskoi shkole,* no. 3 (1930), pp. 180–83.

68. *Programmy fabrichno-zavodskoi semiletki,* pp. 16–24.

69. *UG:* no. 3 (373) (January 9, 1930), p. 4; and no. 38 (408) (April 1, 1930), p. 2.

70. Collegium rejection in *Biulleten' NKP,* no. 12 (April 20, 1930), p. 7; the criticism in *Za kommunisticheskoe prosveshchenie* [henceforth *ZKP*], no. 54 (424) (May 4, 1930), p. 3.

71. *Na Putiakh:* no. 6 (June 1930), pp. 79–81; and no. 7 (July, 1930), pp. 88–90.

72. An incomplete collection of journal-textbooks is at the Library of the Academy of Pedogogical Sciences in Moscow.

73. *Shkol'naia brigada,* no. 2–3 (1931), p. 40.

74. Esipov also served on the editorial board of *Mal'enkie udarniki.*

75. D. Khanin, "Bor'ba za detskogo pisatelia," *Kniga detiam,* no. 1 (January 1930), pp. 1–2.

76. *Pervyi Vserossiiskii s"ezd po politekhnicheskomu obrazovaniiu,* pp. 126–127, 150ff., 231–37, 260–74.

XIV. Slower History

1. Kirienko, "Soveshchanie," pp. 87–89; *VP,* no. 4 (April 1929), pp. 97–98; *Russkii iazyk v sovetskoi shkole,* no. 9 (1929), pp. 143–45; *Na putiakh,* no. 7–8 (July–August 1931), pp. 16–19, 45, 53, 57–58, 62–69. Also *ZKP:* no. 168 (538) (November 28, 1930), p. 3; no. 28 (594) (February 4, 1931), p. 3; and no. 103 (669) (May 4, 1931), p. 3. Also *Za Vseobshchee obuchenie* [henceforth *ZVO*]: no. 6 (1931), pp. 14–15; and no. 8 (1931), pp. 13–14.

2. Chuvashev, "Politekhnicheskoe vospitanie," *NU,* no. 12 (December, 1931), p. 161.

3. *Biulleten' NKP,* no. 32–33 (August 25, 1931), pp. 2–3.

4. *ZKP,* no. 28 (594) (February 4, 1931), p. 3.

5. *KP,* no. 3 (February 5, 1931), p. 5.

6. *Sobr. uzak. RSFSR,* 1930, no. 42, st. 319.

7. *ZKP:* no. 159 (529) (November 18, 1930), p. 3; and no. 28 (594) (February 4, 1931), p. 3; *Biulleten' NKP,* no. 12 (April 20, 1931), pp. 4–6.

8. *ZKP,* no. 159 (529) (November 18, 1930), p. 3.

9. *Pervyi Vserossiiskii s"ezd po politekhnicheskomu obrazovaniiu,* p. 94.

10. *Novye formy i metody prosvetitel'noi raboty,* p. 50.

11. *ZKP,* no. 134 (700) (June 9, 1931), p. 3.

12. *Narodnoe prosveshchenie v SSSR za 1928/29,* pp. 5–8.

13. *Biulleten' NKP,* no. 3 (January 25, 1930), p. 14.

14. *Biulleten' NKP,* no. 17 (June 10, 1930), p. 19; and *Pervyi Vserossiiskii s"ezd po politekhnicheskomu obrazovaniiu,* pp. 237–38.

15. *Biulleten' NKP,* no. 24 (August 20, 1930), p. 22.

16. *Biulleten' NKP,* no. 23 (August 10, 1930), p. 13.

17. *ZKP,* no. 101 (471) (August 20, 1930), p. 1.

18. *Russkii iazyk v sovetskoi shkole,* no. 3 (1929), p. 143; and *Biulleten' NKP,* no. 20 (July 10, 1930), pp. 28–29.

19. Conference on the Project Method, December 17–19, 1930, in *Na putiakh,* no. 1 (January 1931), pp. 50–52; and the Second Republic Conference on the Project Method, April 9–14, 1931, in *Na putiakh,* no. 5 (May 1931), pp. 25–34.

20. *ZKP:* no. 142 (512) (October 28, 1930), p. 2; and no. 177 (547) (December 9, 1930), p. 2. Earlier, *ZKP* complained of general courses taught at pedagogical technicums by "pedagogues of the old school": no. 86 (456) (July 16, 1930), p. 3. Bubnov complained of a failure to teach and use new methods before the Pedagogical Section in April 1931: *KP,* no. 13 (July 5, 1931), p. 18.

21. S. Liubimova, "Vypolnim reshenie TsK VKP(b) 'O nachal'noi i srednei shkole'," *Za kommunisticheskoe vospitanie,* no. 14–15 (1931), p. 10.

22. A. Vladimirsky, "Protsentnaia otsenka pis'mennykh rabot po rodnomu iazyku," *VP,* no. 11–12 (November–December 1928), pp. 86–91.

23. *UG,* no. 5 (232) (January 11, 1929), p. 4.
24. *Na putiakh,* no. 7–8 (July–August 1931), pp. 46–49, 58.
25. *Sistema narodnogo obrazovaniia,* p. 33.
26. *Russkii iazyk v sovetskoi shkole,* no. 4 (1931), p. 181; and *ZKP,* no. 95 (661) (April 23, 1931), p. 4.
27. Krupskaya, *Pedagogicheskie sochineniia,* vol. 5 (Moscow, 1959), pp. 267–68.
28. Pidkasistyi, *N. K. Krupskaia,* p. 29; from a document in the Central Party Archives.
29. *Sistema narodnogo obrazovaniia,* p. 11; N. Krupskaya, "Detskoe samoupravlenie v shkole," *Na putiakh,* no. 10 (October 1930), p. 21; N. Krupskaya, "Samoupravlenie v shkole," *Na putiakh:* no. 4 (April 1931), pp. 25–28; and no. 7–8 (July–August 1931), pp. 15–16.
30. N. Krupskaya, "Obshchestvo pedagogov-marksistov," *Vestnik kommunisticheskoi akademii,* no. 1 (January 1931), p. 39; Ravkin, "V bor'be za leninskii stil'," p. 48.
31. Sovnarkom on February 5, 1929, in *Ezhenedel'nik NKP,* no. 16–17 (April 9, 1929), p. 3; the Party's Central Committee on February 21, 1931, in *NO,* p. 114; Bubnov in *XVI s"ezd Vsesoiuznoi Kommunisticheskoi partii (b)* (Moscow-Leningrad, 1931), p. 184.
32. *Piatiletnii plan,* p. 95.
33. *UG,* no. 112 (339) (September 26, 1929), p. 2.
34. *NO,* pp. 108, 113; *Biulleten' NKP:* no. 30 (October 20, 1930), pp. 5–6; and no. 36 (December 20, 1930), p. 4. In Moscow and Leningrad, Narkompros claimed to provide no more than 40 percent of the pupils with breakfast: *Biulleten NKP,* no. 9 (March 20, 1931), p. 23.
35. *Biulleten' NKP,* no. 9 (March 20, 1931), p. 23.
36. *Narodnoe prosveshchenie v RSFSR v tsifrakh,* p. 41. On distribution: *ZVO,* no. 14 (1931), pp. 14–16; and *UG,* no. 36 (263) (March 27, 1929), p. 2.
37. *Na putiakh,* no. 12 (December 1929), pp. 46–48; *Biulleten' NKP,* no. 17 (June 10, 1930), p. 19; *ZKP,* no. 146 (516) (November 2, 1930), p. 3; *Biulleten' NKP,* no. 7 (March 1, 1931), p. 19.
38. *UG,* no. 110 (337) (September 21, 1929), p. 6.
39. *Na putiakh,* no. 10 (October 1930), pp. 45–47.
40. Ibid., p. 49.
41. *UG,* no. 105 (475) (August 29, 1930), p. 1.
42. *Biulleten' NKP,* no. 24 (August 20, 1930), pp. 38–39; and *ZKP,* no. 105 (475) (August 29, 1930), p. 1.
43. *Narodnoe prosveshchenie v RSFSR v osnovnykh pokazateliakh,* p. 80.
44. *Kul'turnoe stroitel'stvo SSSR,* p. 40.
45. *Pozyvnye istorii: uchenye zapiski VLKSM,* vol. 3 (Moscow, 1973), pp. 163, 165.
46. *IX Vsesoiuznyi s"ezd VLKSM. Stenograficheskii otchet* (Moscow, 1931), p. 385.
47. *Narodnoe prosveshchenie v RSFSR v osnovnykh pokazateliakh,* p. 80.
48. Ibid.
49. Ibid.
50. "Vsesoiuznyi s"ezd rabotnikov prosveshcheniia SSSR," *Na putiakh,* no. 3 (March 1929), pp. 46–47; *ZVO,* no. 2 (1930), pp. 19–21; *XVI s"ezd Vsesoiuznoi Kommunisticheskoi partii,* pp. 184–85; and *NO,* pp. 457–58.
51. *Narodnoe prosveshchenie v RSFSR v tsifrakh,* p. 41.
52. On supplements: *ZVO,* no. 2 (1930), p. 20; and *ZKP,* no. 76 (642) (April 1, 1931), p. 2. On fuel and other products: Danev, *Narodnoe obrazovanie,* p. 209.
53. *ZKP,* no. 193 (760) (August 18, 1931), p. 4.
54. *Nizhegorodskii prosveshchenets,* no. 6–7 (June–July 1931), p. 71.
55. *UG,* no. 36 (263) (March 27, 1929), p. 2.
56. *ZVO,* no. 2 (1930), p. 20; and *XVI s"ezd Vsesoiuznoi Kommunisticheskoi partii,* p. 185.

57. *Ezhenedel'nik NKP:* no. 42 (October 12, 1928), pp. 12–13; and no. 7 (February 8, 1929), pp. 15–17.

58. For example: *UG,* no. 84 (311) (July 23, 1929), p. 4; *ZKP:* no. 164 (534) (November 24, 1930), p. 3; no. 76 (642) (April 1, 1931), p. 2; and no. 193 (760) (August 18, 1931), p. 4; *Nizhegorodskii prosveshchenets,* no. 6–7 (June–July 1931), p. 7.

59. *UG,* no. 147 (365) (December 19, 1929), p. 2.

60. *Na putiakh,* no. 3 (March 1929), p. 46. Some teachers helped organize collective farms: I. A. Klitsakov, "Obshchestvenno-politicheskaia deiatel'nost' sovetskogo uchitel'stva," *Sovetskaia pedagogika,* no. 9 (September 1988), p. 93.

61. *UG,* no. 132 (350) (November 14, 1929), p. 2.

62. *ZKP:* no. 62 (628) (March 16, 1931), p. 4; and no. 66 (632) (March 20, 1931), p. 3. For similar stories: *UG,* no. 4 (374) (January 11, 1930), p. 4; and T. P. Bibanov, "Obshchestvenno-politicheskaia deiatel'nost' uchitel'stva v period sotsialisticheskogo stroitel'stva (1925–1936)," *Sovetskaia pedagogika,* no. 7 (July 1977), p. 110.

63. *NO,* p. 457; *ZVO,* no. 2 (1930), p. 19.

64. *ZVO,* no. 2 (1930), p. 19.

65. *Ezhenedel'nik NKP,* no. 52 (December 14, 1928), p. 38; and *Zakonodatel'stvo o trude,* p. 170.

66. *XVI s"ezd Vsesoiuznoi Kommunisticheskoi partii,* p. 183.

67. *NO,* p. 458.

68. A. Smirnov, "Prichiny vtorogodnichestva," *VP,* no. 11–12 (November–December 1928), pp. 117–25.

69. *UG:* no. 20 (390) (February 18, 1930), p. 3; and no. 34 (404) (March 22, 1930), p. 2.

70. *UG,* no. 5 (375) (January 14, 1930), p. 6.

71. *ZKP,* no. 168 (538) (November 28, 1930), p. 3.

72. *ZKP,* no. 196 (496) (October 9, 1930), p. 3; and *Biulleten' NKP,* no. 18 (March 25, 1932), p. 13.

73. Three articles in *ZKP,* no. 75 (445) (June 20, 1930), p. 3.

74. *ZKP,* no. 75 (445) (June 20, 1930), p. 3.

75. Ibid.

76. *ZKP,* no. 164 (534) (November 24, 1930), p. 3.

77. There were many such reports. For example: *UG,* no. 84 (311) (July 23, 1929), p. 4.

78. *ZKP:* no. 121 (491) (October 3, 1930), p. 3; no. 126 (496) (October 9, 1930), p. 3; and no. 204 (770) (August 30, 1931), p. 2.

79. *Nizhegorodskii prosveshchenets,* no. 11 (November 1931), p. 86; and *Biulleten' NKP,* no. 18 (March 25, 1932), p. 13.

80. *ZKP:* no. 86 (456) (July 16, 1930), p. 3; and no. 87 (457) (July 18, 1930), p. 1.

81. *Kul'turnoe stroitel'stvo SSSR,* p. 40.

82. Ibid., pp. 37–38, 51. For first grade enrollment: *Massovoe prosveshchenie v SSSR (k itogam pervoi piatiletki),* pp. 40–41. On coverage: *Massovoe prosveshchenie v SSSR k 15-letiiu oktiabria,* p. 35.

83. *Massovoe prosveshchenie v SSSR (k itogam pervoi piatiletki),* p. 73. The figure for urban schools was 97 percent, for rural schools 90 percent.

84. Ibid., pp. 6–9.

85. On the FZS: R. Kharitonov, "Fabrichno-zavodskaia semiletka," p. 72 and N. A. Konstantinov, *Istoriia pedagogiki* (Moscow, 1959), p. 388. On the FZU: Philip Lever, "The State Labor Reserves System," unpublished masters thesis (Columbia University, 1948), p. 78. These figures include some schools similar in nature to Factory Apprenticeship Schools. Estimates of the number of apprenticeship schools vary widely because of a lack of clarity regarding definition and geographic area covered.

86. *Narodnoe prosveshchenie v RSFSR v tsifrakh*, p. 26. Similar figures for Moscow province are in *Vseobshchee obiazatel'noe obuchenie*, p. 86.

87. *Massovoe prosveshchenie v SSSR (k itogam pervoi piatiletki)*, p. 69.

88. Ibid., p. 50.

89. Ibid., p. 70. In rural regions, 15 percent of the pupils belonged to the Pioneer organization and another 2 percent to the Octobrists.

90. *Massovoe prosveshchenie v SSSR k 15-letiiu oktiabria*, p. 78.

91. *Na putiakh*, no. 7-8 (July-August 1931), p. 7.

92. *Massovoe prosveshchenie v SSSR (k itogam pervoi piatiletki)*, pp. 58-59.

93. *Massovoe prosveshchenie v SSSR (k itogam pervoi piatiletki)*, pp. 6-9.

94. Ibid., pp. 40-41.

95. A. Fokht, "O kachestve raboty," *Obshchestvovedenie v sovetskoi shkole*, no. 6 (1931), pp. 23-30; and *Biulleten' NKP*, no. 5 (February 10, 1930), pp. 14-15.

96. Fitzpatrick, *Education and Social Mobility*, pp. 186-89.

97. *Ezhenedel'nik NKP*, no. 20-21 (May 17-24, 1929), p. 25.

98. *Biulleten' NKP*, no. 18 (June 20, 1930), pp. 14-15.

99. *UG*, no. 23 (393) (February 25, 1930), p. 4.

100. *UG*, no. 28 (398) (March 8, 1930), p. 4.

101. *NP*, no. 5 (1930), p. 16.

102. Ibid., no. 8-9 (August-September 1930), p. 146.

103. *Biulleten' NKP*, no. 18 (June 10, 1931), p. 7.

104. *Sistema narodnogo obrazovaniia*, p. 24.

105. *Biulleten' NKP*, no. 18 (June 10, 1931), p. 7.

106. *Narodnoe prosveshchenie v RSFSR v osnovnykh pokazateliakh*, p. 11. These figures were for the Russian Republic exclusive of its autonomous republics. See also *ZKP*, no. 6 (572) (January 7, 1931), p. 4.

107. *UG*, no. 146 (516) (November 2, 1930), p. 3; and *Biulleten' NKP*, no. 7 (March 1, 1931), p. 19.

108. *Narodnoe prosveshchenie v SSSR za 1928/29*, p. 59; Fitzpatrick, *Education and Social Mobility*, pp. 177-78.

109. *Biulleten' NKP*, no. 20 (July 10, 1930), p. 28.

110. Samarin, "The Soviet School," p. 29.

111. Veselov, *Professional'no-tekhnicheskoe obrazovanie*, p. 206; *Podgotovka kadrov*, p. 32.

112. Calculations in Osovsky, *Razvitie*, pp. 186, 192, 197; Veselov, *Professional'no-tekhnicheskoe obrazovanie*, p. 314.

113. Osovsky, *Razvitie*, p. 190.

114. Veselov, *Professional'no-tekhnicheskoe obrazovanie*, p. 287.

115. *Na putiakh*, no. 10 (October 1930), p. 47; Veselov, *Professional'no-tekhnicheskoe obrazovanie*, pp. 285-86; Blinchevsky, *Professional'no-tekhnicheskoe obrazovanie*, p. 46; Fitzpatrick, *Education and Social Mobility*, p. 103.

116. Bubnov, *Stat'i i rechi*, pp. 112-72.

117. Cited in Ravkin, "V bor'be za leninskii stil'," pp. 47-48.

XV. Policy Meets Practice, 1931

1. *NO*, pp. 157-58.

2. *NO*, p. 160.

3. *ZKP*, no. 179 (549) (December 11, 1930), p. 2.

4. *Na putiakh*, no. 1 (January 1931), pp. 50-52.

5. *Russkii iazyk v sovetskoi shkole*, no. 1 (1931), p. 178.

6. Ibid.; and *Rezoliutsii tretei sessii Gosudarstvennogo Uchenogo Soveta (27 dekabria 1930 g.-2 ianvaria 1931 g.)* (Moscow-Leningrad, 1931), pp. 8, 11, 13ff.

7. *ZKP*, no. 3 (569) (January 4, 1931), p. 3.

8. *ZKP*: no. 87 (653) (April 14, 1931), p. 4; no. 89 (655) (April 16, 1931), p.

3; and no. 90 (656) (April 17, 1931), p. 3; *Na putiakh,* no. 5 (May 1931), pp. 30–31.

9. *ZKP,* no. 86 (652) (April 13, 1931), p. 4; and *Na putiakh,* no. 5 (May 1931), p. 29.

10. *KP:* no. 4 (February 20, 1931), p. 2; no. 6 (March 20, 1931), pp. 70–74; no. 7 (April 5, 1931), pp. 73–79; and no. 8 (April 20, 1931), pp. 97–101.

11. *ZKP,* no. 93 (659) (April 21, 1931), p. 2.

12. *ZKP:* no. 130 (696) (June 4, 1931), p. 3; and no. 136 (702) (June 11, 1931), p. 3.

13. *Na putiakh,* no. 7–8 (July–August 1931), p. 46–49, 58.

14. L. Skatkin, "K voprosu o metode proektov," *Na putiakh,* no. 8–9 (August–September 1930), p. 57.

15. R. Lemberg, "Znaniia v proektakh nachal'noi shkoly," *Na putiakh,* no. 2 (February 1931), pp. 37–50.

16. *KP,* no. 9 (May 10, 1931), pp. 18–21.

17. *Na putiakh,* no. 7–8 (July–August 1931), pp. 14–15. Also her "Disskussionye voprosy," *Na putiakh,* no. 3 (March 1931), pp. 21–22.

18. As quoted in L. A. Stepashko, *Voprosy aktivizatsii uchebnoi deiatel'nosti shkol'nikov v sovetskoi didaktike (1917–1931 gg.)* (Khabarovsk, 1975), pp. 91–92.

19. *Biulleten' NKP,* no. 12 (April 20, 1931), p. 5.

20. *Russkii iazyk v sovetskoi shkole,* no. 4 (1931), pp. 180–81; *ZKP,* no. 95 (661) (April 23, 1931), p. 4.

21. *Russkii iazyk v sovetskoi shkole,* no. 4 (1931), p. 183; *ZKP,* no. 95 (661) (April 23, 1931), p. 4.

22. *Russkii iazyk v sovetskoi shkole,* no. 4 (1931), p. 183; *Na putiakh,* no. 5 (May 1931), pp. 41–42.

23. *ZKP,* no. 95 (661) (April 23, 1931), p. 4.

24. *KP,* no. 12 (June 20, 1931), pp. 13, 15.

25. Ibid., p. 18.

26. Ibid., p. 19–24; *KP,* no. 13 (July 5, 1931), p. 21.

27. *Russkii iazyk v sovetskoi shkole,* no. 4 (1931), pp. 142, 154–55, 175. On the reevaluation of instruction in literature: Ia. A. Rotkovich, "The History of Literature Teaching in the Soviet School," *Soviet Education,* vol. 22, no. 7–8 (May–June 1980), p. 66.

28. *Obshchestvovedenie v shkole,* no. 3–4 (1931), pp. 3–7.

29. *ZKP,* no. 133 (699) (June 8, 1931), p. 3. The draft curricula emphasized the project method, socialist competition, production instruction, and political agitation as vital components of schooling: *Proekt programmy pervoi stupeni fabrichno-zavodskoi semiletki* (Moscow-Leningrad, 1931), especially p. 10; *Programmy sel'skoi nachal'noi shkoly* (Moscow-Leningrad, 1931), especially p. 15; also *Proekt novykh programm fabrichno-zavodskoi semiletki* (Moscow, 1931), vyp. 3, pp. 5ff., 50, 62ff.

30. Bubnov, *Stat'i i rechi,* p. 189.

31. *KP,* no. 17 (September 5, 1931), pp. 11–17. Summary in *ZKP,* no. 195 (761) (August 19, 1931), p. 3.

32. *KP,* no. 17 (September 5, 1931), p. 16.

33. *ZKP,* no. 201 (767) (August 26, 1931), p. 2; *Fizika, khimiia, matematika, tekhnika v sovetskoi shkole,* no. 6–7 (1931), p. 46. He also identified the method with the notion of a convergence of pupil self-government at school with the Pioneer organization.

34. *ZKP:* no. 181 (747) (August 3, 1931), p. 3; and no. 192 (758) (August 16, 1931), p. 2. *Fizika, khimiia, matematika, tekhnika v sovetskoi shkole,* no. 6–7 (1931), p. 47.

35. *ZKP:* no. 201 (767) (August 26, 1931), p. 1; no. 203 (769) (August 28, 1931), p. 1; and no. 206 (September 1, 1931), p. 1.

Conclusion

1. *XVII s"ezd Vsesoiuznoi partii (b). Stenograficheskii otchet* (Moscow, 1934), p. 564.

2. Ibid., p. 565.

3. Oskar Anweiler, "Der Revolutionaere Umbruch im Schulwesen und in der Paedagogik Russlands," in *Bildung, Politik und Gesellschaft* (Vienna, 1978), p. 262.

4. General education might better prepare pupils for short courses, on-the-job training, specialized education, and retraining that rapidly changing economies require. See *Education and Economic Development,* ed. C. Arnold Anderson and Mary Jean Bowman (Chicago, 1965), especially Philip J. Foster, "The Vocational School Fallacy in Development Planning," pp. 142–66.

5. Roberta Manning, *Government in the Soviet Countryside in the Stalinist Thirties: The Belyi Raion in 1917* (The Carl Beck Papers #301, University of Pittsburgh, 1984); J. Arch Getty, *Origins of the Great Purges: The Soviet Communist Party Reconsidered, 1933–1938* (New York, 1985); Lynne Viola, "The Campaign to Eliminate the Kulak as a Class, Winter 1929–1930: A Reevaluation of the Legislation," *Slavic Review,* vol. 45, no. 3 (Fall 1986), pp. 503–24.

6. Kendall Bailes, *Technology and Society under Lenin and Stalin: Origins of the Soviet Technical Intelligentsia, 1917–1941* (Princeton, 1978); Eugene Huskey, *Russian Lawyers and the Soviet State: The Origins and Development of the Soviet Bar, 1917–1939* (Princeton, 1986).

7. Moshe Lewin, *The Making of the Soviet System: Essays in the Social History of Interwar Russia* (New York, 1985). Also contributions to *Bolshevik Culture:* Jeffrey Brooks, "The Breakdown in Production and Distribution of Printed Material, 1917–1927," pp. 151–74; and Beatrice Farnsworth, "Village Women Experience the Revolution," pp. 238–60.

8. See the contributions to *Cultural Revolution in Russia:* David Joravsky, "The Construction of the Stalinist Psyche," pp. 105–28; and Susan Gross Solomon, "Rural Scholars and the Cultural Revolution," pp. 129–53. Also: Joravsky, *Soviet Marxism and Natural Science;* Susan Gross Solomon, *The Soviet Agrarian Debate: A Controversy in Social Science, 1923–29* (Boulder, 1977); Louise Shelley, "Soviet Criminology: Its Birth and Demise, 1917–1936," *Slavic Review,* vol. 38, no. 4 (December 1979), pp. 614–28; Peter H. Solomon, Jr., "Soviet Penal Policy, 1917–1934: A Reinterpretation," *Slavic Review,* vol. 39, no. 2 (June 1980), pp. 195–217; Richard Taylor, *The Politics of Soviet Cinema, 1917–1929* (New York, 1979).

9. Roger Pethybridge, *The Social Prelude to Stalinism* (New York, 1974), pp. 196–251; Fitzpatrick, *Education and Social Mobility,* pp. 113–205.

10. Pethybridge, p. 239.

11. By Dneprov: "Uchit'sia uchit," *Sovetskaia kul'tura* (November 14, 1987), p. 3; "Vedomstvennoe samovlastie," *Pravda* (February 13, 1988), p. 3. These and other comments by Dneprov have been published by the Provisional Research Collective: E. D. Dneprov, *Shkola na segodnia, zavtra i poslezavtra* (Moscow, 1989).

BIBLIOGRAPHY

I. Archival Sources

Central State Archive of the RSFSR (TsGA RSFSR), Moscow.

Fond 1575 including: materials on the work of the Department of the United Labor School; school curricula and syllabi; reports from and on regular and experimental schools; reports on the training and repreparation of teachers and on the training and activity of inspectors.

Fond 2306 including: Narkompros reports on the state of education; school curricula and syllabi; materials on the activity of various Narkompros departments; Narkompros response to Rabkrin investigations; protocols of sessions of the Narkompros Collegium.

Fond 298 including: reports from various sections and subsections of Narkompros; protocols of sessions of the Pedagogical Section of the State Academic Council.

II. Selected Books and Articles

Western Works

Anweiler, Oskar. *Geschichte der Schule und Paedagogik in Russland vom Ende des Zarenreiches bis zum Beginn der Stalin-Aera* (2nd ed.; Berlin, 1978).

Anweiler, Oskar, and Karl-Heinz Ruffman (eds.). *Kulturpolitik der Sowjetunion* (Stuttgart, 1973).

Bolshevik Culture: Experiment and Order in the Russian Revolution, ed. Abbott Gleason, Peter Kenez, and Richard Stites (Bloomington, 1985).

Eklof, Ben. "Peasant Sloth Reconsidered: Strategies of Education and Learning in Rural Russia Before the Revolution," *Journal of Social History,* vol. 14, no. 3 (Spring 1981), pp. 355–85.

———. *Russian Peasant Schools: Officialdom, Village Culture, and Popular Pedagogy, 1861–1914* (Berkeley, 1986).

Epshtein, Abraham. "The School in Soviet Russia," *School and Society,* vol. 16, no. 406 (October 7, 1922).

Fisher, Ralph T. *Pattern for Soviet Youth: A Study of the Congresses of the Komsomol, 1918–1954* (New York, 1959).

Fitzpatrick, Sheila. *The Commissariat of Enlightenment: Soviet Organization of Education and the Arts under Lunacharsky, October 1917–1921* (Cambridge, 1970).

———. *Education and Social Mobility in the Soviet Union, 1921–1934* (Cambridge, 1979).

Fitzpatrick, Sheila (ed.). *Cultural Revolution in Russia, 1928–1931* (Bloomington, 1978).

Gock, Anna. *Polytechnische Bildung und Erziehung in der Sowjetunion bis 1937* (Berlin, 1985).

Hans, Nicholas and Sergius Hessen. *Educational Policy in Soviet Russia* (London, 1930).

Kline, George L. (ed.). *Soviet Education* (New York, 1957).

Lapidus, Gail Warshofsky. "Educational Strategies and Cultural Revolution: The Politics of Soviet Development," in *Cultural Revolution in Russia, 1928–1931* (Bloomington, 1978), pp. 78–104.

O'Connor, Timothy Edward. *The Politics of Soviet Culture: Anatolii Lunacharskii* (Ann Arbor, 1983).

Stites, Richard. *Revolutionary Dreams: Utopian Vision and Experimental Life in the Russian Revolution* (New York, 1989).

————. "Stalin: Utopian or Antiutopian? An Indirect Look at the Cult of Personality," in *The Cult of Power: Dictators in the Twentieth Century,* ed. Joseph Held (Boulder, 1983).

Stolee, Margaret Kay. "'A Generation Capable of Establishing Communism': Revolutionary Child Rearing in the Soviet Union, 1917–1928," unpublished dissertation (Duke University, 1982).

Soviet Works

Anikst, Ol'ga. "Puti professional'nogo obrazovaniia," *Narodnoe prosveshchenie,* no. 10 (October 1927).

Anikst, Ol'ga. (ed.) *Professional'no-tekhnicheskoe obrazovanie v Rossii za 1917–1921 gg.: iubileinyi sbornik* (Moscow, 1922).

Belousov, S. "'Vtorogodnichestvo' i ego rol' v zhizni nashei shkoly," *Narodnoe prosveshchenie,* no. 4–5 (April–May 1926).

————. "Vtorogodnichestvo v gorodskikh shkolakh," *Vestnik prosveshcheniia,* no. 5 (May 1972).

Belozerov, A. "O sotsial'nom sostave uchashchikhsia sotsvosa," *Narodnoe prosveshchenie,* no. 6 (June 1929), pp. 59–63.

Blinchevsky, F. L. and G. I. Zelenko. *Professional'no-tekhnicheskoe obrazovanie rabochikh v SSSR* (Moscow, 1957).

Bogdanov, I. M. "Kharakteristika sotsial'nogo sostava uchashchikhsia na raznykh stupeniakh obucheniia v sisteme sotsvosa i profobra," *Narodnoe prosveshchenie,* no. 5 (May 1929).

————. "Nominal'nyi i fakticheskii kurs obucheniia v nachal'noi shkole," *Narodnoe prosveshchenie,* no. 1 (1925), pp. 64–75.

————. "Vazhneishie itogi perepisei naseleniia i shkol'noi v prilozhenii k zaprosam prosveshcheniia," *Narodnoe prosveshchenie,* no. 5 (May 1928).

Chuvashev, I. V. "Voprosy trudovoi politekhnicheskogo vospitaniia," *Narodnyi uchitel',* no. 12 (December 1929); no. 1 (January 1930); no. 2 (February 1930); no. 7–8 (July–August 1930); and no. 9–10 (September–October 1930).

Dmitrieva, L. N. *Partiinoe rukovodstvo professional'no-tekhnicheskim obrazovaniem molodezhi (1917–1936 gg.)* (Leningrad, 1978).

Epshtein, M. "Shkola, kak ona est'," *Narodnyi uchitel',* no. 7 (July 1926), pp. 10–22.

Esipov, B. "Voprosy uchitelei po povodu programmy GUS'a," *Na putiakh k novoi shkole,* no. 7–8 (July–August 1924), pp. 78–95.

Gaidovskaia, E. "Pervye shagi," *Narodnyi uchitel',* no. 7 (July 1926).

Goncharov, N. K. (ed.). *V. I. Lenin i problemy narodnogo obrazovaniia* (Moscow, 1961).

Ivanov, A. G. "Ocherki po istorii sovetskoi srednei obshcheobrazovatel'noi shkoly (1917–1925 gg.)," in *Uchenye zapiski. Yaroslavskii gosudarstvennyi pedagogicheskii institut,* vyp. 48 (Yaroslavl', 1961), pp. 5–185.

Iz opyta gorodskoi semiletki; sbornik, ed. E. Kushner and A. Kolpakova (Moscow-Leningrad, 1927).

"Iz raboty Nauchno-Pedagogicheskoi Sektsii," *Na putiakh k novoi shkole,* no. 5–6 (May-June 1926).

Kharitonov, R. "Fabrichno-zavodskaia semiletka i zadachi klassovogo vospitaniia detei rabochikh," *Narodnoe prosveshchenie,* no. 1 (January 1929).

Konovalova, K. "S uchitel'skoi konferentsii," *Narodnyi uchitel',* no. 4 (April 1926).

Konstantinov, N.A., E. N. Medynskii, and M. F. Shabaeva. *Istoriia pedagogiki* (Moscow, 1959).

Korolev, F. F. *Ocherki po istorii sovetskoi shkoly i pedagogiki, 1917–1920* (Moscow, 1958).

————. *Sovetskaia shkola v period sotsialisticheskoi industrializatsii* (Moscow, 1959).

Korolev, F. F., T. D. Korneichik, and Z. I Ravkin. *Ocherki po istorii sovetskoi shkoly i pedagogiki, 1921-1931* (Moscow, 1961).

Lunin, E. "O chem pishet narodnyi uchitel'," *Narodnyi uchitel'*, no. 6 (June 1924).
Lysiakov, L. "Iz grudy uchitel'skikh stikhov," *Narodnyi uchitel'*, no. 5-6 (May–June 1927).
Novye formy i metody prosvetitel'noi raboty. Sbornik (Moscow–Leningrad, 1929).
Osovsky, E. G. *Razvitie teorii professional'no-tekhnicheskogo obrazovaniia v SSSR (1917-1940)* (Moscow, 1980).
Pedagogicheskaia entsiklopediia, 3 vols. (Moscow, 1927-1930).
Pidkasistyi, P. I. *N. K. Krupskaia o soderzhanii v sovetskoi shkole* (Moscow, 1962).
Pistrak, M. "Kak sozdavalis' programmy GUSA," *Narodnoe prosveshchenie*, no. 10 (1927).
———. "Nedopustimye uklony v shkol'nom dele," *Na putiakh k novoi shkole*, no. 11 (November 1927), pp. 8-22.
Prava uchashchikhsia i uchashchikh. Sbornik deistvuiushchego zakonodatel'stva (Moscow, 1925).
Programmy GUS'a i mestnaia rabota nad nim, ed. S. T. Shatsky (Moscow, 1925).
Programmy GUS'a i obshchestvenno-politicheskoe vospitanie, ed. E. Rudneva (Moscow, 1925).
Rabochaia molodezh' i ee shkola (Petersburg, 1922).
Ravkin, Z. I. *Sovetskaia shkola v gody perekhoda na mirnuiu rabotu po vosstanovleniiu narodnogo khoziaistva (1921-1925 gg.).* Akademiia pedagogicheskikh nauk. *Izvestiia, vyp. 22 (Moscow, 1949).*
———. *Sovetskaia shkola v period vosstanovleniia narodnogo khoziaistva, 1921-1925 gg.* (Moscow, 1959).
———. "V bor'be za leninskii stil' raboty Narkomprosa," *Narodnoe obrazovanie*, no. 2 (February 1964), pp. 42-48.
"Shkola II-oi stupeni," *Narodnoe prosveshchenie*, no. 16-17 (November–December 1920).
Shumov, S. "O chem pishet narodnyi uchitel'," *Narodnyi uchitel'*, no. 5 (May 1925).
Sirotkin, V. "Kak rabotaiut shkoly Moskovskoi gubernii," in *Kak rabotaiut shkoly Moskovskoi gubernii. Sbornik* (Moscow, 1925), pp. 12–88.
Svadkovsky, I. F. *Rabochaia kniga po istorii pedagogiki* (Moscow-Leningrad, 1927).
Tolstov, A. "Na rabote po organizatsii trudovoi shkoly," *Narodnoe prosveshchenie*, no. 10 (October 1927).
V pomoshch' organizatoru narodnogo prosveshcheniia: sbornik po voprosam inspektirovaniia i rukovodstva prosvetitel'noi rabotoi (Moscow, 1928).
Vasil'ev, A. "Biudzhet narodnogo obrazovaniia v SSSR," *Narodnoe prosveshchenie*, no. 4 (1928), pp. 120–30.
Veselov, A. N. *Professional'no-tekhnicheskoe obrazovanie v SSSR: Ocherki po istorii srednego i nizshego proftekhobrazovaniia* (Moscow, 1961).
Vospominaniia o Nadezhde Konstantinovne Krupskoi, ed. A. M. Arsen'ev, V. S. Dridzo, and A. G. Kravchenko (Moscow, 1966).
Zakolodkin, "Kul'turnye nozhnitsy," *Narodnoe prosveshchenie*, no. 10 (October 1928), pp. 82-101; no. 11 (November 1928), pp. 103–110; and no. 12 (December 1928), pp. 68-75.
Zakonodatel'stva o trude rabotnikov prosveshcheniia (Moscow, 1931).

III. Statistical Compilations

Regional Surveys

Itogi osnovnogo obsledovaniia sostoianiia narodnogo obrazovaniia v Novgorodskoi gubernii na 1-e noiabria 1920 goda (Novgorod, 1922).
Kul'turnoe sostoianie Nizhe-Volzhskogo kraia (kratkoe opisanie) (Saratov, 1928).
Narodnoe obrazovanie Orlovskoi gubernii za 1910-1917, 1920–23 gg. (Orel, 1924)
Narodnoe obrazovanie v Leningradskoi oblasti za 15 let: sbornik (Leningrad, 1932).
Narodnoe obrazovanie v Pskovskoi gubernii (Pskov, 1921).

Narodnoe obrazovanie v Severno-Dvinskoi gubernii (Velikii-Ustiug, 1922).
Narodnoe obrazovanie v Ul'ianovskoi gubernii za 1914–1924 gg. (Ul'ianovsk, 1927).
Popov, V. A. *Shkoly sotsial'nogo vospitaniia: g. Moskvy i Moskovskoi gubernii. Statisticheskii obzor* (Moscow, 1930).
Shkol'noe obrazovanie na 1-i stupeni obucheniia v Novgorodskoi gubernii po sostoianiiu na 1-e ianvaria 1924 goda (Novgorod, 1924).
Sostoianie i perspektivy razvitiia narodnogo obrazovaniia v Moskve i moskovskoi gubernii (Moscow, 1928).

Surveys of the Russian Republic and USSR

Kontrol'nye tsifry narodnogo prosveshcheniia v RSFSR na 1937 g. (Moscow, 1937).
Kul'turnoe stroitel'stvo Soiuza sovetskikh sotsialisticheskikh respublik: sbornik diagramm (2nd ed.; Moscow-Leningrad, 1932).
Kul'turnoe stroitel'stvo SSSR: statisticheskii sbornik (Moscow-Leningrad, 1940).
Massovoe prosveshchenie v SSSR (k itogam pervoi piatiletki) (Moscow, 1933).
Massovoe prosveshchenie v SSSR k 15-letiiu oktiabria, pt. 1 (Moscow-Leningrad, 1932).
Na poroge vtorogo desiatiletiia: praktika sotsial'nogo vospitaniia (Moscow-Leningrad, 1927).
Narodnoe obrazovanie, nauka i kul'tura v SSSR: statisticheskii sbornik (Moscow, 1977).
Narodnoe obrazovanie v RSFSR (po dannym godovoi statisticheskoi otchetnosti mestnykh organov 1924 goda (Moscow, 1925).
Narodnoe prosveshchenie v RSFSR: statisticheskii sbornik (Moscow-Leningrad, 1928).
Narodnoe prosveshchenie v RSFSR v osnovnykh pokazateliakh: statisticheskii sbornik (1927/28–1930/31 gg., so vkliucheniem nekotorykh dannykh za 1931/32 g.) (Moscow-Leningrad, 1932).
Narodnoe prosveshchenie v RSFSR v tsifrakh za 15 let sovetskoi vlasti (Moscow-Leningrad, 1932).
Narodnoe prosveshchenie v SSSR 1926–1927 uchebnyi god (Moscow, 1929).
Narodnoe prosveshchenie v SSSR. I. Predvaritel'nye itogi shkol'noi perepisi. 15 dekabria 1927 goda. II. Dannye tekushchei statistiki 1927–28 uchebnogo goda (Moscow, 1929).
Narodnoe prosveshchenie v SSSR za 1928/29 (Moscow-Leningrad, 1930).
Narodnyi Komissariat po prosveshcheniiu. 1917-oktiabr'–1920 (kratkii otchet) (Moscow, 1920).
Podgotovka kadrov v SSSR 1917–1931 gg. (Moscow-Leningrad, 1933).
Prosveshchenie v RSFSR v 1926/27 uchebnom godu po materialam: 1) tekushchego obsledovaniia na 1 dekabria 1926 goda; 2) vyborochnogo obsledovaniia biudzheta shkol sotsvosa za 1926/27 uchebnyi god (Moscow, 1928).
Statisticheskii sbornik po narodnomu prosveshcheniiu RSFSR 1926 g. (Moscow, 1927).
Statisticheskii ezhegodnik: sostoianie narodnogo obrazovaniia v SSSR (bez avtonomnykh respublik) za 1924/25 uch. god (Moscow, 1926).
Vseobshchee obiazatel'noe obuchenie: statisticheskii ocherk po dannym shkol'noi perepisi tekushchei statistiki prosveshcheniia (Moscow, 1930).
Vseobshchee obuchenie likvidatsii negramotnosti i podgotovka kadrov (statisticheskii ocherk) (Moscow, 1930).
Vsesoiuznaia perepis' naseleniia 17 dekabria 1926 g. Kratkie svodki. vyp. 5. *Vozrast i gramotnost'. Evropeiskaia chast' RSFSR. Belorusskaia SSR* (Moscow, 1928).

IV. Collections of Documents and Decrees

Danev, A. M. (ed.). *Narodnoe obrazovanie* (Moscow, 1948).
Direktivy VKP(b) po voprosam prosveshcheniia (Moscow-Leningrad, 1930).
Kommunisticheskaia partiia Sovetskogo Soiuza v rezoliutsiiakh i resheniiakh, s"ezdov, konferentsii i plenumov TsK, 10 vols. (8th ed.; Moscow, 1970–1973).
Narodnoe obrazovanie v SSSR. Sbornik dokumentov, 1917–1973 gg. (Moscow, 1974).
Sobranie uzakonenii i rasporiazhenii rabochego i krest'ianskogo pravitel'stva RSFSR (Moscow, 1920–1949).

V. Collected Works

Bubnov, A. S. *Stat'i i rechi o narodnom obrazovanii* (Moscow, 1959).
The Karl Marx Library, ed. Saul Podover, 7 vols. (New York, 1971–1977).
Krupskaya, N. K. *Pedagogicheskie sochineniia*, 11 vols. (Moscow, 1957–1963).
Lenin, V. I. *Polnoe sobranie sochinenii*, 55 vols (5th ed.; Moscow, 1958–1966).
Lunacharsky, A. V. *Lunacharsky o narodnom obrazovanii* (Moscow, 1958).
————. *O vospitanii i obrazovanii* (Moscow, 1958).
————. *On Education: Selected Articles and Speeches* (Moscow, 1981).
Marx, Karl and Friedrich Engels. *Collected Works*, 17 vols. (London, 1975–).
Stalin, I. V. *Sochineniia*, 13 vols. (Moscow, 1946–1951).
Shatsky, S. T. *Pedagogicheskie sochineniia*, 4 vols. (Moscow, 1962–1965).

VI. Soviet Periodicals

Central Journals
Biulleten' Narkomprosa RSFSR (1930–1935)
Biulleten' ofitsial'nykh rasporiazhenii i soobshchenii (1921–1923)
Ezhenedel'nik Narkomprosa RSFSR (1923–1929)
Fizika, khimiia, matematika, tekhnika v sovetskoi shkole (1927–1932)
Istorik-Marksist (1926–1941)
Kommunisticheskoe prosveshchenie (1931–1936)
Kommunisticheskaia revoliutsiia (1920–1935)
Na putiakh k novoi shkole (1922–1933)
Narodnoe prosveshchenie: Ezhenedel'nik Narkomprosa (1918–1922)
Narodnoe prosveshchenie (1918–1930)
Narodnyi uchitel' (1924–1935)
Nauchnyi rabotnik (1925–1930)
Obshchestvovedenie v trudovoi shkole (1927–1932)
Rabotnik prosveshcheniia (1920–1930)
Russkii iazyk v sovetskoi shkole (1929–1931)
Sovetskoi shkole—novyi uchebnik (1925–1928)
Trudovaia shkola (1928)
Vestnik prof-tekhnicheskogo obrazovaniia (1920–1922)
Za Vseobshchee obuchenie (1930–1935)

Provincial Journals
Biulleten' Moskovskogo Otdela Narodnogo Obrazovaniia (1928–1929)
Biulleten' Otdela Narodnogo obrazovaniia (Moscow) (1918–1920)
Ezhenedel'nik Moskovskogo Otdela Narodnogo Obrazovaniia (1926–1928)
Informatsionnyi Biulleten' Otdela Narodnogo Obrazovaniia (Moscow) (1921)
Narodnoe obrazovanie (Tver) (1919)
Narodnoe prosveshchenie (Kursk) (1922)
Nash trud (Yaroslavl') (1922–1929)
Nizhegorodskii prosveshchenets (Nizhnii Novgorod) (1929–1932)
Nizhe-Volzhskii prosveshchenets (Saratov) (1928–1929)
Shkola i zhizn' (Nizhnii Novgorod) (1923–1929)
Vestnik prosveshcheniia (Moscow) (1922–1929)
Vestnik prosveshcheniia (Tambov) (1919, 1922)
Za kommunisticheskoe vospitanie (Moscow, 1930–1935)

Newspapers
Izvestiia

Pravda
Uchitel'skaia gazeta (renamed *Za kommunisticheskoe prosveshchenie* in April 1930)

VII. Conferences and Congresses

Young Communist League *(in chronological order)*
Pervyi s"ezd RKSM, 29 oktiabria–4 noiabria 1918 g. (Moscow, 1934)
Vtoroi Vserossiiskii s"ezd RKSM, 5–8 oktiabria 1919 goda. Stenograficheskii otchet (3rd ed.; Moscow-Leningrad, 1926).
Tretii Vserossiiskii s"ezd RKSM, 2–10 oktiabria 1920 goda. Stenograficheskii otchet (Moscow-Leningrad, 1926).
Chetvertyi s"ezd RKSM, 21–28 sentiabria 1921 g. Stenograficheskii otchet (Moscow-Leningrad, 1925).
Piatyi Vserossiiskii s"ezd RKSM, 11–19 oktiabria 1922 goda. Stenograficheskii otchet (Moscow-Leningrad, 1927).
Shestoi s"ezd Rossiiskogo leninskogo Kommunisticheskogo soiuza molodezhi, 12–18 iiulia 1924 goda. Stenograficheskii otchet (Moscow-Leningrad, 1924).
Rezoliutsii i postanovleniia VI Vsesoiuznogo s"ezda RLKSM (Moscow, 1924).
Sed'moi Vsesoiuznyi s"ezd leninskogo Kommunisticheskogo soiuza molodezhi, 11–22 marta 1926 goda. Stenograficheskii otchet (Moscow-Leningrad, 1926).
Rezoliutsii i postanovleniia VII Vsesoiuznogo s"ezda VLKSM (Moscow-Leningrad, 1926).
VIII Vsesoiuznyi s"ezd VLKSM, 5–16 maia 1928 goda. Stenograficheskii otchet (Moscow, 1928).

On Education
Leonova, E. "Pervaia Vserossiiskaia konferentsiia po uchebnoi i detskoi knige," *Na putiakh k novoi shkole,* no. 7–8 (July-August 1926).
Pervyi Vserossiiskii s"ezd po politekhnicheskomu obrazovaniiu: doklady, preniia, rezoliutsii i dr. materialy (Moscow-Leningrad, 1931).
Piatiletnii plan kul'turnogo stroitel'stva (Moscow-Leningrad, 1929).
Prilozhenie k Biulleteniu VIII s"ezda sovetov (January 10, 1921).
Rezoliutsii piatogo Vserossiiskogo s"ezda zaveduiushchikh otdelami narodnogo obrazovaniia (Moscow, 1926).
Rezoliutsii tretei sessii Gosudarstvennogo Uchenogo Soveta (27 dekabria 1930 g.-2 ianvaria 1931 g.) (Moscow-Leningrad, 1931).
Sistema narodnogo obrazovaniia v rekonstruktivnyi period: soveshchanie Obshchestva Pedagogov-Marksistov pri Kommunisticheskoi akademii 7/II–16/III (Moscow, 1930).
"Tret'e soveshchanie narkomprosov soiuznykh avtonomnykh respublik SSSR," *Narodnoe prosveshchenie,* no. 1 (10) (1924).
Uchitel'stvo na novykh putiakh: sbornik statei, dokladov i materialov Vsesoiuznogo s"ezda uchitelei (Leningrad, 1925).
Voprosy shkoly II stupeni: Trudy Pervoi Vserossiiskoi konferentsii shkol II stupeni 5–10 iiulia 1925 g. (Moscow, 1925).
Vtoroe Vsesoiuznoe partiinoe soveshchanie po narodnomu obrazovaniiu. Stenograficheskii otchet (Moscow, 1931).

VIII. Curricula, Syllabi, and Instructional Materials from Narkompros RSFSR (in chronological order)

1919
Materialy po obrazovatel'noi rabote v trudovoi shkole (Moscow, 1919).

1920
Primernye programmy po istorii dlia skhol II stupeni (Moscow, 1920).
Primernye programmy po izobrazitel'nym iskusstvam dlia shkol I i II stupeni (Moscow, 1920).
Primernye uchebnye plany dlia I-i i II-i stupeni v edinoi trudovoi shkole (Moscow, 1920).

1921

Khudozhestvennaia organizatsiia shkol'noi zhizni (Moscow, 1921).
Programmy semiletnei edinoi trudovoi shkoly (Moscow, 1921).
Rodnoi iazyk v shkole I stupeni (Moscow, 1921).
Tezisy k dokladu s"ezdu Gubernskikh ONO o vyrabotannykh programmakh dlia edinoi trudovoi shkoly I i II stupeni (Moscow, 1921).

1923

Metodicheskie pis'ma. Pis'mo pervoe. O kompleksnom prepodavanii (9th ed.; Moscow, 1925).
Novye programmy dlia edinoi trudovoi shkoly (Moscow-Leningrad, 1923).

1924

Blonsky, P. P. *Novye programmy GUS'a i uchitel'* (Moscow, 1924).
Novye programmy edinoi trudovoi shkoly pervoi stupeni (I, II, III i IV gody obucheniia) (Moscow, 1924).

1925

Avtukhov, I. G. and I. D. Martynenko (eds.). *Programmy GUS'a i massovaia shkola* (2nd ed.; Moscow, 1925).
Metodicheskie pis'ma. Pis'mo tret'e. Ob uchete raboty v shkole I stupeni (Moscow, 1925).
Pis'mo shkol'niku i shkol'nitse 1-i stupeni (Moscow, 1925).
Programmy dlia pervogo kontsentra shkol vtoroi stupeni (5, 6, i 7 gody obucheniia) (Moscow-Leningrad, 1925).

1926

Avtukhov, I. G. (comp.). *Kak prorabatyvat' uchitel'stvu programmy GUS'a: dlia shkol pervoi stupeni* (Moscow, 1926).
Praktika raboty po programme GUS'a: Rabochaia kniga uchitelei I stupeni, pt. 2 (Moscow, 1926).
Programmy GUS'a dlia pervogo i vtorogo godov sel'skoi shkoly I stupeni (s izmeneniiami, sdelannymi na osnovanii ucheta opyta) (Moscow, 1926).
Proekty programm shkoly II stupeni (I kontsentr—5, 6, i 7 gody obucheniia) (Moscow, 1926).

1927

Programmy i metodicheskie zapiski edinoi trudovoi shkoly (Moscow-Leningrad, 1927).
Vypusk 1. *Gorodskie i sel'skie shkoly I stupeni. Programmy*
Vypusk 2. *Gorodskie i sel'skie shkoly I stupeni. Metodicheskie zapiski k programmam*
Vypusk 3. *1-i kontsentr gorodskoi shkoly II stupeni*
Vypusk 5. *2-i kontsentr shkoly II stupeni. Programmy obshcheobrazovatel'nykh predmetov*
Vypusk 6. *2-i kontsentr shkoly II stupeni. Programmy spetsial'nykh predmetov*

1928

Programmy i metodicheskie zapiski shkol krest'ianskoi molodezhi (Moscow-Leningrad, 1928).
Povyshennaia shkola i oborona strany. Sbornik materialov dopolnenii i poiasnenii programmam Narkomprosa (Moscow-Leningrad, 1928).

1929

Programmy edinoi trudovoi shkoly I stupeni. Dlia fabrichno-zavodskoi i gorodskoi shkoly (Moscow, 1929).
Programmy edinoi trudovoi shkoly I stupeni. Dlia sel'skoi shkoly (Moscow, 1929).

1930

Programmy fabrichno-zavodskoi semiletki (Moscow-Leningrad, 1930).
Programmy i metodicheskie zapiski shkol kolkhoznoi molodezhi: programmnye materialy (Moscow-Leningrad, 1930).

Programmy nachal'noi shkoly: gorodskoi variant (Moscow, 1930).
Programmy nachal'noi shkoly: sel'skii variant (Moscow, 1930).

1931
Proekt novykh programm fabrichno-zavodskoi semiletki (Moscow, 1931).
Proekt programm sel'skoi nachal'noi shkoly (Moscow, 1931).
Proekt programmy pervoi stupeni fabrichno-zavodskoi semiletki (Moscow-Leningrad, 1931).
Programmy sel'skoi nachal'noi shkoly (Moscow-Leningrad, 1931).

IX. Curricula, Syllabi, and Instructional Materials from Provincial Departments of Education (in chronological order)

1918–1919
Edinaia trudovaia shkola i primernye plany zaniatii v nei (1-ia stupen'obucheniia) (Viatka, 1918).
Narodnaia edinaia trudovaia shkola. vyp. 2 (Penza, 1919).
Programmy nachal'noi shkoly (s shestiletnim kursom) (Malmyzh, 1919).

1920
Primernaia programma edinoi trudovoi shkoly I stupeni (Moscow, 1920).
Primernye programmy sovetskoi edinoi trudovoi shkoly 1-oi stupeni (Novonikolaevsk, 1920).

1921
Primernye programmy dlia pervoi stupeni edinoi trudovoi shkoly (Kursk, 1921).
Primernye programmy dlia II-i stupeni edinoi trudovoi shkoly (Orenburg, 1921).
Primernyi plan rabot v shkole I-i stupeni (Viatka, 1921).
Primernyi uchebnyi plan shkoly 1-i stupeni (na 1921–22 uchebnyi god) (Tsaritsyn, 1921).
Semiletnaia shkola (Kursk, 1921).

1922
Programma semiletnei trudovoi shkoly (Roslavl', 1922).
Programmy chetyrekhletnei edinoi trudovoi shkoly (V. Ustiug, 1922).
Programmy dlia pervoi i vtoroi stupeni edinoi trudovoi shkoly (Kursk, 1922).
Programmy dlia 1-oi i II-oi stupeni edinoi trudovoi shkoly (Novgorod, 1922).
Programmy dlia shkol 1-i stupeni, Vladimirskoi gubernii (Vladimir, 1922).
Programmy minimum dlia sel'skoi shkoly (Moscow-Leningrad, 1922).
Programmy I-i stupeni edinoi trudovoi shkoly (Saratov, 1922).
Uchebnyi plan i programmy edinoi trudovoi shkoly I stupeni (4-kh letki) (Samara, 1922).

1923
Programma minimum dlia shkoly I stupeni s chetyrekhletnim kursom obucheniia (Ekaterinburg, 1923).
Programmnye materialy dlia edinoi trudovoi shkoly I stupeni (chetyrekhletki) (Samara, 1923).
Programmy dlia shkol pervoi i vtoroi stupeni (Ivanovo-Voznesensk, 1923).
Programmy dlia shkol pervoi stupeni Tul'skoi gubernii na 1923–24 god (Tula, 1923).
Programmy-minimum dlia edinoi trudovoi shkoly 1-i i 2-i stupeni (Petrograd, 1923).
Programmy shkol I i II stupeni (Vladivostok, 1923).
Programmy shkoly 9-letki na 1923–24 uchebnyi god (Orel, 1923).

1924
Informatsionnoe pis'mo po provedeniiu programmy GUS'a i uchetu shkol'noi raboty (Tula, 1924).
Novye programmy 1 i 2 godov obucheniia shkol 1-i stupeni (Nikol'sk, 1924).
Programmy dlia shkol semiletok i pervykh trekh grupp shkol II-oi stupeni (Ekaterinburg, 1924).
Programmy dlia III i IV grupp shkol I stupeni (Ekaterinburg, 1924).

1925

Kompleksnye programmy shkol I stupeni na 1925–26 uchebnyi god (Ust'sy sol'sk, 1925).
Materialy po razrabotke programm GUS'a v massovoi sel'skoi shkole (Novgorod, 1925).
Novye programmy 1, 2, 3 i 4 godov obucheniia shkol I-i stupeni (V. Ustiug, 1925).
Proizvodstvennyi plan sel'skoi shkoly I stupeni (Vladivostok, 1925).
Programmy dlia sel'skikh shkol (Syzran', 1925).
Programmy V, VI i VI grupp shkoly 7-letki gor. Moskvy i Moskovskoi gubernii (Moscow, 1925).

1926

Praktika raboty po programme GUS'a: rabochaia kniga uchitelei I stupeni, 2 vols. (Moscow, 1926).
Programmy dlia pervogo i vtorogo kontsentra shkol-semiletok Riazansko-ural'skoi zheleznoi dorogi (Saratov, 1926).
Programmy dlia vtorogo kontsentra shkoly semiletki (V, VI i VII gody obucheniia) (Moscow, 1926).
Programmy dlia sel'skoi shkoly 1-i stupeni (Penza, 1926).
Programmy edinoi trudovoi shkoly II stupeni (5, 6, 7, 8 i 9 gody obucheniia) (Khabarovsk-Vladivostok, 1926).
Programmy-minimum edinoi trudovoi shkoly (Leningrad, 1925).

1927

Programmnyi material dlia shkol I-i stupeni po III-mu i IV-mu godam obucheniia (Ivanovo-Voznesensk, 1927).
Programmy dlia shkol I-i stupeni Sverdlovskogo okruga (Sverdlovsk, 1927).
Programmy-minimum dlia V, VI, VII godov obucheniia shkoly-semiletki sotsvosa (Moscow, 1927).
Programmy III i IV godov obucheniia dlia sel'skoi shkoly I stupeni (Kursk, 1927).
Rabochie programmy dlia shkol pervoi stupeni g. Moskvy (Moscow, 1927).
Sibirskii variant programm GUS'a (dlia gorodskikh shkol I stupeni sibirskogo kraia) and *(dlia sel'skikh shkol I stupeni Sibirskogo kraia)* (Novosibirsk, 1927).

1929

Programmy GUS'a v sel'skoi shkole: metodicheskoe posobie dlia sel'skikh uchitelei (Moscow-Leningrad, 1929).

1930

Programmy dlia shkol I stupeni v kolkhozakh Sibirskogo kraia (Novosibirsk, 1930).
Programmy dlia gorodskikh shkol pervoi stupeni i mladshikh grupp FZS i ShKS Sibirskogo kraia (Novosibirsk, 1930).

INDEX

Academic failure: continuation of traditional methods, 38–39; frequency in late 1920s, 95; indiscriminate promotion and academic standards, 135

Academy of Sciences: Lunacharsky on rejection of Marxist nominees, 118

Activity method: Narkompros and new curriculum, 10

Akun'kov, A.: educational press and cultural revolution, 116

Aleksev, M.: continuation of traditional methods in Moscow, 42

Aleksinsky, A.: Narkompros and cultural revolution, 122–23

All-Russian Central Executive: abuse of teachers by local authorities, 50

Baturin, N. N.: criticism of Narkompros, 62

Bauer, Ia.: purge of Narkompros, 120

Bem, O. L.: disorganization in Pedagogical Section, 70; Narkompros program and class school, 71; complex method, 80

Berdnikov, A. I.: Gosplan and Narkompros, 115

Biulleten' ofitsial'nykh rasporiazhenii i soobshchenii: continuation of traditional methods, 18; publication and distribution, 70–71; project method, 124

Blonsky, P.: disorganization in Pedagogical Section, 70; defense of new curriculum, 71, 75; complex method, 77, 80; class discrimination and grade repetition, 135

Bolsheviks: ideology of education, 3, 4; differences in visionary thought among, 7; modern culture and visionary thought, 155n

Bubnov, A. S.: replacement of Lunacharsky and cultural revolution, 119–20; occupational training and secondary schools, 122; local authorities and abuse of teachers, 131–32; 1931 report on state of education, 136; project method and content, 138–39, 140; lack of interest in participatory decision-making, 144

Bureaucracy: ineffective and campaign for technical education, 24; departments of education and failure of Narkompros's policies, 45

Center for Pedagogical Innovation: contemporary educational policy, 145–46

Central Institute of Labor: counterproposals for vocational education, 90

Chaplin, Nikolai: Komsomol and secondary education, 84; Komsomol and Narkompros during cultural revolution, 111

Class: Krupskaya on ideology of education, 6; Komsomol's criticism of United Labor Schools, 21; social origins of teachers, 55, 173n; Komsomol and secondary education, 84; lack of progress toward universal education, 97–99; Narkompros and discriminatory policies, 101–102; Narkompros and purging of students during cultural revolution, 113, 114; purging of students and Lunacharsky's resignation, 118–19; social composition of schools in early 1930s, 131; struggle and project method, 137–38; occupation in Russian Republic, 186n. See also Peasants; Working class

Commissariat of Enlightenment. See Narkompros

Committees for School Welfare: changes in structure, 31–32

Communist Party: criticism of Narkompros policies, 22–23, 76; criticism of progressive methods, 62; educational policy and cultural revolution, 110–11; purge and reorganization of Narkompros, 119; dictation of school policy, 137; social dimension of educational policy, 141–42; membership and teachers' unions, 174n

Complex method: Narkompros's policies and expectations, 32–34; curricula, 35–36; teachers and resistance, 39–40, 51; parents and traditional methods, 59; Moscow Department of Education criticism of Narkompros, 75; Rabkrin report on, 77

Councils: centralization of curricular authority, 31

Cultural revolution: effect on intellectual endeavors, 109–10; Communist Party's educational policy, 110–11; debate between Narkompros and Komsomol, 111–12; Narkompros's defense of policies, 112–15; Gosplan and Narkompros, 115–17; removal and replacement of Lunacharsky, 118–20; purge of Narkompros, 120–21; Narkompros and occupational training, 122–23; 1930 curricula, 123–25; adverse impact on education, 145

Curricula: Narkompros and establishment of new system, 9–11; State Academic Council

LARRY E. HOLMES is Professor of History at the University of South Alabama, where he has taught since 1968. He has published articles on Soviet historical literature and education in *Slavic Review, Russian History, CLIO, The History of Education Quarterly,* and *Sovetskaia pedagogika.*